75 Years:
REFLECTIONS OF MY LIFE
AND THE WORLD AROUND ME

75 Years:
REFLECTIONS OF MY LIFE AND THE WORLD AROUND ME

S. Krishnamoorthi

ZORBA BOOKS

ZORBA BOOKS

Publishing Services in India by Zorba Books, 2019

Website: www.zorbabooks.com
Email: info@zorbabooks.com
Copyright © **S. Krishnamoorthi**

ISBN Print Book 978-93-88497-22-0
       E-book 978-93-88497-23-7

All rights reserved. No part of this book may be reproduced or transmitted in any form or by any means, electronic or mechanical, except by a reviewer. The reviewer may quote brief passages, , with attribution, in a review to be printed in a magazine, newspaper, or on the Web—without permission in writing from the copyright owner.

The publisher under the guidance and direction of the author has published the contents in this book, and the publisher takes no responsibility for the contents, it's accuracy, completeness, any inconsistencies, or the statements made. The contents of the book do not reflect the opinion of the publisher or the editor. The publisher and editor shall not be liable for any errors, omissions, or the reliability of the contents of the book.

Any perceived slight against any person/s, place or organization is purely unintentional.

Zorba Books Pvt. Ltd.(opc)
Gurgaon, INDIA

Dedicated to
Everyone and Everything around me

Acknowledgements

My profound thanks are due to my daughter Shyamala who took pains to correct my manuscript word by word. I thank my grandson Joshua Davis for being the first reader of every chapter and for his frank comments. I thank my granddaughter Amenda Davis for providing the synopsis and title of the book. I thank my son-in law Alex for his valuable suggestions and constant support. Padmanabhan, Balasubramanian, Vasantha, Dinky, Rani Mohanraj, Ernest Johnson, Donella, Mathiyazhagan, Pini Paul, Lola Raghavan and Nikita Kapoor are to be thanked for providing data, comments and encouragement.

I thank Zorba Books, my publisher for giving me an insight into the publishing world and for publishing the book under self - publishing category.

I acknowledge Wikipedia as a resource for the data compiled in the sections titled "Around Me". I thank Poonam Sethi, a renowned tarot reader and space healer for writing the forecast in one of the Friday issues of Times of India in February 2015 under the Virgo sign, "You have been doing the same old thing for so many years. Now is the time to start something new". After seeing this I was inspired to pen my autobiography.

I thank "The Remembering Site" for sharing the personal history of Faye James under the topic, "Growing up in Nebraska" which motivated me.

Finally, I thank God, the Almighty, for giving me the strength to write and publish the book successfully.

Preface

"God shuts one door and He opens another."
and
"God has a place where you can be your best for Him."

I was born amidst World War II, grew up during British rule and lived as a citizen of the Republic of India. I was surrounded by the lives of Muhammad Ali, Paul McCartney, Stephen Hawking, Harrison Ford, Joyce Meyer, Bobby Fischer, Margaret Court, Patricia Bath, Rajiv Gandhi, and Amitabh Bachchan but unlike them, I am not famous.

This is my story. I, who became fatherless when I was two years and eight months old, was adopted by God. He cared for me through various people at every stage of my life and also made me give back to society what was given to me. He once saved me when I almost drowned in a river at age 10. Whenever I lacked something, he never failed to reward me with better things. He placed me where I was needed the most and made important things occur around me and involving me.

I can quote what two prominent people have said. Balan Nair, a famous astrologer after casting my horoscope for the first time told me, "Your horoscope says that you are an adopted son of God." Mata Amritanandamayi Devi, during her *darshan*, hugged me and said, "You are the adopted son of God."

Everyone needs a safe birth into this world and a good education for life. Gynaecologists are responsible for the safe birth of a child. Teachers impart education to children and play a role in shaping their future. Henry Adams once said, "Teachers affect eternity; No one can tell where their influence stops." There is a strange coincidence in my life. My grandmother and mother-in-law were involved in childbirth and my granddaughter is specializing in Gynaecology and Obstetrics as well. As teachers, my mother shaped young minds, my daughter is moulding adolescent minds, and I have been training adult minds. When we were all engaged in our professions, my wife, June, took care of us and lent us constant support, encouragement and unconditional love.

This is also a narration of some major events that happened around me in India and the world. My life has been entwined with World War II, the first (hopefully the last) atomic bombing of two Japanese cities, India's independence, wars, the disintegration of the Soviet Union, man's quest for conquering space, computer and knowledge revolution, rampage of diseases like cancer and AIDS, threats of terrorism, climate change, Olympic games, assassinations of world leaders, the presence of simple and straightforward political leaders like Kamaraj, Annadurai and Lal Bahadur Shastri, and the contributions of great souls like Mother Teresa and A.P.J. Abdul Kalam.

I am deeply affected by sufferings during famines, victims tortured by oppressors, helpless old people and the lack of cooperation between countries and within countries. Loneliness, poverty, and pain make a mockery of what human life should be. I long to end the sufferings of everyone but that is impossible. So, in my own small way I help to alleviate the anguish of people around me.

I moved very close to God through Ahilan, but—

Contents

    Prologue 1
1. Birth and Childhood – August 1943 to May 1948 4
2. Elementary School Life – June 1948 to May 1953..................21
3. High School Life – June 1953 to June 1959 30
4. College Life – July 1959 to July 1967 44
5. Love and Marriage – December 1965 to August 1967 67
6. Life in Calicut – October 1967 to July 1974............................76
7. Life in Trichy, Part I – July 1974 to June 1984 101
8. Life in Trichy, Part II – July 1984 to September 1992...........121
9. Life in Trichy, Part III – October 1992 to June 2003 149
10. Research and Administration – July 1984 to June 2003 183
11. Game of Contract Bridge – 1966 to 2018 200
12. Life in Kanchipuram – June 2003 to July 2007 213
13. Life in Gurgaon, Part I – July 2007 to November 2010.........234
14. Death of June – November 6, 2010..253
15. Life in Gurgaon, Part II – November 2010 Onwards.............260
16. My Role in the Success of Others 290
17. My Failures 297
18. My views on Major Events around Me 303
    Epilogue 308

Prologue

I can never forget that fateful day. I was almost washed away while bathing in the River Kudamurutti and I would not be talking to you today but for my cousin Ramdas who saved me. It happened during the Christmas holidays when my mother had taken my sister and me to Tiruvaiyaru village in Thanjavur district, 75 kilometres from my home town Tiruchirappalli (Trichy), in the state of Tamil Nadu, India. It happened in December, 1953, when I was 10 years old, just 90 days after Andhra Pradesh was carved out of Madras State on October 1, 1953. Ramdas still lives in Tiruvaiyaru. He retired from the Indian Postal Service.

That means you are 75 now?

Great and smart! To be precise, 75 years and 1 month.

You don't look a day over 65, more like in your 60's. Your hair is still black and your body is lean without a paunch. What is your secret? Do you practice yoga?

There is no secret. I have never done any yoga. Teaching is my profession and I am surrounded by students between the ages of 18 to 22 for most of my day and most part of my life for the past 50 years. So, I feel young at heart and in body.

What made you write your autobiography? You are not a popular figure known to many people, an admired sportsman, a popular film star, a well-known politician, a philosopher, a successful businessman, a Noble Laureate, a spiritual leader, a writer, a famous singer, a social worker or a prominent public figure.

Hmmm! Yes, you are right. I am not famous, unlike them. There are two famous sayings, "When God shuts one door, He opens another." Also, "God has a place for everyone where you can be your best for

Him!" I have found these two sayings to be true throughout my life. I have had unique experiences which have impacted my life. I feel the need to share these experiences. So, could you please wait till the end for the answer?

Sure. I can wait. What are you doing now?

I retired as Emeritus Fellow from the Department of Civil and Environmental Engineering, the NorthCap University (formerly Institute of Technology and Management University), Gurgaon on May 31, 2016, after working for 8 years since May 9, 2008. I am continuing as visiting faculty in the same university.

What made you move from your home town, Trichy, to Gurgaon?

After my voluntary retirement from Regional Engineering College (REC), now National Institute of Technology (NIT), Tiruchirappalli in 2003 (three months before my retirement age of 60), I worked as Professor and Head, Department of Civil Engineering, Arulmighu Meenakshi Amman College of Engineering near Kanchipuram. In 2007, my daughter, Shyamala and my son-in-law, Alex, invited my wife, June, alias Shanthi, and me to Gurgaon (now Gurugram), Haryana, to help them as my daughter had started a new job. So, we came to Gurgaon on July 14, 2007 after winding up everything in Tamil Nadu, a state where I had spent 64 years of my life and my wife had spent 58 years of her life. Both June and Shyamala thought that I could work in Gurgaon. So, I applied to a few colleges and within 41 days of my arrival, I got a job at Ansal Institute of Technology (now Ansal University) as Deputy Registrar, Examinations. I joined on my 65th birthday, August 24, 2007. Within 8 months I was appointed as an Associate Professor at the Institute of Technology and Management (ITM), Gurgaon on May 9, 2008.

Everything was fine in Gurgaon until the most unfortunate and sad incident happened on the morning of Saturday, November 6, 2010 - my wife, June, who had been with me for 43 years, 2 months and 8 days passed away unexpectedly.

Oh! Sorry about that. How did it happen?

I would have to go back 75 years to the beginning of my life in order to answer that question. Do you have the patience?"

Sir, what a question! I have come to share your experiences and write your autobiography. Shall we proceed in question and answers format?

Yes...I am going to talk not only about myself but also about the events around me in Tamil Nadu, India and the world. I will reveal my vision for an idyllic India and an epitome world.

Wow! That will be something new and unique. Shall we start?

Yes. Sure!

CHAPTER 1

Birth and Childhood - August 24, 1943 to May 31, 1948

Abstract

Me

Basic information about my birth, my childhood, birth of my sister, deaths of my father, paternal grandmother and maternal step grandmother, my paternal grandfather's mental illness and my mother becoming a teacher are presented.

Around Me

In India, the major events were the death of Netaji (1945), India's independence (1947), first Indo-Pakistan War (1947-48) and Mahatma Gandhi's assassination (1948).

In Madras Presidency, the major events were the formation of Dravidar Kazhagam (1944) and C. Rajagopalachari becoming Union Minister and Governor (1946-47).

In the World, the major events were the founding of the Arab League (1945), Truman becoming US President (1945), death of Hitler (1945), atomic bombing of Japanese cities (1945), end of world War II (1945), the birth of the Republic of Vietnam (1945), sale of ball point pens (1945), Clement Attlee becoming Prime Minister of England (1945), the first computer (1946), birth of United Nations (1946), Stalin becoming Chairman of Council of Ministers (1946), UN resolution on Jewish state (1947), Independence of Burma and Ceylon (1948) and birth of Israel (1948).

Me

Basic Information

Can you introduce yourself?

My name is S. Krishnamoorthi. S stands for Subramanian, my father's name. My mother was A. Dharmambal. I like my name because it is the name of Lord Krishna with whom I share my birth star. My nick name is Kittu. I was born on August 24, 1943 in Cuddappa. I am the eldest child and I have a younger sister, Vasantha. I lived in Tiruchirappalli (Trichy) town for 46 years and so I consider it as my home town or native place.

Tiruchirappalli, also called Trichy or Tiruchi, is a city in Tamil Nadu, India. Located 322 kilometres south of Chennai and 379 kilometres north of Kanyakumari, Tiruchirappalli sits almost at the geographic centre of the state. The most prominent historical monuments include the Rockfort, perched on a massive rocky outcrop which rises abruptly from the plains towering over the city, the Ranganathaswamy Temple at Srirangam, and the Jambukeswarar Temple at Thiruvanaikaval. The river Cauvery runs through the city with an ancient dam Kallanai (Grand Anicut), constructed in the 2nd century A.D., across it. The city is an important Educational and Industrial centre. A major road and railway hub of the state, the city has an international airport which operates flights to Southeast Asia and the Middle East.

I have a Bachelor of Engineering (BE) degree in Civil Engineering from College of Engineering Guindy, University of Madras (1965) and Master of Engineering (ME) degree in Hydraulics and Hydraulic structures from Indian Institute of Science (IISc), Bangalore (1967).

I married June on August 30, 1967. Shyamala is our only child and she married Dr. Joseph Alexanand Davis on February 10, 1992. I have a granddaughter, Amenda, who is currently doing her M.D. and a grandson, Joshua, who is in 12th standard.

I was in the teaching profession as a faculty in Civil Engineering from October 16, 1967 at Regional Engineering College, Calicut until I retired on May 31, 2016 from the NorthCap University (NCU), Gurgaon. Now, I serve as visiting faculty at NCU.

I live in the city of Gurgaon.

I am right- handed, 165 cm tall, 60 kg in weight and the colour of my eyes is black. I have been wearing corrective eye glasses from the age of 37 and recently cataract operation was done on my right eye in the All India Institute of Medical Sciences (AIIMS), New Delhi. My blood group is O+ and I am not allergic to anything.

Birth and Childhood

When and where were you born?

I was born on Tuesday, August 24, 1943 at 5.00 a.m., in Cuddappa (now Kadapa), Madras province, now in Andhra Pradesh. The whole world was in turmoil due to World War II which had started in 1939. At the same time, India was struggling for her freedom from British rule. I added one more to India's population of 398 million.

Without being aware of the tumultuous world around, I was growing up in a small space, under the protection of my parents and grandparents, demanding their attention to feed, bathe, and dress me and to pacify me when I cried. In return, I probably made them happy with my smiles and efforts to crawl and speak. The world sighed with relief when World War II ended in September, 1945. India's fight for freedom ended successfully in 1947— a double sigh of relief for Indians.

Please share the names and occupations of your parents and close relatives. How did you address them?

My mother was A. Dharmambal and my father, P. R. Subramanian. We addressed our mother as "Amma" and father as "Appa". My paternal grandfather was D. Rathinaswamy and my grandmother was Gangamirtham. My maternal grandfather was A. Arumugam and my grandmother was Chinnammal. My maternal step grandmother (nana) was Dr. Daisy. We addressed our grandparents as "Thatha" and "Patti". Gangamirtham was the sister of Arumugam and Subramanian was her son.

Arumugam worked as a Post Master in the Postal Department, Government of India. Rathinaswamy worked as a Station Master in the Indian Railways. Subramanian worked as a clerk in the Indian Railways. Daisy was a doctor who had specialised in Gynaecology and obstetrics. My mother worked as a teacher after my father's demise. My grandmothers were housewives.

You mentioned your maternal step grandmother Dr. Daisy, tell me more about her.

Daisy was a doctor in a government hospital in Kumbakonam town. She was my grandmother's Gynaecologist. My grandfather and

Dr. Daisy got acquainted during that time. When Chinnammal died within seven days of delivering her third child, Dr. Daisy, who was a spinster, offered to raise Arumugam's three children. Arumugam and Daisy got married and decided not to have any children of their own. My grandfather worked in Trichy and he visited Kumbakonam during the weekends.

You said your home town is Trichy. Then, how is it you were born 500 kilometres away from Trichy?

As the due date for the delivery neared, my maternal step grandmother, Dr. Daisy, who was working in Cuddappa Government Headquarters Hospital, took my mother there for her delivery and confinement.

__Kadapa__ (formerly known as __Cuddappa__) is a city in the Rayalseema region of the south-central part of Andhra Pradesh, India and is also known as the "Heart of Rayalaseema". It is the district headquarters of Kadapa district. It is located 8 kilometres south of the Penna River. The city is surrounded on three sides by the Nallamala and Palkonda Hills lying on the tectonic landscape between the Eastern and Western Ghats. The city is nicknamed "Gadapa" ("threshold") since it is the gateway from the west to the sacred hills of Tirumala.

Do you have brothers and sisters? What are their names? When were they born? Do you remember the first time you saw them?

I have a sister, Vasantha. She was born on July 3, 1945. I don't remember the first time I saw her.

Tell me about your aunts and uncles. Did they play an important role in your life when you were growing up? Do you remember any special people?

I have 2 maternal uncles who are younger to my mother, A. Govindarajan and A. Padmanaban. Since I was born around the same time as Lord Krishna, there was a belief that my maternal uncles should not set their eyes on me when I was brought to Tiruchirappalli in November, 1943. They first saw my image in water. My aunts were Mangayarkarasi, wife of Govindarajan and Shantha, wife of Padmanaban. They played an important role in my life which I will discuss later. I had one paternal aunt, Savithri and an uncle, Muthiah (Savithri's husband). Govindarajan was an ophthalmologist and Padmanaban a lawyer. Muthiah was an auditor in the Indian Railways. All my aunts were housewives.

Was yours a religious family?

We follow Hinduism and worship God in different forms and names. We are staunch believers in the miracles of prayer and God.

Village deities (Kula Deivam, meaning Family God) are the patron deities or gramadevata of the village. They do not belong to the Vedic-Agamic-pantheon of Hinduism which is practiced in almost all the villages throughout India, and Andhra Pradesh and Tamil Nadu in particular. They are generally recognized by various communities, sects and clan groups as part of the lineage through which they trace their origin through the centuries. Most of these village deities have their shrines on the periphery of the village as a representation of their position as the village guardian. These are either represented by a huge, fierce statue or a simple stone. Most of these temples are not closed premises but are simple and small worship areas. Ayyannar, Muniyappan, Veera Maha Kali, Madurai Veeran, Karuppanaarswamy, and Pappathi Ammal are some of the deities.

Were you considered rich, poor, or middle class? Were times ever tough for all of you or was it always smooth sailing? Did you have to go without things that your friends had?

Middle class. We had all the basic necessities to lead our life. I can say we had a smooth sailing life.

How did World War II and the freedom struggle affect your family?

I don't know much about it except for one thing told by my mother. Whenever there was a siren we used to lie down fearing bomb attacks.

How was your relationship with your parents? Would you describe it as warm, formal, loving, stern or demonstrative?

As I lost my father when I was about 3 years old, my mother, my sister and I stayed in my maternal grandfather's house. There, my mother and grandfather took care of us. My grandfather was strict with everyone but not with my sister and me because we were fatherless. My mother was strict when we made mistakes but it was otherwise a loving relationship.

Can you talk a bit more about your parents?

My mother was born on November 1, 1922. She had two younger siblings Govindarajan (May 28, 1927) and Padmanaban

(June 7, 1931). After the death of her mother, Dharmambal had to take care of both her brothers. She had to perform the duties of a mother when she was just 9 years old. My parents and my uncles studied in Town High school, Kumbakonam, about 85 kilometres from Trichy. My father was 2 years older than my mother and he completed the Secondary School Leaving Certificate (SSLC), consisting of 11 years of schooling, in 1936 and my mother completed hers in 1938. My uncles were fond of my father and called him "Athan" (paternal aunt's son). As soon as my mother completed her SSLC, my grandfather wanted her to marry Subramanian. My father ran off to join the army but returned at the insistence of my grandfather. He was recruited as a clerk in the Indian Railways and was posted in Jolarpettai soon after. My parents got married in Kumbakonam, in July, 1942, the year in which the Quit India Movement (Civil Disobedience or August Movement) was launched.

Shifting from Kumbakonam to Trichy

After their marriage, my parents settled in Jolarpettai. Dr. Daisy was transferred to Cuddappa in June, 1943, and my grandfather urged his sons to settle in Trichy with him. My uncles joined St. Joseph's College High School, Trichy to complete their schooling.

My Short Life with My Father

My father worked in the Indian Railways as a clerk in the Good Shed Yard in Jolarpettai. He was transferred to Erode in June, 1944. Very soon my father had an attack of TB.

__Tuberculosis__ (TB) is a deadly and dreaded infectious disease caused by the bacteria Mycobacterium tuberculosis. Tuberculosis generally affects the lungs, but also other parts of the body. Albert Calmette and Camille Guérin achieved the first genuine success in immunization against tuberculosis in 1906, using attenuated bovine-strain tuberculosis. It was called Bacille Calmette–Guérin (BCG). The BCG vaccine was first used on humans in 1921 in France but received widespread acceptance in the US, Great Britain, and Germany only after World War II. One-third of the world's population is thought to be infected with TB. New infections occur in about 1% of the population each year.

It was detected in January, 1945 and my mother had recently conceived their second child. In those days TB was a dreaded disease with no proper medicines to treat it.

So, my family shifted to Trichy to my grandfather's house and my father was separated from us. He lived alone in a house next to his sister's, just 500 metres away from us. Food was sent from our house for my father. Every day in the evening my mother and I would go to my father's house. We would stand outside and I would try to catch glimpses of him through a window. In the meantime, my sister was born on July 3, 1945 in Trichy.

My Father's Bereavement

Since suitable medicines for treating TB were not available, my father passed away on April 22, 1946. He was just 26 years old. My mother was 24. I was 2 years 8 months and my sister was only 9 months old. Normally, the eldest son performs the last rites of his father according to Hindu customs. Since I was a small boy, I was not permitted to do the last rites and I am not sure who performed the last rites for him.

I doubt I would have cried over my father's death then. But, I can't hold back my tears now when I see a scene in a movie or read a passage in a novel describing a father's cremation or burial.

My mother never shared her feelings or discussed anything about my father's death thinking that we might feel sad. After I grew up I also made a mistake and did not think of asking her about a loss that must have affected her deeply. I must confess that we started performing annual rituals for my father very late.

After my father's death, my paternal grandmother, Gangamirtham, and my maternal step grandmother, Dr. Daisy, passed away in quick succession the same year. In between, my paternal grandfather became mentally ill and was relieved from his position as station master. A series of calamities struck my family that year.

Do you remember anything about your father?

I was very young when he died and most of the time we never lived together as a family. I was not allowed to go near him fearing I may contract TB (although, later, I got it). So, I don't remember anything about my father.

Do you miss your father?

> A father is respected because
> He gives his children leadership...

> Appreciated because
> He gives his children care...
> Valued because
> He gives his children time...
> Loved because
> He gives his children the one thing
> they treasure most - himself.

In a way, big **YES**. Even though I have been well taken care of by my grandfather, mother, uncles, aunties, foster mother-in-law, wife, daughter, son-in-law, grandchildren and many well-wishers, I definitely missed all what a father can give. I missed being carried by him, holding his hand and walking, hearing stories from him, fearing him, arguing with him, lying to him. I missed the joy he would have felt about my studies, job, marriage and becoming a grandfather. I miss caring for him in his old age and performing his last rites. My teachers used to tell me that I lacked life in me. My sister, mother and I were like nomads unable to stay in our own house.

What was your grandfather's role in modelling your life?

Victor Hugo says, "There are fathers who do not love their sons; there is no grandfather who does not adore his grandson."

My grandfather gave me everything my father could have given me or maybe even more. He shaped my character. He was the one who made me pursue an under-graduation degree in engineering from the College of Engineering, Guindy, the oldest and one of the best colleges in India and a post-graduation degree in engineering from IISc, Bangalore which is a premier institute even today. I could not fulfill his desire to acquire a doctorate in engineering. Even though I have done some good research, I have not been able to convert it into a Ph.D. degree.

Indira Gandhi said, "My grandfather once told me that there were two kinds of people: those who do the work and those who take the credit. He told me to try to be in the first group; there was much less competition."

Kevin Johnson said, "My role model was my grandfather. He instilled in me the feeling that no matter how successful you are, you have a responsibility to help others."

These two quotes have influenced me a lot and I think I belong to the first group and I have tried to help others throughout my life.

How did your mother cope with the situation of becoming a widow at the age of 24 with two children?

My mother's life was really tragic. She became motherless at 12 and a widow at 24. My mother was bold like her father and aspired to pursue medicine and perhaps find a cure for TB. Unfortunately, my uncles did not want her to be separated from the family. She sacrificed her ambition and decided to become a school teacher. My mother did her teacher training while taking care of the family and completed it through sheer hard work. God closes one door but opens another. There was a doctor, Shafiulla, practicing in Palakkarai, just two kilometres from our house. Since he was a paediatrician, my mother used to take my sister and me to him when we fell ill. When he came to know that my mother had completed the teacher training course, he offered her the post of a teacher in Majli-sul-Ulama Elementary School, which had been started by a Muslim Trust for poor people. He was the Chairman of the Trust. She accepted the offer, after consulting her father, and became a teacher in June, 1948. I started attending school at the same time as well. What a coincidence! Teaching in school is the best profession for women, especially for widows. The school was far away from the house but she coped by taking the bus. Through her hard work, she became the headmistress of the school and retired in the year 1980 at 58 years of age.

How was the household run after your mother started to work?

We required two things: Money and someone to cook and look after the household. Money was managed through my grandfather's pension, my mother's salary, and Dr. Daisy's savings. My grandfather was an influential man in our community and he brought Savithri, a distant relative, from our native village, Kabistalam, to do the house work including cooking.

Can you describe the house in which you were brought up?

I lived in a small rented house at No.9 Marsingpet Road, Beemanagar, Trichy until I was 16. It was in the middle of a series of five houses which we called a store. It was around 500 sq. ft. and it had two floors. It had a dry latrine and when we were young we relieved ourselves in the gutter outside.

It had a hall-cum-dining room, a bedroom, a kitchen, a small space adjacent to the kitchen leading to the toilet and washroom, a passage way in the front to enter the hall and to go to the first floor and a veranda in the front. It had a bedroom and balcony on the first floor. There was a small sump in the front to store water, a tap to collect municipal water and no overhead tanks. The rent was Rs. 15 per month.

We had a cot and dining table which was used by my grandfather. All male members used the bedroom on the first floor. I slept on the floor in my grandfather's room. My favourite place was under the cot.

The kitchen had an oven made of brick and mud which we called a fire pit. Stacks of bricks were cemented on the kitchen floor making a cooking pit which stood one foot high above the ground. A burning fire was the energy source. Women would fan the fire by blowing through a black hollow metal pipe. Much of rural India still uses this method for cooking. It was hard work for the women of the house gathering wood, being constantly surrounded by smoke and always blowing into the fire. There were shops which sold firewood exclusively. If they were wet, we had to dry them before using them. To aid burning we would also add broken pieces of *ratti* (dried cow dung tapped into a round shape). We had a boiler for hot water.

Unknowingly, we had sown the seeds of air pollution due to the release of smoke and environmental degradation due to cutting down trees for firewood contributing to the present day environmental crisis.

There was no telephone, fan, radio or car. We had one bicycle.

Security was not a problem but we locked the doors during the night when we slept. From a young age, I had the habit of checking and locking the doors and even today I have taken the responsibility of locking the doors at night.

On full moon nights, we would have dinner on the open terrace on the first floor with friends and neighbours. My mother used to make tasty food like mutton biryani, tamarind rice and bagalabath (curd rice).

The houses were arranged very close and we used to jump from one balcony to another.

My grandfather used to eat on the dining table in the hall. The rest of us sat cross legged on the floor in the veranda adjoining the kitchen or in the hall to eat our meals. Idli, dosa, and poori were some of our favourite items served for breakfast or dinner.

Since there was no radio or television, we communicated a lot with each other. Many relatives and friends from nearby villages stayed in our home either for their education or to help us cope with the housework. Now, communication among family members is dwindling due to television, mobile phones and the internet.

Unity in Diversity

We embraced national integration in the true sense. The 5 houses consisted of 3 Hindu families belonging to Tamil Nadu, Andhra Pradesh and Kerala, a Christian family and a Muslim family. We also had a Bengali family living nearby. All the families lived in harmony and we would celebrate festivals together and support each other in times of need.

What kind of chores did you have to do for the family?

Not much except go to the butcher shop on Sundays to buy meat.

If you could move back into the house you grew up in, just the way it was then, would you? Why or why not?

I wonder how we were able to stay in such a small house with a dry latrine. But it was joyful in the sense that there were fewer problems. However, afterwards, for the rest of my life I have lived in better and bigger homes with all the modern amenities and gadgets. I am afraid I would not dare to go back.

Do you remember August 15, 1947?

When the whole nation was celebrating the bitterly won Independence, my family was engaged in performing the death anniversary ceremonies of my father, paternal grandmother and maternal step grandmother. In Hindu religion, Shraddha, an annual ceremony is very important for the departed souls.

Three deaths in a row in one year and three death anniversaries shook the very core of our family. If not for my grandfather, who was a courageous man, we would not have come out of these tragedies unscathed.

You were born during World War II and India's struggle for freedom. Within two years of your birth, the war ended and within four years India became independent. I feel all those born during your time must be lucky to have brought peace to the world and India.

Hmmm. Maybe!

What type of transportation was there?

We would mostly walk or use bullock carts for local travel. Buses and trains were used for long distance travel.

Tell me about some of your childhood memories?

I remember two things as told by my mother. When my maternal grandmother died, my family members were all busy preparing for her cremation. But I was creating a tantrum because I wanted to eat idlis (rice cake). Even today everybody laughs when the incident is narrated.

One of my nails, on the middle finger on my left hand got dislodged while playing with a small stone which we used as a door stopper. Even now, I do not have that nail. It is a good ID mark. Can you see it? Whoever meets me for the first time never fails to ask about my missing nail.

Yes. What did you learn from your mother and grandfather?

Honesty, selflessness, patience, kindness, hard work, calmness and generosity.

What about your preparations to enter school?

There was no pre-school, LKG or UKG in those times. There were no registrations or interviews for parents and not much was at stake. Unlike today's children we spent long years of childhood at home. Decision making was easy and simple. There was direct entry to first standard at the completion of five years of age. If there was no birth certificate, the age was decided by a child's ability to touch their nose by putting their hand around the head. There was no need to search for schools because there was an elementary school run by the Trichy Municipality (called Municipal School) behind my house, just 200 steps away. My uncle, Govindarajan, who was 16 years old, took me to the school and admitted me. He made two mistakes while giving the particulars in the application form. He gave my date of birth as August 24, 1942 instead of 1943 and my community as Pillai (forward caste) instead of Moopanar (backward caste). Often, in India, people give a false date of birth so that they can retire later. The two mistakes were corrected by my grandfather before I completed my schooling. Everyone was eager for me to start schooling.

Around Me

Let us go through the major events that took place during this period.

India

Politics

Death of Subhas Chandra Bose, 1945 - The consensus of scholarly opinion is that the death of Subhas Chandra Bose, freedom fighter, occurred from third-degree burns on August 18, 1945 after his overloaded Japanese plane crashed in Japanese occupied Formosa (now Taiwan).

Independence of India and Pakistan, 1947 - The Labour party came to power in July, 1945 in the United Kingdom. In 1946, the Labour Government, its treasury exhausted by World War II, realised that it had neither the mandate at home nor the reliability of native forces to control an increasingly restless India. It was increasingly losing international support as well. In February 1947, Prime Minister Clement Attlee announced that the British government would grant full self-governance to British India by June 1948. The new Viceroy, Lord Mountbatten, advanced the date, believing the continuous contention between the Congress and the Muslim League might lead to a collapse of the interim government. He chose the second anniversary of Japan's surrender during the second world war, August 15, as the date of the transfer of power. Maybe, at that time numerology was not popular. The British government announced on June 3, 1947 that it had accepted the idea of partitioning British India into two states; the successor governments would be given dominion status and would have the right to separate from the British Commonwealth. On August 14, 1947, the new Dominion of Pakistan came into being. Muhammad Ali Jinnah was sworn in as the first Governor General in Karachi. The Constituent Assembly of India met for its fifth session at 11 p.m., on August 14 in the Constitution Hall in New Delhi. The session was chaired by President Rajendra Prasad. Jawaharlal Nehru delivered the 'Tryst with Destiny' speech proclaiming India's independence at 12.00 a.m., on August 15, 1947.

Mahatma Gandhi's Assassination, 1948 - After a previous failed attempt to assassinate Gandhi at Birla House, Nathuram Godse and Narayan Apte returned to Delhi on January 29, 1948 to make another attempt. Godse approached Gandhi on January 30, 1948 during the evening prayer at 5.17 p.m. When Godse bowed, Abha Chattopadhyay, who was supporting Gandhi, said, "Brother, Bapu is already late," and tried to put him off, but he pushed her aside and shot Gandhi in the chest thrice at point-blank range. Gandhi died a few hours later. Godse himself shouted, "Police," and surrendered. It is said that Gandhi invoked God saying, "Hey Ram," as he was assassinated.

War

First Indo - Pak War, 1947- 48 - The Indo-Pakistani War of 1947–1948, or the First Kashmir War, was fought over the princely state of Jammu and Kashmir from 1947 to 1948. Pakistan triggered the war a few weeks after formally gaining independence by launching tribal *lashkar* (militia) from Waziristan to secure Kashmir. The inconclusive result of the war still affects the geopolitics of both countries. A formal cease-fire was declared on the night of January 1, 1949.

Madras Presidency

Formation of Dravidar Kazhagam, 1944 - After E. V. Ramasamy Naicker (Periyar)) became the leader of the Justice Party in 1944, he merged the Justice Party and his own Self Respect Movement and named it Dravidar Kazhagam.

C. Rajagopalachari as Union Minister and Governor, 1946 - 47 - C. Rajagopalachari became a Minister for Industry, Supply, Education and Finance in the Interim Government of India in 1946 and then the Governor of West Bengal from 1947.

World

Politics

Harry S. Truman as President, 1945 - Truman, Democratic Party, became the 33rd President of USA on April 12, 1945 when President Franklin D. Roosevelt died on April 12, 1945.

Hitler's Suicide, 1945 - Adolf Hitler was the leader of the Nazi Party, Chancellor of Germany from 1933 to 1945, and Führer ("Leader") of Nazi Germany from 1934 to 1945. He shot himself on April 30, 1945 in his Führer bunker in Berlin.

Arab League, 1945 - To oppose the establishment of a Jewish state, the Arab League was formed in Cairo on March 22, 1945 with six members: Egypt, Iraq, Transjordan (renamed Jordan after independence in 1946), Lebanon, Saudi Arabia, and Syria. Yemen joined as a member on May 5, 1945.

Clement Attlee, PM, England, 1945 - Clement Attlee became the Prime Minister of England on July 26, 1945 after Winston Churchill (1940 to 1945).

Republic of Vietnam, 1945 - On September 2, 1945, Ho Chi Minh proclaimed the independent Democratic Republic of Vietnam in Hanoi's Ba Dinh square.

Birth of United Nations, 1945 - The United Nations was born on October 24, 1945 as a better means of mediating international conflict and negotiating peace than the old League of Nations. Negotiating and maintaining the peace was the responsibility of the new U.N. Security Council, made up of the United States, Great Britain, France, the Soviet Union, and China. Each would have veto power over the other.

Joseph Stalin, 1946 - When the Chairman of the Council of People's Commissars, Soviet Union was changed to Chairman of Council of Ministers (Premier), Joseph Stalin became the first Chairman of Council of Ministers from March 15, 1946.

UN Resolution, 1947 - On November 29, 1947, the U.N. General Assembly adopted a resolution recommending the creation of independent Arab and Jewish States and the Special International Regime for the City of Jerusalem.

Burma became Independent, 1948 - On January 4, 1948, the nation which had previously been under British rule became an independent republic. It was renamed the Union of Burma, with Sao Shwe Thaik as its first President and U Nu as first Prime Minister.

Ceylon became Independent, 1948 - The Sri Lankan Independence Movement was a peaceful political movement aimed at achieving independence and self-rule for Sri Lanka, (then Ceylon) from the British Empire. Ceylon was granted independence as the Dominion of Ceylon in 1948. Dominion status within the British Commonwealth was retained for 24 years until May 22, 1972 when it became a Republic and was renamed Republic of Sri Lanka.

Birth of Israel, 1948 - On May 14, 1948, in Tel Aviv, Jewish Agency Chairman, David Ben-Gurion proclaimed the State of Israel, establishing the first Jewish state in 2000 years.

War

Atomic Bombings of Hiroshima and Nagasaki in Japan - August 6 & 9, 1945 - Harry S. Truman, President of USA with the consent of the United Kingdom, as laid down in the Quebec Agreement, dropped nuclear bombs on the Japanese cities of Hiroshima (Little Boy) and Nagasaki (Fat Man) on August 6 and 9, 1945 respectively to force Japan to surrender during the second world war. Within the first two to four months the acute effects of the atomic bombings killed 90,000–146,000 people in Hiroshima and 39,000–80,000 in Nagasaki; roughly half of the deaths occurred on the first day. During the following months, large numbers died from the effect of burns, radiation sickness, and other injuries, magnified by illness and malnutrition.

End of World War II, August 15, 1945 - World War II, a global war lasted from 1939 to 1945, although related conflicts began earlier. It involved many nations including all the great powers which formed two opposing military alliances: The Allies and the Axis. It was the most widespread and deadliest war in history, and involved more than 100 million people from over 30 countries. It resulted in 50-85 million fatalities. Germany, Japan and Italy were the main countries in the Axis and USA, Soviet Union, UK, and France were the main countries in the Alliance. The war in Europe concluded with an invasion of Germany by the Western Allies and the Soviet Union, culminating in the capture of Berlin by Soviet and Polish troops and the subsequent surrender by Germany on May 8, 1945. Japan surrendered on August 15, 1945 and thus ended the war in Asia, strengthening the total victory of the Allies. World War II altered the political alignment and social structure of the world.

Science and Technology

Sale of Ballpoint Pen, 1944 - The first man to develop and launch a ballpoint pen was the Hungarian László Jozsef Bíró (1899-1985) from Budapest, who, in 1938, invented a ball-point pen with a pressurized ink cartridge. Sales of ballpoint pens began in 1944.

First Computer Built, 1943 to 1945 - Electronic Numerical Integrator And Computer (ENIAC), built between 1943 and 1945 was the first large-scale computer to run at electronic speed without being slowed by any mechanical parts. ENIAC was designed by John Mauchly and J. Presper Eckert of the University of Pennsylvania, USA.

CHAPTER 2

Elementary School Life - June 1948 to May 1953

Abstract

Me

The details of the first five years of my elementary school education are given.

Around Me

In India, the major events were nationalisation of Reserve Bank of India (1949), ceasefire of Indo-Pakistan War (1949), London Declaration (1949), Indo-Pak Karachi Agreement (1949), the hanging of Mahatma Gandhi's assassins (1949), India's recognition of People's Republic of China (1949), Indian Constitution (1946-50), *Jana Gana Mana* as National Anthem (1950), unification of India and India becoming Republic (1950), States and Union Territories (1950), first President (1950), death of Vallabhbhai Patel (1950), Liaquat-Nehru Pact (1950), Indo-Nepal Treaty (1950), birth of Bharatiya Jana Sangh (1951), first general elections in the Indian Republic and first (1952) and the first Backward Class Commission (1953).

In Madras Province, the major events were the birth of Dravida Munnetra Kazhagam, (1949), first State Assembly elections (1952), first Chief Minister (1952) and M.G. Ramachandran joining DMK (1953).

In the World, the major events were First Arab-Israeli War (1948), crisis in Germany (1948), birth of the Republic of South Korea (1948), Apartheid in South Africa (1948), Jinnah's death (1948), Truman's second term as US President (1949), formation of FRG and GDR

(1949), birth of People's Republic of China (1949), first President and Prime Minister of China (1949), independence of Indonesia (1949), Korean War (1950), Colombo Plan (1950), 22nd amendment in USA (1951), China-Tibet Treaty (1951), Churchill becoming Prime Minister of UK (1951), assassination of Liaquat Ali Khan (1951), detonation of Hydrogen bomb (1952), Eisenhower becoming US President (1953), death of Stalin and Melenkov becoming Chairman, Council of Ministers, USSR (1953) and first ascent of Mount Everest by Tenzing Norgay and Edmund Hillary (1953).

Me

Where and when did you complete your elementary school education?

When I completed 4 years and 9 months of age in June 1948 my maternal uncle, Govindarajan, admitted me to the class 1 in a municipal school just behind my house.

The school had two small campuses on either side of a small lane. One campus had classes I to V and the other had forms I to III (classes VI to VIII) with a small playground. All the classrooms had tiled roofs. Every morning the bell would ring thrice at intervals of 5 minutes each and I would run to school after the second bell. It would take just 2 minutes. There were no uniforms. It was a Tamil medium school. There was an assembly every day.

At that time, there were no play schools or nursery schools. We spent most of our childhood at home unlike children of today who have to go to school once they complete 3 years.

Like any other child, I too cried every morning before going to school. Both my uncles pacified me and helped me to go to school. One of my teachers was Dharmambal, who shared the same name as my mother and the Head Master was Irudhayaraj.

I studied from classes I to V from June 1948 to May 1953. I do not remember many things about that time. It was just routine activity and I never had any difficulty in learning my lessons.

During my second year of schooling, there was an incident in which I was falsely accused of wrong doing. One of the boys who lived in a house on the street opposite ours hurt his eye. His parents complained to my mother that I threw a stone at his eye. My mother also punished me without giving me a chance to explain. On the same day, the boy told his parents that it was not me and luckily whatever bad impression had been created was erased.

Another incident that happened in class III, which got me a thrashing from my uncle Govindarajan, was when I accompanied my mother to her friend's house inappropriately dressed.

When I entered class IV, I started to learn to ride a bicycle and I succeeded in perfecting it in class V.

I was not a topper but an average student.

When I went to visit the school in 2015, I found residential apartments instead. On enquiring, I came to know that it had been shifted to another place.

I used to come home during the lunch break. In the evenings, light snacks like wheat appam or uppuma (wheat or rice) or murukku would be awaiting me. There was a famous confectionery shop in Palakkarai and my grandfather used to buy milk halwa and wheat halwa from there frequently.

Our favourite games involved marbles and tops. I slowly learnt to play football.

Where did you continue your education after completing class V?

Actually, my grandfather was contemplating admitting me to Ramakrishna Tapovanam situated in Tirupparaitturai, about 30 kilometres from Trichy.

Sri Ramakrishna Tapovanam, founded by Swamiji Chidbhavananda Maharaj in 1942, is an institution working for the educational, spiritual, moral and cultural advancement of the southern region of the Indian peninsula.

When my mother came to know about this, she told him, "Appa he is the only son I have and I do not want him to stay in a hostel." My grandfather did not wish to hurt my mother and did not propose the idea again. All of us were eagerly awaiting my results.

In the meantime, one of my classmates, Venkatesan, informed my grandfather that St. Joseph's College High School was issuing application forms for form I (Class VI). Grandfather requested him to get an application form. I wrote the entrance examination and was selected for admission. Unfortunately, Venkatesan could not get through and he joined E.R. High School. Now, my new school was 5 kilometres away from home. This was a drastic change from attending school just a stone's throw away.

New, big and reputed school, new surroundings and transportation to school made us all anxious at home.

Around Me

Let us go through the major events that took place around me during this period.

India

Politics

London Declaration, 1949 - India issued the London Declaration on April 28, 1949, enabling it (and, thereafter, any other nation) to remain in the British Commonwealth despite becoming a Republic, creating the position of 'Head of the Commonwealth' and renaming the organisation as the 'Commonwealth of Nations'.

Hanging of Gandhi's Assassins, 1949 - Nathuram Godse and Narayan Dattatraya Apte, Mahatma Gandhi's assassins, were executed by hanging on November 15, 1949, at Ambala Jail.

Constitution of India, 1950 - B.R. Ambedkar was the Chairman of the Drafting Committee of the Constitution of India which was adopted by the Constituent Assembly on November 26, 1949, and came into effect on January 26, 1950.

Sardar Patel's Role - Sardar Vallabhbhai Patel accomplished the task of bringing around 565 princely states, big and small, ruled by powerful sovereigns protected by treaties of alliance with the British Crown into the Indian Republic to integrate the country into one nation.

Recognition to PRC, 1949 - The government of India extended recognition to the People's Republic of China (PRC) in December, 1949. India became the first non-socialist country to establish diplomatic relations with the People's Republic of China in April 1950. K. M. Panikkar was appointed India's first Ambassador to China.

Reserve Bank Nationalized, 1949 - The Reserve Bank of India is the central banking institution, which controls the monetary policy of the Indian rupee. It commenced on April 1, 1935 during the British Rule in accordance with the provisions of the Reserve Bank of India Act, 1934. Following India's independence on August 15, 1947 the RBI was nationalized on January 1, 1949.

National Anthem, 1950 - *Jana Gana Mana,* the national anthem of India is the Hindi version of a song composed in Bengali by poet Rabindranath Tagore. It was adopted by the Constituent Assembly of India as the National Anthem on January 24, 1950.

India became a Republic, 1950 - India became a Republic on January 26, 1950 when the 34th and last Governor General of India, Chakravarti Rajagopalachari, read out a proclamation announcing the birth of the Republic of India.

First President of India, 1950 - The Constituent assembly elected Dr. Rajendra Prasad as the first President of the Indian Republic at a special session on January 24, 1950, in accordance with the Constitution. The new Republic was declared to be a "Union of States".

Union of States, 1950 - The constitution of 1950 distinguished between three main types of states: There were 9 states under part A, 8 under part B, 10 under part C and 1 under part D.

Indo - Nepal Treaty, 1950 - The India - Nepal Treaty (July 31, 1950) of Peace and Friendship, a bilateral treaty established a close strategic relationship between the two South Asian neighbours.

Death of Sardar Patel, 1950 - Sardar Vallabhbhai Patel, born on October 31, 1875, died on December 15, 1950 in Bombay. He was the Founding Father of the Republic of India.

Birth of Bharatiya Jana Sangh, 1951 - The Bharatiya Jana Sangh (BJS), commonly known as Jan Sangh, was a nationalist political party, started by Syama Prasad Mookerjee on October 21, 1951 in Delhi in collaboration with the Rashtriya Swayamsevak Sangh (RSS), as an alternative to the Indian National Congress.

First General Elections and First Prime Minister - Jawaharlal Nehru became the first Prime Minister of India after the first Indian general elections held from October 25, 1951 to February 21, 1952 to elect the first Lok Sabha. Indian National Congress (INC) won 384 out of 489 seats, Communist Party of India (CPI) 16 seats and Bharatiya Jana Sangh (BJS) 3 seats.

Backward Classes Commission, 1953 - Adhering to Article 340 of the Constitution of India, the First Backward Classes Commission was set up by a Presidential order on January 29, 1953 under the Chairmanship of Kaka Kalelkar to determine the criteria in considering other sections of the people in addition to the SC and

ST as socially and educationally backward classes and to prepare a list of such classes, setting out their approximate members and their territorial distribution.

War

Ceasefire in First Indo-Pak War, 1949 - A formal ceasefire was declared at 11.59 p.m. on the night of January 1, 1949 in the first Indo-Pakistan War which started from October 22, 1947 and continued for one year and two months.

The Karachi Agreement, 1949 - The Karachi Agreement was signed by the military representatives of India and Pakistan on July 25, 1949 under the supervision of the United Nations Commission to establish a cease-fire line in Kashmir following the Indo-Pakistani War.

The Liaquat–Nehru Pact or Delhi Pact, 1950 - The Liaquat–Nehru Pact was a bilateral treaty between India and Pakistan to guarantee the rights of minorities in both countries after the Partition of India and to avert another war between them. It was signed in New Delhi by Prime Ministers Jawaharlal Nehru and Liaquat Ali Khan on April 8, 1950.

Madras Province

Formation of Dravida Munnetra Kazhagam (DMK) Party, 1949 - Due to growing differences between Periyar and his followers, Annadurai, on September 17 (Periyar's date of birth), 1949 along with V.R. Nedunchezhiyan, K.A. Mathiazhagan, K. Anbazhagan, N.V. Natarajan, E.V.K. Sampath, and thousands of others announced the formation of the Dravida Munnetra Kazhagam (DMK) in Robinson Park, Royapuram, Madras. The name of the party Dravida Munnetra Kazhagam (DMK) was announced by Kudanthai Perunthagai K.K. Neelamegam.

First Assembly Elections, 1952 - The first Legislative Assembly elections were held in March 1952. The total number of seats were 375. INC won 152 seats, CPI won 62 seats and independents won 62 seats. No single party obtained simple majority to form an independent government.

First Chief Minister - Indian National Congress formed the government with support of few independents and

C. Rajagopalachari (Rajaji) of the Indian National Congress became the Chief Minister on April 10, 1952.

MGR Joins DMK, 1953 - In 1953, popular actor M. G. Ramachandran (MGR) joined the DMK and popularised the party flag and symbol by displaying them in his movies.

World

Politics

Crisis in Germany, 1948 - At the end of the Second World War, US, British, and Soviet military forces divided and occupied Germany. The United States, United Kingdom, and France controlled the western portions of the city, while Soviet troops controlled the eastern sector. The crisis started on June 24, 1948, when Soviet forces blockaded rail, road, and water access to Allied controlled areas of Berlin. The United States and United Kingdom responded by airlifting food and fuel to Berlin from Allied airbases in Western Germany. The crisis ended on May 12, 1949, when Soviet forces lifted the blockade.

The First Republic of Korea, 1948 - The First Republic of Korea was established on August 15, 1948, with Syngman Rhee as the first President. The 38th parallel was established as the boundary between Soviet and American occupation zones. It divided the Korean peninsula roughly in the middle. In 1948, this parallel became the boundary between the Democratic People's Republic of Korea (North Korea) and the Republic of Korea (South Korea).

Death of Muhammad Ali Jinnah, 1948 - Muhammad Ali Jinnah, the first Governor General of Pakistan died on September 11, 1948.

Apartheid in South Africa - The system of racial segregation in South Africa known as apartheid was implemented and enforced by a large number of laws. This legislation served to institutionalise racial discrimination and dominance by white people over other races. This legislation was enacted after the election of the National Party government in 1948.

Harry S. Truman as US President, 1949 - Truman continued as President of US for the second term from January 20, 1949.

Formation of West and East Germany, 1949 - On May 23, 1949 the West German Parliamentary Council met and declared the establishment of the Federal Republic of Germany, partly occupied by the French, British, and Americans. The Soviets reacted adversely by announcing the establishment of the German Democratic Republic (East Germany) in October 1949. These actions in 1949 marked the end of any talk of a reunified Germany.

Birth of PRC, 1949 - On October 1, 1949, after a near complete victory by the Communist Party of China (CPC) in the Chinese Civil War, Mao Zedong proclaimed the People's Republic of China (PRC) from atop the Tiananmen monument. Mao Zedong became the first President and Zhou Enlai the first Prime minister on October 1, 1949.

Indonesia's Independence, 1949 - The Indonesian National Revolution involving armed conflict and diplomatic struggle between Indonesia and the Dutch Empire, along with international pressure, made Netherlands recognise Indonesian independence on December 29, 1949.

Colombo Plan, 1950 - The Colombo Plan was born in the Commonwealth Conference of Foreign Ministers, held in Colombo, Sri Lanka, in January 1950. The objective was to promote international cooperation efforts to raise the standards of people in the region. It has grown from a group of seven Commonwealth of Nations - Australia, Britain, Canada, Ceylon, India, New Zealand and Pakistan - into an international governmental organisation of 27, including non-Commonwealth countries.

Twenty Second Amendment in USA, 1951 - The Twenty-Second Amendment of the United States Constitution set a term limit (two) for election and overall term of service to the office of President of the United States. It was proposed on March 24, 1947 and ratified on February 27, 1951.

China-Tibet Agreement, 1951 - The delegates of the 14th Dalai Lama, Sovereign of the State of Tibet, reached an agreement in 1951 with the Central People's Government of the newly established PRC on upholding Chinese sovereignty over Tibet.

Churchill becoming Prime Minister of UK, (1951) - Churchill became Prime Minister of UK on October 26, 1951 for the second time after Clement Attlee.

Assassination of Liaquat Ali, 1951 - Nawabzada Liaquat Ali Khan, the first Prime Minister of Pakistan was assassinated by a hired assassin, Sa'ad Babrak, on October 16, 1951.

Detonation of Hydrogen Bomb, 1952 - The United States detonated the world's first thermonuclear weapon, the hydrogen bomb, on Eniwetok atoll in the Pacific on November 1, 1952.

Dwight D. Eisenhower became US President, 1953 - Eisenhower of the Republican Party, became the 34th President of USA on January 20, 1953 after Harry S. Truman.

Death of Stalin, 1953 - Joseph Stalin died on March 5, 1953 after a cerebral haemorrhage. Georgy Malenkov became the Chairman of the Council of Ministers (Premier) on March 5, 1953.

Ascent of Mount Everest, 1953 - Sir Edmund Percival Hillary was a New Zealand mountaineer, explorer and philanthropist. On May 29, 1953, Hillary and Nepalese Sherpa mountaineer Tenzing Norgay became the first climbers to reach the summit of Mount Everest.

War

Arab-Israeli War, 1948 - The 1948 Arab-Israeli War or the First Arab–Israeli War was fought from May 15, 1948 between the State of Israel and a military coalition of Arab states after the Israeli Declaration of Independence.

The Korean War, 1950 - The Korean War was between North and South Korea, in which a United Nations force led by USA fought for the South, and China fought for the North, assisted by the Soviet Union. The conflict regarding the boundary escalated into open warfare when North Korean forces supported by the Soviet Union and China invaded South Korea on June 25, 1950.

CHAPTER 3

High School Life - June 1953 to June 1959

ABSTRACT

Me

The details of my education at St. Joseph's College High school, Trichy from June, 1953 to June, 1959 are presented.

Around Me

In India, the major events were the birth of Indian Airlines (1953), birth of Andhra Pradesh state (1953), formation of States Reorganisation Commission (1953), annexation of Dadra and Nagar Haveli from Portuguese (1954), agreement between India and China on Tibet (1954), Zhou Enlai's first visit to India, trade agreement between India and China, Nehru's visit to China (1954), birth of the State Bank of India (1955), passing of the Bill and list of reorganised States (1956), second Indian general elections, Nehru continuing as Prime Minister, Rajendra Prasad continuing as President (1957), first Communist government in Kerala (1957), Zhou Enlai's visit to India and Vice President Radhakrishnan's visit to China (1957).

    In Madras State, the major events were Kamaraj replacing Rajagopalachari as Chief Minister (1954), Ariyalur train accident and resignation of Railway Minister Lal Bahadur Shastri (1956), resignation of C. Rajagopalachari (1957), second Assembly elections (1957), Kamaraj continuing as Chief Minister (1957), launching of Neyveli Lignite Corporation Ltd (1958) and initiation of Swatantra Party by Rajagopalachari (1959).

    In the World, the major events were birth of the Republic of Egypt (1953), Korean Armistice Agreement (1953), detonation of Hydrogen bomb by Soviet Union (1953), "Atoms for Peace" talk by Eisenhower (1953), Nikita Khrushchev becoming General Secretary, USSR (1953), nuclear powered submarine (1954), Geneva Conference (1954), sovereignty to East Germany (1954), resignation of Churchill as Prime Minister (1955), sovereignty to West Germany (1955), Nasser becoming President of Egypt (1955), Anthony Eden as Prime Minister of UK (1955), Asian-African meet (1955), Morocco's independence (1956), Suez Canal Crisis (1956-57), Macmillan becoming Prime Minister of England (1957), launching of Sputnik I (1957), Eisenhower continuing as US President (1957), launching of Explorer I (1958), Khrushchev becoming Premier of Soviet Union (1958), De Gaulle becoming President of France (1959), Fidel Castro becoming Prime Minister of Cuba (1959), Dalai Lama's asylum in India (1959) and Liu Shaoqui becoming Chairman of China (1959).

Me

How did you like your new school?

I was very nervous on the first day. My grandfather took me to school and walked me to my classroom.

St. Joseph Boys Higher Secondary School, Tiruchirappalli has been run by the Society of Jesus since 1862 in the campus of St. Joseph's college, Tiruchirappalli.

St. Joseph's College High School was very big compared to my elementary school. The main building was very long and had three floors. The playgrounds were very big. There were probably about one thousand students from Form I (standard VI) to Form VI (standard XI). Each form had at least four sections.

Definitely, I liked my school which was among the top schools not only in Trichy but also in Madras state.

What was the medium of instruction?

It was a Tamil medium school.

Can you please talk about the academic aspects of your high school education?

It took some time for me to adjust to the new environment, new teachers and new classmates.

Forms I, II and III were common to all of us. But Forms IV, V, and VI had three streams out of which a student could choose any one stream. One was general and the other two were called bifurcated streams.

Bifurcated streams

The state board, in addition to the general stream, introduced two bifurcated streams from Form IV to Form VI. If a student was not interested in these two streams, he/she could choose the general stream. One stream was Engineering and the other, Commerce. The idea behind this was to help students choose their future career. I took the Engineering stream since my mother wanted me to become an engineer. I have never studied biology. The General stream included subjects like Physics, Chemistry and Biology.

I had first language (Tamil), second language (English), Mathematics, Social Studies, Engineering paper I (General science and Drawing) and Engineering paper II (Applied science and practical).

My final practical examination in Form VI was for seven hours at a stretch. We had a break for 30 minutes to have lunch in the laboratory itself. My practical examination included electrical circuits, plumbing, fitting, smithy and welding.

How about your teachers?

All the teachers were very good. I cannot forget Vedamuthu Sir who taught me English and Social Studies. He was known as "boxer" among the students as he would box us whenever we made any mistake or could not answer a question. He would throw the duster and chalk on us if questions on maps were not answered. But all of us liked him. Another person whom I cannot forget is the Headmaster, Fr. Thambi, who was very strict but at the same time very kind. Another person who played an important role was the new Headmaster, Fr. Maruthanayagam, who helped me secure Pre-University Course admission.

Did you go for any school trips?

In Form IV we went on a local tour to see Rock Fort and Srirangam. I was afraid to walk on the Cauvery Bridge because it had wooden sleepers with gaps and I could see the water in the river below me. I had vertigo then itself. During Form V, we went to Coimbatore for three days. We stayed in St. Michael's High School.

What about your transport and lunch arrangements?

I went to school by train. I boarded at Palakkarai Station and got off at the ensuing Fort Station. The journey was enjoyable even though it only lasted 5 to 10 minutes. Some students used to board and de-board while the train was still in motion. It was a thrill for them. I cannot forget how one student lost his leg due to this. Sometimes when there was no train service, we had to walk along the railway track. In those days, the train had to cross two manually operated railway gates, one in Palakkarai and other in Tennur. Now, over-bridges have been constructed to bypass them.

My lunch was brought by a lady from home in a tiffin carrier. In those days, many women took lunch boxes and tiffin carriers in bamboo baskets to schools and offices. Each lady would cater to about 10 people so that she could earn her living. Some of them used to sell the uneaten food to the needy and hungry people. During Forms V and VI, my grandfather was posted as Postmaster in the Teppakkulam Post Office which was close to my school. Lunch would be brought to the post office for my grandfather and me, and two of his colleagues would join us as well. They used to share non-vegetarian food with me since I relished it a lot. This was something I really enjoyed. My grandfather was a vegetarian.

Did you become ill at any time?

Yes. I cannot forget two things.

In Form III, during the annual examination I got fever brought on by a blister in the right foot by an ill-fitting slipper. My uncle, Padmanaban, took me to school in a rickshaw to inform the Headmaster, Fr. Thambi, and apply for leave. But the Headmaster called the attender and asked him to carry me to the examination hall on the third floor. I tried to attempt the examination but could not go through with it and after attending school the whole day my friend, Hasheem, took me home in a rickshaw. My fever increased and I also started suffering from nausea. I was so tired and weak that I collapsed on my grandfather's bed. My mother came from school and was shocked to see me with a high fever of 104 degrees. Immediately, my mother went to my uncle Govindarajan, an MBBS student who was studying in the room upstairs and asked him to do something for me. He came down and gave me an injection. I was delirious the whole night and though I gradually began to feel better, I could not write the examination the next day.

During the annual holidays of Form IV, when I was 14 years, I went to our village with some of my relatives. A small girl of about six or seven years, Karuna, was also with us. I was carrying her in my arms and playing with her. I did not know she had serangu (impetigo). When I reached Trichy, I got a bout of serangu which was restricted to my unexposed body parts. I was shy and did not tell anyone about it. It became very unbearable and I had to tell my mother. Immediately she took me to Kerala Warrier. With diet control and medicines, I was completely cured.

What would you like to forget?

A few things.

In Form IV, I was riding a bicycle and when I saw a police man, I got down and started pushing the bicycle because I did not have a flashlight. In those days, every bicycle had to have a light. The police man booked a case against me and the next day I had to go to a court and pay a small fine.

In Form VI, the last year of school an unfortunate event occurred. Without informing anyone in the house, I went to see a Tamil movie "Annaiyin Anai". My mother's colleague saw me in the theatre and informed my mother. That evening my mother slapped me in the kitchen and asked me not to repeat the act again.

On another occasion, I had to buy a cigarette for my uncle Padmanaban and had to tell the truth when caught by my grandfather. My uncle was reprimanded by my grandfather and so he sarcastically commented that I was Harishchandra who never uttered a lie in my life.

Did any incident occur which surprised you?

During my final year, my grandfather and I were alone in the house and I asked my grandfather's permission to go to a Tamil movie "Nadodi Mannan". That day was my 15th Birthday in 1958. To my surprise he gave me permission and money. Why the surprise? Because he never watched movies and he didn't like others doing so. I went to Wellington theatre but I could not get a ticket. More than me, my grandfather was disappointed that I could not watch the movie.

What are the things you would like to cherish?

Uncle Govindarajan's Visit to Singapore

My uncle Govindarajan did his MA in Presidency College, Madras and completed his MBBS from Madras Medical College, Madras in the year 1957. He was the first doctor in our community. Later, he went to Singapore to work as a doctor for a year in January, 1957. My sister and I went to Madras with my mother to send him off by ship. We stayed at my mother's close friend Baby aunt's house. It was my first trip to Madras and we were delighted to see the Marina Beach, the Zoo and of course the harbour with so many ships. Baby aunty and uncle were surprised to see my sister and me fighting. My grandfather did not come because he did not like send offs.

Uncle Govindarajan's Return from Singapore

When Govindarajan returned from Singapore, he brought us our first radio (National Ekco) and our first table fan (TDK) which thrilled my sister and me.

Uncle Govindarajan's Marriage

Before Govindarajan could return, my mother wanted to select a bride for him. She started her search and selected Mangayarkarasi, who was the eldest daughter of Lakshmana Moopanar, a school teacher in Ombalapadi, Kabistalam village. My mother sent my sister and me to gather first-hand information about the family and the girl. After preliminary talks between the two families, Govindarajan and Mangayarkarasi got engaged and the wedding was solemnised on February 10, 1958 in Trichy.

To accommodate the new couple, my grandfather took another house close by where my uncle Padmanaban, my grandfather Hari, our cook Ramasamy and I would sleep at night and do the daily chores in the morning.

Since Savithri, our cook, went back to her village to get married, we brought Ramasamy from another village. He was a very good cook and whenever he prepared masala dosa or poori or some other favourite of mine, he would inform me earlier so that I could eat hot tasty food. I used to eat about 10 dosas or 12 pooris. While getting ready for bed, he would tell stories.

Playing with My Friends

During the holidays, I would go to Mohammed Ali's house which had a lot of open space. We would continue to play even after 1.00 p.m., without caring about lunch. My sister would come and say, "Anna, come home soon. They are waiting for you. You will get a nice thrashing." I would run back to the house before her. On seeing everyone sitting and eating in the hall, I would swiftly cross them and sit near the kitchen to have my lunch. Nobody would say anything.

My notable friends were Hasheem, Thamba, Venkatesan, Jagannathan, Sherfuddin, Mohammed Ali, Aslam and Nagaraj. Aslam would make everyone laugh with his conversations and mannerisms. One day, after talking to him I came home at 6.30 p.m., which was very late and my uncle Govindarajan became very angry and slapped me.

Summer Holidays

During the Summer holidays, I used to go to Kabistalam village to stay with Savithri akka's parents and brothers. Savithri Akka's father had a small eatery that sold idlis. Her mother would make idlis and chutney. Her younger brother, Ramalingam, would carry them to the shop. The Idli and chutney were very tasty. We used to bathe in the well and sleep in the front veranda (Thinnai). No fan was needed and there was no worry of mosquitos.

Preparations for Uncle Padmanaban's Marriage

After my board exam in form VI, I was waiting for my result.

In the meantime, my mother was planning my uncle Padmanaban's marriage. After seeing three or four girls she chose Shantha, daughter of a Zamindar in Kabistalam village, as the bride. As usual, my mother sent my sister and me to their house. The family liked both of us and asked us to stay for two days. In those two days, Shantha's elder brother Anantha Padmanaban, who was a very reserved man, surprised his family by two acts. When we were playing shuttle cock, my toe got injured and he personally nursed it. Also, he went and brought Viral fish from their pond especially for us. After preliminary talks the marriage was fixed for September, 1959.

Change of House

My mother searched for a bigger house and to our luck we got a very big house in Salai Road, Woriyur, which was 4 kilometres from the present house. By the last week of June, we shifted to the new house, vacating the house which I had lived in for 15 years. I was happy to go to a new big house but was very sad to leave all my friends

My result came and I passed, scoring an average of 61%.

What was your plan for higher studies?

My grandfather wanted to put me in a three-year diploma programme offered by a polytechnic institute.

He said to my mother, "See, Dharma, can I get an application form for admitting Kittu in a polytechnic which requires only 3 years of study? He can study in Trichy itself and the expenses would be manageable."

But my mother wanted me to study in a five-year degree programme and become an engineer.

So, she said, "Appa, I want him to become an engineer."

"But Dharma it will be very expensive. He has to do one year Pre-University here in Trichy and 5 years in an engineering college while staying in a hostel. Where would we go for money?"

As they were talking, my mother started to sob and my uncle Govindarajan heard her and came to her and asked, "What is the problem Akka?"

My grandfather explained the whole problem and my uncle immediately said, "Akka, don't worry, if he studies well and gets a seat in an engineering college, I will pay all the expenses for his education."

My uncle was just starting his career and family life and he had no savings to back him. My mother was very happy and quite relieved as though I had already become an engineer. My grandfather got an application form for admission in the Pre- University Course in St. Joseph's College, Trichy.

When I went to submit the form, I faced a new problem.

What was the problem?

Fr. Erhart, Principal, St. Joseph's college refused to accept my application saying that all those who took engineering bifurcated stream should go for 3-year diploma programme in polytechnic directly and not apply for 1 year Pre - University programme. All of us, who took the engineering bifurcated scheme were highly disappointed and ran to the Headmaster, Fr. Maruthanayagam, of our school which was in the same campus. We requested him to intervene in the matter and help us. He asked us for a days' time. I could not sleep that night wondering what would happen.

Next day, I reached the school with a worried and anxious face and stood outside the headmaster's room along with my other classmates. Within a short time, the headmaster came out and said that we could go and submit our forms. We did not wait to say thanks; we just ran off to the college and submitted our forms.

The list of admitted students was displayed on the same day and I was very happy to see my name on it.

So, God saved you from two problems - Financial and Admission.

Yes.

What were your feelings when you had to go to college and study in an English medium course?

Well. In those days, we were living within four walls and there was less awareness about many things. But, I was not nervous about the college because I had already studied in that campus for 6 years. I was not worried about English medium of instruction because I was good in English.

Around Me

Let us go through the major events that took place around me during this period.

India

Politics

Founding of Indian Airlines, 1953 - Indian Airlines Corporation was established from June 15, 1953 to cover domestic routes and several International services to neighbouring countries in Asia. Eight pre-Independence domestic airlines were merged to form the new domestic National carrier, Indian Airlines Corporation.

Creation of Andhra State, 1953 - Andhra state was created on October 1, 1953 from the Telugu speaking districts of Madras, with its capital at Kurnool as a result of deterioration of law and order after the death of Potti Sriramulu, who went on a hunger strike from October 10, 1952.

Annexation of Dadra and Nagar Haveli from the Portuguese, 1954 -The Indian Annexation of Dadra and Nagar Haveli was the conflict in which the territories of Dadra and Nagar Haveli passed from Portuguese rule to Indian Union rule on August 11, 1954. The territories were subsequently merged into the Indian Union in 1961.

China-India Relationship, 1954 - On April 29, 1954, India and China signed an eight-year agreement on Tibet based on Five Principles of Peaceful Coexistence or Panchsheel. In June 1954, Zhou Enlai, after attending a meeting in Geneva, visited New Delhi for the first time and an official banquet was arranged for him. It was during this visit that the Panchsheel agreement was formulated. The governments of the Republic of India and China reached an agreement for trade on October 14, 1954 on the basis of equality and mutual benefit. In October 1954, Jawaharlal Nehru visited China with his daughter Indira Gandhi. Premier Zhou Enlai visited India in January, 1957 and received an honorary doctorate from Calcutta University. Indian Vice President Dr. S. Radhakrishnan visited China in September 1957. The popular catch phrase of India's diplomacy with China in the 1950's was *Hindi-Chini bhai-bhai* (Indians and Chinese are brothers).

Formation of SBI, 1955 - The Imperial Bank of India, the oldest and the largest commercial bank was transformed into the State Bank of India (SBI) on April 30, 1955.

Reorganisation of States, 1956 - Based on the States Reorganisation Commission report, the states of Andhra Pradesh, Kerala and Mysore were created on November 1, 1956.

Second General Elections, 1957 - Jawaharlal Nehru continued as the Prime Minister after the second general elections were held from February 24 to March 14, 1957 to elect the second Lok Sabha. Out of 494 seats, INC secured 371, BJS 4, CPI 27 and independents 41. Rajendra Prasad continued as President for a second term.

First Communist Government in India, 1957 - Communist Party of India won the elections in Kerala in 1957 and E. M. S. Namboodiripad became the first Chief Minister.

Madras State

Kamaraj as Chief Minister, 1954 - In 1953, Rajagopalachari introduced a new education scheme known as the "Modified System of Elementary Education". According to this scheme students would spend three hours in school and learn their family vocation the rest of the time. It conveyed that every child should follow the family vocation and not aspire for other professions. The plan received sharp criticism and aroused strong protests from Dravidian parties. The rising unpopularity of his government forced K. Kamaraj to withdraw his support for Rajagopalachari who resigned as Chief Minister on April 13, 1954, citing poor health, and Kamaraj was sworn in as Chief Minister on April 13, 1954.

Train Accident in Ariyalur, 1956 - The Tuticorin (Thoothukudi) Express slipped off the rails at about 5.30 a.m., on November 23, 1956, while crossing the Maruthaiyar Bridge, which was submerged due to floods in the river, at about 3 kilometres from Ariyalur Station and about 50 kilometres from Trichy. The accident left 142 passengers dead, 110 injured, an estimated 200 people buried in the debris and many missing, their bodies never to be recovered. Lal Bahadur Shastri, who was the Minister of Railways and Transport in the Central Cabinet, resigned accepting moral and constitutional responsibility for the accident. Nehru stated that he was accepting the resignation because it would set an example in constitutional politeness and not because Shastri was in any way responsible for the accident.

Launching of Neyveli Lignite Corporation Limited (NLC), 1956 - Neyveli Lignite Corporation Limited (NLC) was formed as a Corporate Body in 1956 in Neyveli town, Cuddalore, Tamil Nadu. It is a government-owned lignite mining and power generating company administered through Ministry of Coal. The presence of lignite in the area was discovered by C. Jambulingam Mudaliar when he dug a bore well in his land for irrigation. He donated his land to the government free of cost so that it could be used for power generation and benefit the people.

Resignation of Rajagopalachari, 1957 - Rajagopalachari resigned from the Indian National Congress and along with other dissidents, formed a new party known as the Indian National Democratic Congress in Madurai on September 28–29, 1957.

Second Assembly Elections, 1957 - Kamaraj continued as Chief Minister after the 1957 elections. The second Legislative Assembly elections were held on March 31, 1957, the first after the linguistic reorganisation of Madras state in 1954. The Indian National Congress and its leader K. Kamaraj won the election, and defeated Dravida Munnetra Kazhagam. This election saw future DMK leaders, M. Karunanidhi and K. Anbazhagan winning their first MLA seats. INC won 151 seats, independents including DMK (13) 41, Congress Reforms Committee 9 and CPI 4. The Total number of seats were 205.

Birth of Swatantra Party, 1959 - On June 4, 1959, after the Nagpur session of the Indian National Democratic Congress, Rajagopalachari, announced the formation of the new Swatantra Party as a right-wing alternative to the Congress.

World

Politics

Egypt became a Republic, 1953 - Egypt was declared a Republic on June 18, 1953, with Muhammad Naguib as Egypt's first President.

Nikita Khrushchev, General Secretary, Communist Party of Soviet, 1953 - Nikita Khrushchev became the General Secretary, Communist Party of Soviet Union on September 7, 1953 after Joseph Stalin.

Sovereignty of East and West Germany, 1954–1955 - Sovereignty of East Germany was granted by the Soviet Union on March 23, 1954 and that of West Germany was granted by France, the United Kingdom, and the United States on May 5, 1955.

Asian-African Meet, 1955 - The first large scale Asian-African Meet was a convention of mostly newly independent Asian and African states, from April 18–24, 1955 in Bandung, Indonesia. It was attended by representatives of twenty-nine countries. The aims were to promote Afro-Asian economic and cultural cooperation and to oppose colonialism or neo-colonialism by any nation. The conference was an important step toward the Non-Aligned Movement.

Retirement of Churchill, 1955 - Sir Winston Leonard Spencer Churchill, the British leader who guided Great Britain and the Allies through the crisis of World War II, retired as Prime Minister of Great Britain on April 5, 1955.

Sir Anthony Eden, Prime Minister of UK, 1955 - Sir Anthony Eden became the Prime Minister of UK on April 6, 1955 after Churchill.

Nasser became President of Egypt, 1956 - Gamal Abdel Nasser Hussein was elected as the second President of Egypt on June 23, 1956.

Suez Canal Crisis, 1956–57 - Due to differences in the agreement between UK and Egypt in Suez Canal and the conflict with Israel, Nasser unilaterally announced the nationalisation and closure of the Suez Canal on July 26, 1956. It would be a great loss for UK, France and Israel if the trade was not permitted. They hatched a plan to attack and invade Egypt. After the Israeli attack began on October 29, 1956, Britain and France issued an ultimatum calling for an end to hostilities. Despite a withdrawal of Egyptian forces, the Anglo-French invasion commenced. Nasser requested diplomatic assistance from the US on November 1, 1956. The emergency special session of the UN was convened on the same day and it called for an immediate ceasefire. By April 24, 1957 the canal was fully reopened to shipping.

Independence of Morocco, 1956 - Morocco gained independence in 1956 after more than 40 years as a French protectorate (though Spain had controlled the northern third of the country as well as the Western Sahara).

Harold Macmillan as Prime Minister of England, 1957 - Harold Macmillon became the Prime Minister of England on January 10, 1957 after Sir Anthony Eden.

D. Eisenhower, President of US, 1957 - D. Eisenhower continued as President of US for the second time from January 20, 1957.

Emergence of Khrushchev, 1958 - Nikita Sergeyevich Khrushchev became the Chairman of the Council of Ministers, or Premier, Soviet Union on March 27, 1958.

Emergence of De Gaulle, 1959 - Charles André Joseph Marie de Gaulle, a French General, writer and statesman founded the Fifth Republic and was elected as the 18th President of France on January 8, 1959.

Emergence of Fidel Castro, 1959 - The Cuban communist revolutionary and politician Fidel Castro took part in the Cuban Revolution from 1953 to 1959. On February 16, 1959, Fidel Castro was sworn in as Prime Minister of Cuba after leading a guerrilla campaign that forced right-wing dictator Fulgencio Batista into exile.

Asylum to Dalai Lama, 1959 - The spiritual leader of Tibet, the Dalai Lama, crossed the border at the Khenzimana Pass into

India after an epic 15-day journey on foot from the Tibetan capital, Lhasa, over the Himalayan mountains. He was offered asylum in India and settled in Dharamsala in northern India.

Liu Shaoqui, Chairman, Central Committee, Communist Party of China, 1959 - Liu Shaoqui became Chairman of the Central Committee of the Communist Party of China after Mao Zedong on April 27, 1959.

War

The Korean Armistice Agreement, 1953 - The Agreement signed on July 27, 1953, ended the Korean War.

Detonation of First Hydrogen Bomb by Soviet Union, 1953 - The detonation of the first hydrogen bomb by the Soviet Union on August 12, 1953 at the Semipalatinsk test site, Kazakhstan steppe, allowed them to draw even in the arms race.

Speech by Eisenhower on Atoms, 1953 - President Dwight D. Eisenhower delivered the "Atoms for Peace" speech to the UN General Assembly, New York City on December 8, 1953.

First Nuclear-Powered Submarine, 1954 - USS Nautilus (SSN-571) was the world's first nuclear-powered submarine, launched on January 21, 1954.

The Geneva Conference, 1954 - This produced a peace treaty and left Vietnam divided with Ho Chi Minh's Communist government ruling the North from Hanoi and Ngo Dinh Diem's regime, supported by US, ruling the South from Saigon (later Ho Chi Minh City).

Space Technology

Sputnik 1, 1957 - The Soviet Union launched Sputnik 1, the first artificial earth satellite into an elliptical low Earth orbit on October 4, 1957 during the International Geophysical Year. Sputnik provided scientists with valuable information, even though it was not equipped with scientific instruments.

Explorer I, 1958 - Satellite 1958 Alpha was the first United States earth satellite, launched for the International Geophysical Year 1957-1958 on January 31, 1958 by the Jupiter-C vehicle. The discovery of the Van Allen Belts by the Explorer satellites was considered to be outstanding.

CHAPTER 4

College Life - July 1959 to July 1967

Abstract

Me

Details of my eight years of college education and my sister's marriage are presented.

Around Me

In India, the major events were birth of Maharashtra and Gujarat states (1960), annexation of Goa, Diu and Daman (1961), third Indian general elections (1962), Nehru continuing as Prime Minister (1962), conversion to Metric system (1962), Radhakrishnan becoming President (1962), Sino-Indian War (1962), Kamaraj becoming President of INC (1963), Nehru's death (1964), Nanda becoming interim Prime Minister (1964), Shastri becoming Prime Minister (1964), birth of Vishva Hindu Parishad (1964), Indo-Pak War (1965), Tashkent Agreement and death of Shastri (1966), Nanda as interim Prime Minister (1966), Indira Gandhi becoming Prime Minister (1966), birth of Shiv Sena (1966), birth of Haryana state (1966), Mihir Sen's world record (1966), Reita Faria becoming Miss World (1966), fourth general elections (1967), Indira Gandhi continuing as Prime Minister (1967), Zakir Hussain becoming President (1967) and Naxalite uprisings (1967).

In Madras state, the major events were third Assembly elections (1962), Kamaraj continuing as Chief Minister (1962), introduction of Noon Meal Scheme (1962), voluntary resignation of Kamaraj (1963), Baktavatsalam becoming Chief Minister (1963), anti-Hindi agitations (1965), establishment of Madurai University (1966), fourth Assembly elections (1967), DMK coming to power (1967) and Annadurai becoming Chief Minister (1967).

In the World, the major events were arrival of Beatles (1960), American U-2 spy plane incident (1960), Brezhnev becoming Chairman, Supreme Soviet (1960), collapse of Four Power Summit (1960), Kennedy becoming President of USA (1961), Yuri Gagarin, first man in space (1961), Bay of Pigs Invasion (1961), erection of Berlin Wall (1961), Hydrogen bomb testing by USSR (1961), John Glenn, first American in space (1962), Cuban Missile Crisis (1962), Nuclear Test Ban Treaty (1963), hotline between Washington and Moscow (1963), assassination of Kennedy (1963), Johnson becoming President of USA (1963), Alec Douglas becoming England's Prime Minister (1963), Brezhnev becoming General Secretary of USSR (1964), Alexie Kosygin becoming Premier of USSR (1964), Harold Wilson becoming England's Prime Minister (1964), Independence of Singapore (1965), first spacecraft to orbit the moon (1966), death of 3 astronauts (1967) and Arab-Israeli War (1967).

Me

Tell me about your college education.

I went through eight years of college education during which time I finished a one-year Pre-University Course, required for pursuing any degree programme, a five-year Bachelor of Engineering programme in Civil Engineering and a two-year Master of Engineering programme in Hydraulics and Hydraulic Structures.

Pre-University Course (PUC) - July 1959 to June 60

I joined Pre-University Course (PUC) in July, 1959 at St. Joseph's college Trichy, the Alma Mater of great personalities like Dr. Abdul Kalam. It is one of the best colleges in South India even now.

St. Joseph's College, Tiruchirappalli in Tamil Nadu, India, was established in 1844 by the Society of Jesus (Jesuits) in Nagapattinam, Tamil Nadu. It was affiliated to University of Madras in 1866. It was transferred to Tiruchirappalli in 1869. It is currently an affiliated First Grade College of Bharathidasan University. It was awarded Heritage College status, along with 12 other colleges, by the Government of India in 2016.

I took up Mathematics, Physics, Chemistry, Economics, and Logic, along with English and Tamil as languages. There were 6 sections which had around 600 students. Fr. Erhart was the Principal. He was an authoritarian and students were in awe of him. It took some time for me to settle into academics since I had changed from Tamil to English medium. The new house which we moved to was in Salai Road, Woriyur and it was 2 kilometres from my college. I used to go to college by bicycle or on foot. We wrote our examinations and English compositions in Lawley Hall which could accommodate nearly 600 students. We used to write in "pin-drop silence". I can still remember Banumoorthy, our English teacher and Asirvatham, our Economics teacher.

In the quarterly, half yearly and revision examinations I scored very well and was among the top 15 students. I used to get up every day at 5.30 a.m., and study. I put in a lot of hard work to score well in the final examination and get admission into engineering college.

I attempted the Pre-University examination very well and expected to pass with first class but I was very much disappointed when the results came. In those days results were announced in the newspapers in both the evening and morning editions. My uncle Padmanaban went to buy an evening edition but came back around 11 p.m. By that time, I was in bed half asleep. As he entered the house, I could hear him say, "What is this? Kittu got only second class." I had no inclination to get up and see the paper. Even though I could not sleep, I pretended to be asleep but was crying under the bedsheet. I did not get up even when the clock struck 7.00 a.m., the next morning. My grandfather was telling the others, "See, he is not interested in his result." I got up reluctantly and when they informed me about the result I did not show any expression. No one scolded me, instead all consoled me.

If I had received Ist class in PUC it would have been easier to get admission to engineering even though the selection was also based on interview marks. We all had our fingers crossed because of my result. My admission into engineering college was in jeopardy.

Padmanaban Uncle's Marriage

My uncle Padmanaban got married on September 14, 1959 to Shantha. My mother chose a bride for uncle Govindarajan from a middle-class family but for uncle Padmanaban she chose a rich family. The logic behind this was Govindarajan was a doctor and could earn well and he was prudent. Padmanaban was a lawyer and in those days, it was believed that lawyers could not earn well. Padmanaban was also known for spending money lavishly. So, it was wise to choose a girl with an inheritance.

My sister and I played a key role in their marriage. I was 16 and my sister was 14.

Shantha's father, Nagaraja Moopanar, was a well-known landlord in Kabistalam village, Thanjavur district. His brother, Govindasamy Moopanar was also a landlord in that area. His son was G. K. Moopanar a well-respected political figure. Shantha had two older brothers and a younger sister. Shantha's mother Ammani Ammal was from Kerala and the second wife of Nagaraja Moopanar. Their house was palatial and no women could enter through the front door. After Nagaraja's death, Shantha's elder brother, Raja Anantha Padmanaban took over the management of the property and the house. Shantha and her sister Sarasu got married on the same day.

I could not attend the marriage as I had my PUC quarterly examination. I stayed back with my paternal grandfather, Hari Thatha. As mentioned earlier, he was afflicted with a mental disorder. He spent time applying for job positions. He said that he did not know money-magic otherwise he would have a lot of money. Only now I have understood the meaning of money-magic. I had to buy food for both of us from a nearby restaurant as neither of us knew how to cook.

Bachelor of Engineering (B.E.) Degree Programme – July, 1960 to January, 1965

About Engineering Programme

From the academic year 1959, the duration of the engineering programme was changed to 5 years since the 2-year Pre-Degree intermediate programme was reduced to 1 year Pre-University Course and it was called an integrated programme. It had an annual pattern of examinations conducted at the end of each academic year. Only certain courses had sessional (internal) component. Grades were given instead of marks. H was 100%, D plus 85% to 99%, D 75% to 84%, A plus 65% to 74%, A 60% to 64%, B plus 55% to 59%, B 50% to 54%, C plus 45% to 49%, C 40% to 44% and F denoted failure that is less than 40%. The first two years were devoted to basic science and foundation courses like Mathematics, Physics, Chemistry,

English and Engineering Arts and Science. The next three years were devoted to courses of engineering branches like Civil, Mechanical and Electrical.

There were six engineering colleges in the Madras state.

Engineering Admission - July 1960

We had to give three choices of engineering colleges in the application form. Since my grandfather wanted me to study in the College of Engineering, Guindy, Chennai, which was and is one of the oldest and the best technical institutions, I gave it as first choice, even though my mother wanted Alagappa Chettiar College of Engineering, Karaikudi as first choice which was nearer to my native town Trichy.

After submitting the form, we waited for the interview call. When the call for interview was received, my grandfather was contemplating whether to seek any recommendation. He came to know that one of the committee members, Dr. Panchanathan, in the interview panel was the son of his colleague in the postal department. My uncles and he decided to put in a word to favour my interview. My aunty Shantha was pregnant at that time. Combining her checkup and my interview, my grandfather, my uncles, my aunty and I came to Madras three days earlier and stayed at a friend's house. Next day they asked me to go to the venue of the interview and enquire about the procedure from participants. It was my first time venturing alone in a big city like Madras and somehow, I completed the task. On the same day, my grandfather went to meet Dr. Panchanathan. After hearing about my credentials, Dr. Panchanathan told my grandfather "Sir, your grandson has to perform well in the interview which alone will ensure a seat. All the best." In the evening Dr. Govindarajan conducted a mock interview and I did not perform up to his expectation. When he started scolding me, Padmanaban intervened and said that I would be fine at the interview. Next day I performed very well because the pattern of questions was similar for all the students. There were four members in the interview panel and each of them interviewed and evaluated the candidates separately. After the interview, the selected students list was released and we were all happy to find my name against the College of Engineering, Guindy.

College of Engineering, Guindy a public Engineering College in Chennai (formerly Madras), India, is one of the oldest technical institution. Founded in 1794, this college is a perfect example of an esteemed British Indian Educational Institution. Its architecture in white cut stone, red sandstone and brick is not matched by any other structures and sets this bicentennial college apart. Now it is under Anna University.

Chennai *(formerly Madras) is the capital of the Indian state of Tamil Nadu. Located on the Coromandel Coast off the Bay of Bengal, it is one of the biggest cultural, economic and educational centres in South India. From the early ages, Chennai had a cosmopolitan society. It has various famous temples, churches and mosques. The Chennai Metropolitan Area is one of the largest city economies of India. It is "The Detroit of India", with more than one-third of India's automobile industry in the city. There are a number of educational and research institutions which are world famous. Chennai has a very good transportation system with two big railway stations, electric trains, metro rail, a harbour and an airport connecting it to the other cities of India and cities of the world. It also houses the biggest Tamil film industry.*

My mother was worried that I was going so far to stay in a hostel and study for five years. Like any other mother, she prayed that I should not fall into vices like smoking and drinking. At that time, Madras was a dry state and there was no chance of buying alcohol.

We packed my clothes in a steel box. We purchased a hold-all which served as a mobile bed and packing box.

My grandfather and I left Trichy on Sunday July 31, 1960 by Tuticorin Express and reached Egmore next day early in the morning. After reaching the college, we completed all the formalities. We moved to my hostel room no. 9 in F block. We purchased a camp cot made of coir. After spending two days with me, my grandfather left for Trichy.

I did not put in any hard work in the first two years because of the new environment, new city, new friends and new experiences. For the first time, I was alone by myself and totally independent. More chances to go astray. Luckily nothing happened. My average in the first two years was consistently low at around 54%. A second class in PUC in spite of my hard work was always a sore point for me. There was lack of motivation to put in hard work as I felt it did not pay off. What a wrong thought! In addition, in the first 2 years only basic science and foundation courses were taught which made me even less motivated.

From the third year, students were allotted different branches of Engineering as per their performance in the first two years and choice. I was good in Electrical Engineering and could solve the problems very easily and opted for Electrical Engineering from the IIIrd year but I was given Civil Engineering. My uncle and grandfather asked me whether I wanted to change my branch. I said no because I always take the first opportunity that is given to me. From a young age, I used to think that everything is **GOD's design**.

From the third year, courses of Civil Engineering were taught and we all got motivated and I started to put in hard work.

I passed my B.E. degree with first class achieving third rank (out of 40) in my class and seventh rank in the University of Madras (out of 250).

What are the memories you cherish?

My Sister's Wedding

My sister, Vasantha, was studying PUC in Holy Cross College, Trichy during 1961-62 while staying at my uncle Padmanaban's house in Trichy. My mother wanted my sister to become a doctor. Unfortunately, she failed in Advanced English in the PUC examination and my mother's dream was shattered. My sister was preparing to write the supplementary examinations, staying at Pudukkottai. We did not have a house of our own and shuttled between my uncle's houses. Since my mother was working in Trichy, she always stayed with my uncle Padmanaban. My grandfather wanted to get my sister married while he was still alive. He started searching for a bridegroom. He found Ramaiyan who was working in the Municipal office at Thanjavur. After completing various formalities, the marriage was fixed within fifteen days. My sister has not even seen Ramaiyan's photograph. My sister's marriage with Ramaiyan took place on September 5, 1963 (Birthday of Dr. S. Radhakrishnan, former President of India celebrated as Teacher's day) in the bridegroom's home town, Thanjavur.

When I applied for leave, the Head of the Department sanctioned only 3 days against my request for 7 with a warning that I would be punished if I exceeded the sanctioned number of days. So, I went as a guest to my sister's wedding and did not contribute in any way towards the preparations. Of course, I came back on time to the college.

I have to tell about one important incident during the marriage function. My uncle Govindarajan's 3-year-old son Kumararaj was about to be electrocuted and Ramaiyan saved him by his presence of mind, risking his own life.

Survey Camp

A survey camp was organized in Tiruneermalai for 10 days in the fourth year. We set up our own tents shared by 4 students from each batch. It was an adventurous experience of getting up at 4.30 a.m., doing morning chores in the open, surveying from 6 a.m., to 2 p.m., then doing office work followed by cultural programs in the evening. We had taken cooks, provisions and utensils from the hostel. There is a famous Lord Ranganatha in Tiruneermalai and every day, we had dharshan of Lord Ranganatha after climbing about 110 steps.

Faculty

I should pay tributes to Prof. Sadasivam (Astronomical Surveying), Prof. Subramania Pillai (Hydraulic Machinery), Prof. Viswanathan (Strength of Materials), Prof. Sankaralingam (Structural Engineering.), Prof. Kothandaraman (Engineering Drawing), Prof. Ilango (Electrical Engineering), Prof. Pundarikanthan (Hydraulics), Prof. John (Surveying lab), Prof. Sriramulu (Design of Steel Structures), Prof. Kumaresan (Design of Concrete Structures) and Prof. P. S. Natarajan (Theory of Structures). Prof. Natarajan would not carry any notes or books with him. He would derive equations, dictate and solve numericals all from memory. Later I worked under Prof. Ilango at REC Trichy from 1990 to 1995.

Campus and the City of Madras

The campus was very big and nice even though it lacked modern amenities.

There were no mosquitoes. Sometimes, there would be a water problem. Adyar River was close by. We moved into the new hostel in the fourth year.

We enjoyed samosas, Ceylon egg parotta, tea from Buhari's and biryani and non-vegetarian thali from Ponnusamy Hotel on Mount Road.

Entertainment

Movies in 16 mm, mostly English, were screened in the college auditorium at 7 p.m., every Friday. That day variety rice would be on the menu and we would have dinner early and go for the movie. Every year Arts Festival, an intercollegiate cultural competition, open to all colleges was celebrated. We would be excited and wait in anticipation for the event because girls from colleges like Queen Mary's, Ethiraj, etc., would also take part.

Final year students used to have an all India tour but our batch did not have it as a punishment for the strike. Annual elections for student body were an interesting event. The canvasing styles were amusing. A student even appealed for votes with the accordion as accompaniment.

Notable Classmates

Suresh (Chairman, Hudco), Shanmugam (Professor, National University of Singapore), Shantha Kumar (Professor, College of Engineering, Guindy), Rangarajan (Design Engineer, STUP consultant), Vaithilingam (Chief Engineer PWD, WRO) and Muthiah (Chairman, SPIC) were some of my notable classmates.

The famous Indian cricketer S. Venkatraghavan was 2 years junior to me.

My Close Friends

Rangarajan (who is no more), Sherfuddin, Sundararajan, Perumal, Vaithilingam, Nallusamy, Elango and Narayanasamy were my close friends.

Canteen Omelette

The canteen was famous for bread omlette and there would be a long queue to buy them. Funnily the cook's head also looked like an omelette.

Movies

We saw a lot of movies. My roommate Sundarrajan and I saw the movie "Pavamannippu" eleven times in the Shanthi Theater.

Visits by my uncle Govindarajan and my Sister

In the third year, my uncle Dr. Govindarajan stayed in my room for a week to attend a conference in Chennai. At the time, my roommate was Narayanasamy (later son-in-law of actor Sivaji Ganesan). My uncle was not happy because our room was unkempt and untidy.

After her marriage, my sister Vasantha and her husband Ramaiyan visited me and stayed in my hostel for 3 days in November, 1963. They wanted to tour Chennai. One day, I took them to Mount Road to have dinner. Other times they went on their own for sightseeing. It could be called their honeymoon.

New Things Learned

I learned to play table tennis, tennis ball cricket and chess.

In chess, I shined to the extent of defeating Annamalai, the defending champion of our college.

What are the memories you would like to forget?

Mild Attack of TB (July 1961 to June 1962)

As the annual examinations for the 2nd year were approaching, I got sick. Luckily, I had prepared all the courses beforehand. The sickness was due to an allergy to cats. A cat was a common visitor to our mess and whenever I saw her I could not eat at all. I did not share this with anyone and I became very weak and thin. In the surveying practical, I could not even stand in the sun. But the examiner was kind enough to consider my condition. Somehow, I finished all the exams and went home for the Summer Vacation to Pudukkottai where my uncle Govindarajan was a government doctor. After conducting all the tests, they found that I had a mild attack of TB, which had snatched my father earlier. My mother and grandfather became worried. Dr. Ramachandran was the specialist at the time and he treated me. I was admitted to the government hospital and my mother also came to Pudukkottai to take care of me since it was the Summer holidays. I was given a very nourishing diet consisting of mutton soup, mutton liver and eggs. My uncle's sons, Kumararaj and Anandaraj, used to visit me daily. They were just 2 years and 1 year old respectively. I started reading English novels for the first time. They were by Erle Stanley Gardener and Agatha Christie, given to me by a nurse. After 15 days of bed rest and a nourishing diet, I was declared free of TB. But I was asked to continue the medication for one year and to have one raw egg daily for six months. I followed the instructions strictly in the hostel in my third year. After a year, there was no need for further medication.

I cleared the second year successfully without failing in any course.

Nasty and Shameful Incident - 1

When I was doing my 2nd year, we had students belonging to 2 different regulations. The batch belonging to old regulations (4-year degree) was in the final year and the first batch of integrated programme were in the IIIrd year and we, the second batch of the integrated programme, were in the IInd year. We had to go through the mess of the final years to reach our mess and in doing so some students started heckling and teasing the seniors.

The same night around midnight, the seniors came to our hostel, picked up the students involved in the incident, took them to the ground and paraded them naked for some time. When the wardens came, the seniors ran away. The affected students were pacified. Somehow the problem was dissipated.

In the IInd year, my roommate Sherfuddin's father visited us one day early in the morning. We were singing a vulgar Tamil song. He got offended and asked us to wash our dirty mouths.

Nasty and Shameful Incident - 2

The second one took place when we were in the final year. During the annual elections, the student supported by final years won the President post, which angered the IVth year students. When the final year students went for a movie to celebrate, some of the IVth year students came to the final year hostel and mockingly shook hands with a few students in the hostel. When the majority of the final year students returned after watching the film, the humiliated students reported the incident in an exaggerated manner. Immediately, all the final years gathered and decided to attack the IVth year students. Armed with sticks and stones, the operation started around 11 p.m., and I was forced to accompany my classmates but I did not use sticks or stones. The hostel wardens arrived after half an hour and the final year students argued with them. Sensing punishment for their offence, the final year students announced a strike starting the next day. The strike was not a success as the IVth year students did not join it. We took a procession to the office of Directorate of Technical Education (T. Muthian) to give our memorandum of grievances which had 10 demands. Muthian was a tough man and he made us call off the strike with the help of college authorities and the parents. He conducted an enquiry and punished a few students. We lost the Arts Festival and all India tour as punishment.

Why did your BE degree programme end in January instead of June 1965?

As a consequence of the Sino-India War in 1962, a state of emergency was declared from October 26, 1962 to January 10, 1968 "the security of India" having been declared "threatened by external aggression". One of the decisions made was to accelerate the engineering degree programme by six months, to increase the intake and to permit B.Sc. degree holders to enter the third year of B.E. programme. The sole purpose was to produce more engineers.

How did you finance your studies?

All the tuition fees, examination fees, mess fees, and my maintenance expenses were paid by my uncle Govindarajan for all the five years. My grandfather would send a money order for Rs.100 in the first week of every month. In addition, I received a scholarship of Rs. 600 every year on the basis of my belonging to a backward community and being the son of a school teacher. Neither my uncle nor grandfather asked for the scholarship money. I lavishly spent it on books and entertainment.

Did you feel homesick at all?

We never felt homesick. We went home only once a year, during summer vacation. The only source of communication was through postal services.

What were your plans after graduation?

While doing my B.E. degree, somehow, I got interested in a teaching position rather than a field job in government departments. The motivation might have been my mother's dedication as a teacher. The normal choice for majority of Civil Engineering students was to join the Public Works Department (PWD). This was because the government employed them as soon as they passed out. No higher qualifications were required. One could get to the top level of Chief Engineer since promotions were given according to vacancy and seniority.

I had applied for Senior Technical Assistant (STA) at IIT, Madras and Technical Teacher Trainee Programme of the central government. In both positions, one could work, get a stipend and obtain a master's degree within three years.

Also, I had applied for two-year Master's Degree programme at IISc Bangalore which also offered a stipend. The admission was based on the marks obtained in Bachelor degree programme. Since I had better marks in Hydraulics compared to Structural and Soil Mechanics, I was offered a seat in Hydraulics specialization. It was the first offer I received.

My grandfather decided that I should join IISc Bangalore. So, I did not attend the other two interviews. As always, I took the first offer.

M.E. - Indian Institute of Science (IISc), Bangalore - August 1965 to July 1967

My grandfather always wanted me to study in the best schools and colleges. I studied in St. Joseph's High School, Trichy, St. Joseph's College, Trichy and College of Engineering, Guindy. Now, he wanted me to join the Indian Institute of Science (IISc) Bangalore (now Bengaluru), which was and is one of the best institutions for post-graduation studies and research.

***Indian Institute of Science** is a public university for scientific research and higher education in Bangalore, India. It was established in 1909 with support from Jamshedji Tata and H. H. Sir Krishnaraja Wodeyar IV, the Maharaja of Mysore. The establishment was endorsed by Vivekananda. It is locally known as the "Tata Institute". It acquired the status of a Deemed University in 1958. IISc is ranked the top university in India.*

***Bengaluru** (formerly Bangalore) is the capital of the Indian state of Karnataka. It is the third most populous city and fifth most populous urban agglomeration in India. Bangalore is referred to as the "Silicon Valley of India" (or "IT capital of India") because it is the nation's leading information technology (IT) exporter. Like any other metropolitan city, Bangalore also has many great temples and churches. It also houses many educational institutions of repute and industrial organizations.*

I studied well and scored very high marks in all the courses in the first semester.

In the Instrumentation course, I was the only student to have passed out of 36 students.

My design project on "Design of Dams" was quite good. I completed all the assignments well in advance and most of my classmates would come to my room early in the morning and copy them. Some of them like Rangasamy and Ramanujam went to USA and became millionaires.

My seminar and dissertation project did not go well. My seminar was on "Weirs" and I read it from written notes and marks were deducted. My dissertation project was on "Quadrant Edge Orificemeter". I continued the work of Ramamoorthi who had completed his Ph.D. and left to join Thiagarajar College of Engineering, Madurai. Without an appropriate guide and my non-pushy nature, I suffered. Even Prof. Lakshmana Rao who was fond of me got angry with me for not progressing as expected. Somehow, I completed the project and viva-voce.

Because of the low marks in the dissertation project, I dropped from 1st to 3rd rank.

I secured first class with distinction with an overall average of 73.1%.

My childhood friend Hasheem also joined Aeronautics cancelling his admission (losing the fees) at PSG college of Technology, Coimbatore in spite of his admission in Structural Engineering which was and is the most sought-after specialization in Civil Engineering just to be with me and became my roommate.

What new things did you learn there which you cherish even now?

I learnt French.

I learnt to play bridge, billiards and tennis. In tennis, I won the runner up cup once.

In bridge, I became an international champion, thanks to Zahoor Ahmed.

We used to play cricket with playing cards during lunch time. One day Zahoor Ahmed, our classmate from Aeronautics Department told us that he would teach us a nice game called bridge using the cards. I entered a tournament in Bowring Institute, a posh club in Bangalore and an English lady was attracted by my game and appreciated me.

I was introduced to beer by Zahoor Ahmed and when about 10 of us went to the bar for the first time we all felt shy as though we were entering a forbidden place.

How was the campus and Bangalore?

Bangalore city was beautiful with a pleasant climate, tasty restaurants, cinema theatres, Majestic Circle, Cantonment area, Brigadier Road, Malleswaram area, night clubs (cabaret dances) and bars.

IISc campus was equally good with excellent hostel facilities, gymkhana club, library and tasty food in messes. There was a man called Bhasker in the mess who treated students from Tamil Nadu and Kerala nicely with hot masala dosas. Sunday night was self-service and we had an unusual combination of biryani and rasam. We saw a lot of English movies.

My uncle Govindarajan came with my aunty and my cousins to stay in our guest house. My uncle Muthiah (Savithri aunty's husband) came twice to my hostel. He was a big fan of Thiagaraja Bhagavadar, who used to act and sing in movies. Muthiah uncle had a gramophone and was fond of playing vinyl records of Thiagaraja Bhagavadar.

I would like to pay my tributes to my faculty Prof. Govinda Rao, Prof. Lakshmana Rao, Prof. Ramprasad, Prof. Swaminathan, Prof. Sharma and Prof. Ranganath.

How did you manage your finances?

I got a monthly stipend of Rs. 250 which was sufficient for my expenditure in Bangalore.

What new things happened in your personal life?

Birth of Chandrasekar

Chandrasekar (Sekar) was born to my sister on August 30, 1965.

Birth of Selvaraj

Selvaraj (Selvam) was born on July 1, 1967. He is the second child of my sister.

What were your plans after getting M.E. degree?

Ideally a person would be interested in pursuing a job or continuing with a Ph.D. either in India or abroad. Some of my friends planned to go to USA for a Ph.D. which was the major attraction for Indians, even though all of them had lower ranks than me. Somehow, I was not attracted by foreign degrees. I always wanted foreigners to come to India. I attended an interview at Trivandrum for the post of Associate

Lecturer at NSS College of Engineering (private) Palghat, Kerala, along with five of my classmates. Even though I was ranked No. 1, except me everyone else got the appointment. **God had other designs for me.**

In addition to my career problem, I had another problem, my love affair with June.

Wow! That must be very interesting. Please go ahead.

Around me

Let us go through the major events, which took place, during this period.

India

Politics

Birth of Maharashtra and Gujarat States, 1960 - Following protests by Samyukta Maharashtra Movement and Maha Gujarat Movement, Bombay state was dissolved with the formation of Maharashtra and Gujarat states on May 1, 1960.

Annexation Goa, Daman and Diu, 1961 - India annexed Goa, Daman and Diu which had been under Portuguese occupation for more than 450 years by armed action, code named Operation Vijay, involving air, sea and land strikes for over 36 hours.

IIIrd General Elections, 1962 - Jawaharlal Nehru continued as Prime Minister after the third general elections held during February 19-25, 1962 to elect the third Lok Sabha. INC won 361 seats, Bharatiya Jana Sangh 14, CPI 29, Swatantra 18 and DMK 7. The total number of seats were 494.

Conversion to Metric System of Units, 1955-62 - India's conversion to the metric system, based on the International System of Units (SI), occurred in stages between 1955 and 1962.

Radhakrishnan became President of India, 1962 - Sarvepalli Radhakrishnan became the second President of India on May 14, 1962 after Rajendra Prasad.

Kamaraj became President, INC, 1963 - Kamaraj was elected President, Indian National Congress, on October 9, 1963 with Nehru's support.

Prime Minister Nehru's Death, 1964 - Nehru's health began declining after 1962, and he spent months recuperating in Kashmir throughout 1963. He complained of back pain on the night of May 26, 1964 and collapsed. His death was announced to the Lok Sabha at 2.00 p.m., local time on May 27, 1964. On May 28, Nehru was cremated in accordance with Hindu rites at Shantivan on the banks of Yamuna River. Gulzarilal Nanda was interim Prime Minister from May 27 to June 9, 1964.

Shastri became Prime Minister, 1964 - Lal Bahadur Shastri was sworn in as Prime Minister on June 9, 1964 after Nehru's daughter Indira Gandhi turned down the Congress President Kamaraj's offer. This was acceptable to many who wanted to prevent the ascent of conservative right winger Morarji Desai.

Birth of VHP, 1964 - The Vishva Hindu Parishad (VHP), an Indian right wing Hindu nationalist organisation was founded on August 29, 1964 by M. S. Golwalkar and S. S. Apte in collaboration with Swami Chinmayananda.

Tashkent Agreement, 1966 - A meeting was held in Tashkent in the Uzbek SSR, USSR (now Uzbekistan) from January 4-10, 1966 to try to create a more permanent settlement between India and Pakistan. The Soviets, represented by Premier Alexei Kosygin, moderated between Indian Prime Minister Lal Bahadur Shastri and Pakistani President Muhammad Ayub Khan. The Tashkent conference, under United Nations, American and Soviet pressure, compelled India and Pakistan to abide by their previous treaty obligations and accept *Status quo ante bellum* – to give away the conquered regions of each other and return to the 1949 ceasefire line in Kashmir.

Death of Shastri, 1966 - Lal Bahadur Shastri died in Russia, on the next day (January 11, 1966) of signing the Tashkent Agreement under mysterious circumstances, which is unsolved even today after 52 years. Gulzarilal Nanda was interim Prime Minister from January 11 to 24, 1966.

Indira Gandhi became Prime Minister, 1966 - Indira Gandhi took over as India's third Prime Minister on January 24, 1966 when the Congress Legislative Party elected Indira Gandhi over Morarji Desai as their leader.

Birth of Shiv Sena, 1966 - Shiv Sena, an Indian far right regional political party, was founded on June 19, 1966 by political cartoonist Bal Thackeray. It is based on pro - Marathi ideology and Hindu nationalism (Hindutva).

Birth of Haryana, 1966 - By accepting the demands of the Akalis to reorganize Punjab on linguistic lines, the Hindi speaking southern half of Punjab became a separate state, Haryana, on November 1, 1966.

Crossing the English Channel, 1966 - Mihir Sen was a famous long-distance swimmer, the first Indian to conquer the English Channel from Dover to Calais in 1958 and the only man to earn the distinction of swimming the oceans of the five continents in one calendar year (1966).

Miss World, 1966 - Reita Faria Powell won Miss World 1966 becoming the first Asian woman to do so.

IVth General Elections, 1967 - Indira Gandhi became Prime Minister the second time after the Indian general elections were held during February 17 to 21, 1967 to elect the 4th Lok Sabha. INC won 283 seats, Swatantra party 44, Bharatiya Jana Sangh 35 and DMK 25. The total number of seats were 520.

Zakir Hussain became President, 1967 - Zakir Hussain became the third President of India on May 13, 1967 after S. Radhakrishnan.

Uprisings of Naxalites, 1967 - India saw the violent uprisings of Naxalites from November 27, 1967. There was an armed struggle to distribute land to landless.

War

Indo-China War, 1962 - Unable to reach political agreement on disputed territory along the 3,225 kilometres long Himalayan border on the new Indian maps, the Chinese launched simultaneous offensives in Ladakh and across the McMahon Line on October 20, 1962. Chinese troops advanced over Indian forces capturing Rezang la in Chushul in the western theatre and Tawang in the eastern theatre. The war ended when the Chinese declared a ceasefire on November 20, 1962, and announced its withdrawal.

Indo-Pakistan War of 1965 - The Indo-Pakistan War of 1965 was a result of clashes that took place between August and September, 1965. It started following Pakistan's Operation Gibraltar, to penetrate forces into Jammu and Kashmir on August 5, 1965 to precipitate an insurgency against rule by India. India launched a full-scale military attack on West Pakistan. The seventeen-day war caused thousands of casualties on both sides and the largest tank battle since World War II. The hostilities ended after a ceasefire was secured by the United Nations Security Council on September 22, 1965 following diplomatic intervention by the Soviet Union and USA. Soviet Union Premier, Alexei Kosygin, hosted ceasefire negotiations in Tashkent (now in Uzbekistan), where the Tashkent Agreement was signed.

Madras State

IIIrd Assembly Elections, 1962 - K. Kamaraj of INC was sworn in as Chief Minister of Madras state on March 15, 1962 after the Legislative Assembly elections on February 21. Dravida Munnetra Kazhagam emerged as the second party for the first time by winning 50 seats. INC won 139 seats, DMK 50 and Swatantra, 17. The total number of seats were 206.

Noon Meal Scheme, 1962 - Madras was the first state to introduce the Noon Meal Scheme for the primary school children under Chief Minister Kamaraj in the academic year 1962-63. He introduced the scheme first in the city of Madras and then extended it to all the districts of Madras state.

Resignation of Kamaraj, 1963 - On Gandhi Jayanti, October 2nd, 1963, Kamaraj resigned from the Chief Minister post. He suggested to Nehru that senior Congress leaders should leave ministerial posts to take up organisational work. This suggestion came to be known as the Kamaraj Plan. Minjur Kanakasabhapathi Bhaktavatsalam became the Chief Minister of Madras state on October 2, 1963.

Anti - Hindi Agitation, Jan 26, 1965 - The Anti - Hindi agitations happened during both pre and post-Independence periods. The first was launched in 1937, in opposition to the introduction of compulsory teaching of Hindi in the schools of Madras Presidency by the first INC government led by C. Rajagopalachari. The second agitations started on January 25, 1965 which involved several mass protests, riots, student and political movements opposing the use of Hindi as the sole official language from January 26, 1965. The riots subsided after Prime Minister Shastri's assurance that English would continue to be used as the official language as long as the non-Hindi speaking states wanted.

Founding of Madurai University, 1966 - Madurai University, a public university, was inaugurated on February 6, 1966, at Madurai. In 1978 the name was changed to Madurai Kamaraj University to honour K. Kamaraj.

IVth Assembly Elections, 1967 - The Dravida Munnetra Kazhagam (DMK) United Front defeated the Indian National Congress in the fourth Legislative Assembly elections held during February 5 to 21, 1967. DMK won 179 seats (52.6% of total votes polled). The Congress Party, which won in the 1952, 1957 and 1962 elections, secured only 51 seats. The total number of seats were 234. C. N. Annadurai was sworn in as Chief Minister of Madras state on March 5, 1967, the first Chief Minister of the Dravidian parties.

World

Politics

U-2 Spy Plane Incident and Collapse of Four Power Summit, 1960 - The US Government was forced to admit that they had sent spy planes to the Soviet Union when they came up with the captured pilot of a U-2 plane. Tensions from the U-2 incident were high when Eisenhower and Khrushchev arrived in Paris on May 16, 1960 for a Four Power Summit. Any hope of East-West reconciliation was doomed as heads of state--Eisenhower, Nikita Khrushchev, General de Gaulle and Harold Macmillan-- never got beyond preliminary procedural meetings. The collapse of the May 1960 summit meeting was a blow to those in the Soviet Union and the United States who believed that a period of peaceful coexistence between the two superpowers was on the horizon.

Brezhnev became Chairman, Supreme Soviet, 1960 - Brezhnev became Chairman, Supreme Soviet on May 7, 1960.

Kennedy became President of USA, 1961 - John Fitzgerald Kennedy (JFK) of the Democratic Party became the 35th President of USA on January 20, 1961 after D. Eisenhower.

The Bay of Pigs Invasion, 1961 - It was a failed military invasion of Cuba undertaken by the USA during April 17-19, 1961.

Erection of Berlin Wall, 1961 - Walter Ulbricht, First Secretary of the Socialist Unity Party and GDR State Council Chairman signed the order to close the border and erect a wall between the borders of East and West Germany. At midnight on June 13, 1961, police and units of the East German army began to close the border.

Firing of Hydrogen Bomb by USSR, 1961 - AN602 hydrogen bomb or Big Ivan or Tsar Bomba, was fired on October 30, 1961 under Nikita Khrushchev. It was 57 Megatons which is 1,400 times the bombs that were dropped on Hiroshima and Nagasaki combined and ten times the entire combined fire power expended in WWII.

The Cuban Missile Crisis, 1962 - The Cuban Missile Crisis, was a 13-day (October 16–28, 1962) confrontation between the United States and the Soviet Union concerning Soviet ballistic missiles positioning in Cuba. It was the closest the Cold War came to growing into a full-fledged nuclear war. In response to the failed Bay of Pigs Invasion of 1961, and the presence of American Jupiter ballistic missiles in Italy and Turkey against the USSR, Nikita Khrushchev agreed to Cuba's request to place nuclear missiles in Cuba to discourage future harassment of Cuba. After negotiations, an agreement was reached between Kennedy and Khrushchev. Publicly, the Soviets would dismantle their weapons in Cuba and return them to the Soviet Union, subject to United Nations verification, in exchange for a US public declaration and agreement never to invade Cuba without direct provocation. Secretly, the US also agreed to dismantle US built Jupiter IRBMs in Turkey and Italy.

Nuclear Test Ban Treaty, 1963 - Nuclear Test Ban Treaty or Treaty Banning Nuclear Weapons Tests in the atmosphere, in outer space and underwater was signed in Moscow on August 5, 1963, by United States, Soviet Union, and United Kingdom that banned all tests of nuclear weapons except those conducted underground. The origins lay in worldwide public concern over the danger posed by atmospheric radioactive fallout.

Hot Line between Washington and Moscow, 1963 - On August 30, 1963, John F. Kennedy became the first US President to have a direct phone line to Kremlin in Moscow. The "hotline" was designed to enable communication between the US President and

Soviet Premier to reduce the risk of war occurring by accident or miscalculation.

Alec Douglas Home became England's Prime Minister, 1963 - Alec Douglas Home became England's Prime Minister on October 18, 1963 after Harold Macmillan.

Assassination of Kennedy, 1963 - John Fitzgerald Kennedy was assassinated by bullet shots on November 22, 1963 in Dallas, Texas while in a moving car. A ten-month investigation from November, 1963 to September, 1964 by the Warren Commission concluded that Kennedy was shot by Oswald acting alone, and that Jack Ruby acted alone when he killed Oswald before he could stand trial.

Lyndon Baines Johnson, US President 1963 - Lyndon Baines Johnson became 36th President of USA on November 22, 1963 after the assassination of John F. Kennedy.

Brezhnev became General Secretary, 1964 - Leonard Ilyich Brezhnev became the General Secretary of the Communist Party of Soviet Union on October 14, 1964, after Nikita Khrushchev.

Harold Wilson as Prime Minister of UK, 1964 - Harold Wilson became the Prime Minister of England on October 10, 1964 after Alec Douglas Home.

Alexei Kosygin Chairman Council of Minister, 1964 - Alexei Kosygin became the Chairman, Council of Ministers, Soviet Union on October 15, 1964 after Nikita Khrushchev.

Singapore's Independence, 1965 - On August 9, 1965, Singapore separated from Malaysia to become an Independent and Sovereign state.

War

Six Day Arab-Israeli War, 1967 – The Six Day Arab-Israeli War, took place during June 5–10, 1967, and was the third one. Israel's victory included the capture of the Sinai Peninsula, Gaza Strip, West Bank, Old City of Jerusalem, and Golan Heights. The UN Security Council called for a cease-fire on June 7 and the war ended on June 10, 1967.

Space Technology

First and Second Human in Space, 1961 - Yuri Alekseyevich Gagarin was a Russian Soviet pilot and cosmonaut. He was the first human to journey into outer space, when the Vostok 1 spacecraft completed an orbit of the Earth on April 12, 1961. John Herschel Glenn, Jr. became America's first astronaut to orbit the earth on February 20, 1962 when he flew the Project Mercury spacecraft of the Friendship 7 mission. He orbited three times in 4 hours 55 minutes.

Luna 10 Spacecraft, 1966 - The Luna 10 spacecraft was launched towards the Moon from an Earth orbiting platform on March 31, 1966. It completed its first orbit on April 4. Luna 10 was battery powered and operated for 460 lunar orbits and 219 active data transmissions were made before radio signals were discontinued on May 30, 1966.

Death of 3 Astronauts, 1967 - Apollo I was the first manned mission of the US Apollo program and a cabin fire during a launch rehearsal test on January 27, 1967, killed all three crew members - Command Pilot Virgil I. "Gus" Grissom, Senior Pilot Edward H. White II, and Pilot Roger B. Chaffee and destroyed the Command Module.

Music

Arrival of the Beatles, 1960 - The Beatles were an English rock band, formed in Liverpool in 1960 by John Lennon (vocals and rhythm guitar), Paul McCartney (vocals and rhythm guitar), George Harrison (vocals and lead guitar), and Ringo Starr (drums). They became regarded as the foremost and most influential act of the rock era in the early 1960s. Their enormous popularity emerged as "Beatlemania".

CHAPTER 5

Love and Marriage - December 1965 to August 1967

Abstract

Me

The details of my falling in love with June and getting married to her are presented.

Me

How did you fall in love?

First meeting

> "Love isn't something you find. Love is something that finds you."
>
> -Loretta Young

I was doing my M.E. in IISc Bangalore from August 1965. At the end of the first semester, we had a short vacation in December. I went to Chennai to meet one of my school friends and should have gone back to Bangalore from Chennai. But I changed my mind and proceeded to Trichy, instead, to see my family. I came to Trichy on December 26, to stay at my uncle, Dr. Govindarajan's, rented house at 45, Heber Road, Beemanagar, Trichy. Even though I had lived in that house for six months before going to Bangalore in August 1965, I had no idea about any of my neighbours. The houses were separated by 5 feet high compound walls. Our house had an open space in the front with a Neem tree. Nothing happened during the first two days. On December 28, around 6 p.m., as I was standing in the open space waiting for my friend, I accidentally peeped towards the neighbour's house on the right side. A beautiful girl was standing on the steps leading to the house. The house also had a big open space in the front.

Until then, I had not spoken to any girl other than relatives and family friends. In those days, we did not have a girlfriend - boyfriend culture.

But **destiny** gave me the courage to call her to the compound wall and she came as well. We had a small chat over the compound wall, fearing the wrath of our family members in case they saw us. Her name was June. She was 16 years old and I was 22. Since it was winter, darkness was setting in quickly. Ten to fifteen minutes into our conversation, suddenly I held her face, leant over the wall and planted my first kiss on the lips of the most beautiful girl. She did not resist either. I cannot forget that first kiss even today. Meeting her everyday either near the compound or on the terrace continued for four days. Then I had to leave Trichy on January, 1 for Bangalore since my second semester was starting from January, 2. When I shared my experience with some of my friends in Trichy, they cautioned me, saying that she was Anglo Indian with a culture quite different from mine.

I was distracted and thoughts about her slowed down my academic progress. I did not do well in my seminar. My next visit to Trichy was supposed to be at the end of the second semester during the summer vacation in June, 1966.

Tashkent Declaration and My Second Meeting!

But **destiny** gave me an unexpected chance to visit Trichy in February, 1966. Lal Bahadur Shastri became Prime Minister of India in 1964 after the death of Mr. Jawaharlal Nehru on May 27, 1964. When Lal Bahadur Shastri died in Russia on January 11, 1966, after signing Tashkent Agreement, leave was declared to mourn his death and that gave me an unexpected chance to visit Trichy to see my girl.

Let me tell you something about her. She belonged to an Anglo-Indian family. June was the eldest daughter of Rachel Mary and Lionel Aloysius Narcis. She had a younger brother, Rodney, aged 13 and a younger sister, Eugenia (Dinky), aged 10. Her father was working in the Railways and her mother was working as staff nurse in the Nalwazhi Hospital along with her sister Gladys Amelia.

The Nalwazhi hospital was owned by Dr. Thomas and it was next to June's house. Since June's aunty, Amelia, was a spinster, she agreed to foster June and Eugenia. Rodney was also with Amelia for some time but later went to stay with his parents. June had her grandmother, Mabel, at home to cook and look after the girls. June was studying in VIIIth standard at St. Joseph's Anglo-Indian Girls High School, one of the best schools in Trichy for girls. Earlier she studied in St. John's Vestry High School. She was very good in athletics. She was selected to represent her school but her aunty Amelia refused her permission to participate.

I spent two days silently communicating through eye contact. In those days, communicating through eyes was the best way of showing love. I then left for Bangalore.

Growing Love

During the summer holidays, I came to Trichy and I was invited to her house. I visited her home almost daily in the evening from about 7 p.m. to 8 p.m., as advised by her aunty. We used to sit on the sofa in the hall. June's vigilant grandma would be in the hall, kitchen or in her room. I do not remember now what we talked about every day.

The closeness, the privacy and frequency of visits expanded our love leaps and bounds. I went to Dindigul with June, her aunty Amelia and Dr. Thomas for two days for a tennis tournament. Once, accidentally, we ended up going for different movies. I went to a Tamil movie and she went to a Hindi movie "Waqt" with her sister and grandmother. Even though I did not share anything with my family, they suspected that I was up to something. But they did not question me directly. As any other parent and grandparent, they thought I was a good boy and would not do anything which was not approved. I was well known for telling the truth all the time like Harischandra, a mythological character. But everyone forgets that love can make you lie to your own family. It can change anyone.

> *"To love is nothing. To be loved is something. But to love and be loved, that's everything."*
>
> **-T. Tollis**

During my second year of study (August, 1966 to July, 1967) we exchanged letters everyday by Express Delivery which is similar to speed post now. We might have exchanged about 200 letters. We both reluctantly destroyed those letters when I first retired in 2003, after keeping them for 37 years.

There is no surprise that I fell in love with her because she was so beautiful but it is a mystery why she fell in love with me because I was neither good looking nor had good physique. They say "Love is blind."

> *"The greatest happiness of life is the conviction that we are loved; loved for ourselves, or rather, loved in spite of ourselves."*
>
> *- Victor Hugo*

Sensing that I was in love with June, in April 1967, my mother and my brother-in-law came to Bangalore and advised me to forget June saying that our cultures were completely different.

My mother said "Look here Kittu. There are so many reasons why you should not marry this girl. First and foremost, they are Anglo Indians and Christians. Their customs, culture and beliefs are poles apart from ours. Healthy association between the two families may not be possible. What eligibility you have to marry without a job, money and a house to stay? You should make yourself eligible for marriage by securing a job and saving some money for the next three years. The girl is also studying in school and is only 18. What does she know about marriage and life? You both are not ready for marriage now. Later, we ourselves will take necessary steps for your marriage. I hope you understand." But **destiny** did not allow me to understand their advice.

How did you decide to get married?

Marriage

As mentioned earlier I did not get the job as Associate Lecturer at NSS College of Engineering at Palghat. This again was God's plan. Five of my classmates, who joined that college, suffered for the next six years, sometimes without salary also. **HE** saved me as usual.

Seeing my disappointment, my Head of the Department, Prof. Seetharamiah asked whether I wanted to do Ph.D., in USA or in IISc itself. But my thoughts were with June and I told him that I would think about it. After finishing all the formalities at IISc, I reached Trichy in the first week of July 1967. I opened the topic of marrying June. **Destiny** made me forget that I neither had a job nor a house to look after my wife after marriage. I never had enough clothes (maybe two sets of pants and shirts) and my bank account was nearly zero. My mother and grandfather did not have much money either.

My sister spoke to me about this, "Anna, why are you doing this? How much mother, grandfather and I would have imagined about your marriage. They are not only of a different caste but also of a different religion. You know our mother became a widow at such an early age and she struggled to bring us up and it is your duty to make her happy. We can't take part wholeheartedly and people say that if the blessings of parents are absent, then the married couple would suffer. But I don't want that to happen. Think about it and take a good decision." She could not stop the tears from her eyes. But I was not in a position to understand because when destiny decides no one can change its course.

It was stupid of me to write a letter to my grandfather asking him why I could not marry an Anglo Indian when he had married one. I am ashamed now thinking about it. I must have hurt him. How could I do this to a person who did everything for me?

"Being deeply loved by someone gives you strength, while loving someone deeply gives you courage."

-Lao Tzu

Understanding the situation, my uncle Govindarajan and aunty Mangayarkarasi took up the matter, pacified my mother and grandfather and spoke to June's family regarding our marriage. My uncle Padmanaban and aunty Shantha were also willing for our marriage. June's aunty Amelia and Dr. Thomas agreed to sponsor the marriage expenses. Our marriage was fixed on Wednesday, August 30, 1967 between 10.30 a.m., and 12.00 noon after consulting the Panjangam, which is a Hindu calendar and almanac. (She was 18 and I was 24).

Since she was a Catholic Christian and I was a Hindu, there was confusion regarding how to conduct the marriage. Then my uncle resolved it by saying that the marriage would be conducted by him as a Self-Respect marriage.

The Self-Respect Movement *was founded in 1925 by E. V. Ramasamy (Periyar) in Tamil Nadu, India. The aim of such a movement was to achieve a society where backward castes have equal human rights, and to encourage backward castes to have self-respect in the context of a caste-based society that considered them to be the lower end of a hierarchy. One of the major sociological changes was the self-respect marriage system, which encouraged inter-caste* marriages, without being officiated by a Brahmin priest, replacing arranged marriages by love marriages that are not controlled by caste. Tamil Nadu became the first and only state to legalize Hindu marriages conducted without a Brahmin priest. This was the first file signed by Chief Minister Annadurai when the DMK gained power in the 1967 Madras assembly elections, that too after our marriage.

There was a *Mangalsutra (Thali)* to satisfy Hindu custom and a ring and oath taking to satisfy Christian custom. Ashby Hotel, Trichy was fixed as the venue for the marriage.

I wore a silk dhoti and a white silk shirt and June wore a gold silk saree. On the dot of 10.30 a.m., we were made to sit on a sofa in the hall. My uncle started the function by welcoming all the guests. Then my grandfather garlanded both of us. My uncle read out the oath which was repeated first by me and then by June. The oath goes like this.

"I, _____, take you, _____, to be my lawfully wedded (husband/wife). I promise to be true to you in good times and in bad, in sickness and in health. I will love you and honour you, all the days of my life until death do us part."

After the oath taking, I tied the *thali* around June's neck.

Mangalsutra *(Thali in Tamil) literally means "an auspicious thread" which is knotted around the bride's neck. Usually, the groom ties 3 knots and in certain communities, the groom ties the first knot while his sister ties the other two knots. Adi Shankara in his famous book Soundarya Lahari says that, according to Hindu tradition, the mangalsutra is worn for the long life of the husband. There are different interpretations for the three knots. One of them says, "Father protects (her) in childhood, husband protects (her) in youth, and sons protect (her) in old age. A woman cannot be left unprotected."*

Since my sister did not attend the marriage due to some misunderstanding, my aunty Shantha tied the other two knots. A basket that had been hung just above us was pulled open by Rodney and we were showered with flowers. We felt as though God was showering us with blessings. Then we exchanged our garlands and rings. Finally, I proposed a toast.

Only close friends and relatives numbering around 200 from both sides attended. The executive Director of BHEL (Bharat Heavy Electricals Limited) and the General Manager of Small Arms Factory were among the guests.

Immediately after the marriage ceremony, we went to the Registrar Office for registration of the marriage and then to Vayaloor Murugan Temple in the afternoon. Most of the rituals associated with either Hindu or Christian weddings were not followed.

June missed her Christian wedding and I missed my Hindu wedding.

*In **Hindu weddings**, an engagement function is arranged during which the date and time of the wedding is fixed and announced to close relatives. This forms the agreement for the wedding. Then Pandakal Muhurtham is performed just 2 or 3 days before the wedding date, to pray for God's blessings for the successful conduct of the wedding. On the eve of the wedding, a reception is arranged in which rituals are carried out for both bride and the groom separately by close relatives. Next day an hour before the tying of the mangalsutra, the wedding rituals are started by the Panditji. First it is performed for the bride and next for the groom. Then, they change into their traditional wedding attire and come to the pandal and take their position together either on the floor or on a bench. The pandit performs a homam and conducts rituals for both. The mangalsutra is circulated among the guests for their blessings and atchadai (rice mixed with turmeric and flowers) is given to all. When the Panditji gives his acceptance for the right time, the groom ties the mangalsutra around the bride's neck. All the guests throw the atchadai to bless them. After this main event is over, the bride and groom have to follow some more rituals including going around the homam nine times. Homam is a Sanskrit word that refers to a ritual, wherein any religious offering is made into fire. A Homam is sometimes called a "sacrifice ritual" because the fire destroys the offering, but a Homam is more accurately a "contractual ritual". The fire is the agent, and the offerings include those that are material and symbolic such as grains, clarified butter, milk, incense and seeds.*

*In **Christianity, weddings** are conducted in churches. The girl is generally dressed in white. She is taken to the altar by her father where she joins the bridegroom. The awaiting priest offers them best wishes. He then reads psalms from the Holy Bible, which is followed by a sermon called Homily on the sacredness of the wedding. Following this, he questions the bride and the groom regarding their consent for the marriage. The couple makes promises to stay with* *each other through thick and thin and exchange rings. These rings are blessed by the priest first, to instil love and faith between the two. In some cases, the bridegroom ties a gold thali (mangalsutra) to the bride. In some cases they kiss each other. After this the couple is blessed by the gathering and the priest. The wedding concludes by signing in a marriage register and the couple walks down the aisle, arm in arm. A copy of the signed page is later sent to the Registrar of Marriages.*

So, you had a combination of a Hindu and a Christian marriage in the form of Self-Respect marriage. It was not only inter-caste but inter-religion and inter-racial one. It was really a revolutionary marriage. All of you have to be appreciated.

Yes, all the guests liked our wedding and some talk about it even now.

They arranged the nuptials for the same night in June's house and Amelia aunt's family friends, Balu, a tennis player and his wife Kausalya, made the preparations for it.

Where did you stay after your marriage?

We could not stay with my uncle Govindarajan due to lack of space. My uncle Padmanaban offered a place in his house. When we conveyed this to Amelia and Dr. Thomas, they asked us to stay in Amelia's house until I got a job. So, we started to stay in June's house.

Did you go on a honeymoon?

No.

***Honeymoon** is the period when newlyweds take a break to share some private and intimate moments that helps establish love in their relationship. This privacy in turn is believed to ease the comfort zone towards a physical relationship, which is one of the primary means of bonding during the initial days of marriage. The earliest term for this in English was honymoone, which was recorded as early as 1546.*

How could I have thoughts about a honeymoon under the circumstances wherein my mother and my grandfather were emotionally wounded and were still accepting my marriage? They were magnanimous to go through the wedding at least without creating any problems, bravely burying their own sorrow. Moreover, I never had any money of my own. One trip which we had after the wedding was when I brought June to REC guest house in Calicut in

December 1967 and by that time she was pregnant. Can we call it a family honeymoon with three of us?

Did you have any chance of interacting with a girl before you met June?

I told you earlier that there was no boyfriend and girlfriend culture at that time. But every teenage boy would have indulged in covertly looking at a girl. During my V form, when I stayed in Marsingpet road, I used to stand on the first floor waiting to catch glimpses of a Muslim girl who would pass by in a bullock cart. Once when I was 15 years old my mother and I went to see a bride for my uncle Padmanaban, in a village called Ettarai. The girl's sister bought a drink for me and we just looked at each other. Then our fingers touched and it gave me a strange feeling. My mother's close friend Baby had four daughters and she used to tease my mother and me that I should marry one of the girls. My mother got upset and asked me not to go to their house. I talked and played with them as I did with my sister Vasantha. All this happened before I could complete my high school. When I came home during my vacation to Pudukkottai, in 1963, I had a chance to befriend a girl Malathi who was my neighbour.

Did you share this with your wife? What was her reaction?

Not early in our life. But later on, after we became mature enough I shared this.

Actually, she said in anger that I should have married one of them.

You married the girl you loved! Fine. What about your plans for your job?

Regarding my job, after my wedding an interview call came from Regional Engineering College (REC) Calicut which was 350 kilometres away from Trichy. I attended the interview at Calicut and joined as Associate Lecturer in the Department of Civil Engineering on October 16, 1967.

CHAPTER 6

Life in Calicut - October 1967 to July 1974

Abstract

Me

The details of my first stop-gap job in Tamil Nadu PWD (Public Works Department) (1965), first teaching job as Associate Lecturer at Regional Engineering College, Calicut (1967), birth of my only daughter, Shyamala (1968), my promotion as Lecturer (1970), deaths of uncle Thomas (1970), my maternal grandfather Arumugam (1971) and my paternal grandfather Rathinasamy (1973) and rise and fall of our own dream house (1970) are presented.

Around me

In India, the most important events were Indo - China border fight (1967), Indian National Congress split (1969), nationalization of banks (1969), introduction of Rajdhani Express (1969), V. V. Giri becoming President (1969), birth of Himachal Pradesh (1971), 5th general elections (1971), Indira Gandhi continuing as Prime Minister (1971), cyclone in Orissa (1971), Indo-Pakistan War and birth of a new nation, Bangladesh (1971), birth of Manipur state (1972), Indo - Bangladesh Treaty of Friendship (1972), Indo-Pakistan Shimla Agreement 1972), renaming of Mysore state as Karnataka (1973), first nuclear bomb blast (1974) and railway strike (1974).

In Tamil Nadu, the most important events were Kilvelmani Massacre (1968), Madras state renamed as Tamil Nadu (1969), death of Annadurai (1969), Nedunchezhiyan as interim Chief Minister (1969), Karunanidhi becoming Chief Minister (1969), invocation of Tamil Goddess (1970), 5th Assembly elections (1971), Karunanidhi continuing as Chief Minister

(1971), birth of ADMK (1972), death of Rajagopalachari (1972), first victory for ADMK in Lok Sabha by-election (1973) and first victory for ADMK in Assembly by-election (1974).

In the World, the most important events were death of Gagarin (1968), Dong Biwu becoming President of China (1968), Nixon becoming US President (1969), Armstrong on the moon (1969), the breakup of Beatles (1970), death of Nasser (1970), Heath becoming Prime Minister of UK (1970), Sadat becoming President of Egypt (1970), birth of microprocessor (1971), birth of Greenpeace (1971), Nixon's historic visit to China (1972), starting of Watergate scandal (1972), Munich Olympics and massacre (1972), Christmas bombing of North Vietnam (1972), ending of America's role in Vietnam War (1973), fourth Arab-Israeli conflict (1973), Paris Peace Accord (1973) and birth of mobile phone (1973).

Me

Perhaps, you are one of very few people who get married without a job, a place to live and without any financial resources! Tell me about your job at REC, Calicut.

I must tell you about my first job before I joined IISc Bangalore in August 1965.

Junior Engineer, PWD, Trichy (April-June 1965)

In those days, Civil Engineers were offered appointment order from the Government (then Madras), within 15 days of completion of degree. I was posted to work in the division VI of Ordnance Factory project office in Trichy.

Ordnance Factory, Tiruchirappalli (OFT) is a defence company based in Tiruchirappalli, Tamil Nadu, functioning under the Ordnance Factories Board of the Ministry of Defence, Government of India. OFT is the largest small arms manufacturing company of India. It was inaugurated on July 3, 1966 by the Prime Minister Indira Gandhi. It was established to increase the small arms production in the country.

I joined as a Junior Engineer on April 1, 1965. I checked the design of a hospital building and the water supply and sewerage scheme for the Ordnance Factory.

I worked till June 1965 and resigned to pursue my post graduate studies.

Now, I will tell you about my regular job.

Associate Lecturer, Department of Civil Engineering, Regional Engineering College (REC), Calicut, Kerala - October 16, 1967 to August 9, 1970

After my wedding on August 30, I attended an interview on September 13, 1967 for the post of Associate Lecturer in the Department of Civil Engineering, REC (now National Institute of Technology, NIT), Calicut. Actually, they gave two dates for interview, one on August 28, and the other on September 13. Since my wedding was held on August 30, the second date of interview suited me. It is **God's design.** Does anyone give two dates for interview?

Regional Engineering College (REC), Calicut was the outcome of the second five-year plan (1956–60), during which a number of industrial projects were contemplated. To ensure enough supply of trained personnel to meet the demand for these projects, a decision was taken to start the Regional Engineering Colleges (RECs), at the rate of one per each major state. Thus, seventeen RECs were established from 1959 onwards in each of the major states. Each was a joint and cooperative enterprise of the central government and the state government. REC Calicut was started from July 1961. The campus is located about 22 kilometres towards the north-east of Calicut (Kozhikode) city.

Kozhikode (Calicut) is a city in the state of Kerala in Southern India on the Malabar Coast. The city lies about 275 kilometres west of Bangalore. Kozhikode city continues to be a centre of flourishing domestic and international trade for pepper, coconut, coffee, rubber, lemon grass oil etc. It is about 350 kilometres from Trichy.

The journey from Trichy to Calicut was very long, lasting about 15 hours. As I was travelling in the train, I was contemplating whether I should join such a far-off place. But **Destiny** made me take the post on October 16, 1967 because I had no other choice. I joined along with V.J. Kurien, Babu T. Jose, D.P. Isaac, Chandrasekara Nadar and Md. Ashraff. Except me, all of them were bachelors and undergraduates. We were given bachelor accommodation and in our leisure time we played cards. We were engaged in routine teaching. For open house in college, I designed a model of an airport.

Our first Diwali (known as Thalai Diwali), was fast approaching. *There are many mythical and historical reasons why **Diwali**, the Festival of Lights is a great time to celebrate. One of the two major* *reasons are the birthday of Goddess Lakshmi (Goddess of wealth) and the other is the killing of the demon king Narakaasur by Lord Krishna and rescuing of 16,000 women from his captivity.*

For celebrating our first Diwali (November 1, 1967) in Trichy, I was waiting at the Calicut Railway Station for the train to Trichy and I got severe chest pain. I was sweating but I did not have any idea that I might be having a heart attack. After two or three minutes, it stopped and never occurred again. We celebrated Diwali nicely at my uncle Govindarajan's house and I did not tell anyone about this pain.

Next came Christmas on December 25, 1967. I went to June's house and celebrated by going to church, wearing new clothes, and having a sumptuous lunch and dinner.

Death of June's Brother Rodney - May 27, 1968

During the vacations between April to June 1968, I came to Trichy and spent the holidays with June. That time, an unfortunate thing happened. June's only brother Rodney committed suicide on May 27, 1968, allegedly due to love failure. It was a very sad moment for all of us. He was denied a place in the cemetery and we had to bury him in a waste land a little away. Later on, we were able to shift his remains so that he could rest with his parents and relatives.

Became a Father, Birth of Daughter - July 3, 1968

June was expecting our baby in July 1968. She put on a lot of weight and sometimes had swelling in her legs. My aunties were a bit worried and asked her to do blood and urine tests but the results of the tests showed that everything was normal. She did not have regular check up with a Gynaecologist. Her aunty, who was only a trained nurse, took care of her. June was a very bold girl and she never made any fuss. On the afternoon of Wednesday, July 3, 1968 around 2.45 p.m., she complained of some pain and she was taken to Nalwazhi Hospital next door and without causing any anxiety or trouble to anyone, June gave birth to a beautiful girl at about 3 p.m.

I left on July 5, Friday to see my daughter. As I entered the house around 6 a.m., June's grandmother greeted me by saying, "Kittu, you have a beautiful daughter. Go and see her after drinking this coffee." I ran to the hospital, next door. June got up on hearing my footsteps and I was very happy to see my beautiful daughter. I was afraid to carry her because I had never carried a 3-day old baby until then. But my mother-in-law put my daughter in my lap and my awkwardness disappeared.

I felt nervous about being a father since I did not have a dad growing up. I didn't think I could love another person as much as I loved my wife. However, once I saw the baby, all that nervousness went away immediately. Basically, I am a person who doesn't expose my feelings whether they are happy ones or sad ones. My chest pain which occurred to me earlier in the station made me withhold my feelings further thinking that if anything happened to me, they should not miss me too much. I know it was a foolish thought but that's how I am.

June was discharged from the hospital on the fifth day, (Sunday) and I stayed for two more days then left Trichy on Tuesday night. My daughter's cries (mostly) and laughter were new experiences for me. I was hopeless in taking care of my baby. I just watched how June managed my daughter whenever she cried. From her piercing wails, it was difficult to know whether they were due to hunger, cold, dirty diaper, or just the need to be picked up and cuddled.

As I was exiting the house for Calicut, my daughter started to cry and everyone thought that she was crying because I was leaving her behind.

June wanted to name our daughter Shyamala and my mother wanted to name her Mohanambal which was the name of a heroine in a Tamil movie "Thillana Mohanambal". The film had the famous pair of Sivaji Ganesan and Padmini and Padmini's name was Mohanambal in that movie. My mother did not insist on it and as usual she sacrificed her wish.

__Namkaran__ (naming of new born baby) is the occasion where one has the opportunity to decide the name of a baby. The ceremony is significant as namakaran means giving identity to a child. It is done within two weeks after the birth of the baby on a good day and time as per Panjangam. Parents invite relatives, neighbours and well-wishers to extend their blessings to the new born. Baby names are not just quoted randomly. It requires astrological interference. It is selected based on the baby's birth star and the position of planets and stars at the time of birth. Now, people take numerology into consideration as well while deciding the name.

It is also known as Thottil (Cradle) ceremony in Tamil Nadu. After selecting the name, the baby is put in the cradle and the maternal uncle first utters the name of the baby into its ears thrice followed by parents, grandparents and others. In some places, the name is written on rice first. The significance of this ceremony is to bless the baby for a good and prosperous life

Our First Family Quarters in Calicut

I was allotted family quarters F-3, a two-bedroom house in July 1968. But June had to wait for three months to come to Calicut.

In October 1968, all our household things were transferred by lorry to Calicut along with Ramu. June and Shyamala came with my mother and grandfather by train.

Here, I should tell you about Ramu. He was working in the Golden Rock Workshop as a *kalasi* (Labourer) and was known to my mother's close friend Baby. Through Baby, Ramu became a part of our family. He used to offer all kinds of help to our family and Baby's family. He was very honest and dependable. My mother selected a girl for him and he married her.

We unpacked everything and slowly settled in our quarters to start life in Calicut. We used a kerosene stove for cooking. On the first day, when we were in the kitchen we saw a girl of about 14 years standing near the exit door of the kitchen. I tried to speak to her with whatever little Malayalam I knew, and we came to understand that her name was Kanchana and she wanted to work as a maid servant. We all liked her and asked her to come for work. Next day she came with her mother Saroja and started to work for us. They were with us till we left Calicut in 1974. Kanchana looked after Shyamala very well and she herself got married in 1973.

After staying for a week, my mother and grandfather left for Trichy and my grandfather, who usually doesn't express his appreciation openly, praised June saying that her cooking was very good. June used to learn anything quickly and her execution would be perfect as well. After every one left, June and I were alone with Shyamala (of course along with the invisible God) in a place new to both of them. The college was situated in a village called Chathamangalam about 18 kilometres from the city of Calicut. Our neighbour was Vaidyanathan from the Physics Department and they had a son who was three years old. When Shyamala completed one year, he used to ride his tri-cycle with Shyamala seated happily at the back. June became friendly with Mrs. Vaidyanathan who also knew Tamil.

In the meantime, I found out that some of my colleagues played bridge and we started playing at my house with Krishnasamy, Ramasamy and Vaidyanathan. Slowly we taught the game to other faculty members and within a year the number of bridge players in the campus rose to about 20. The game helped us to bond closely with each other.

My Paternal Grandfather's Problem – 1968 to 1969

My paternal grandfather was mentally sick and he stayed near his daughter Savithri's house for a long time. But when Savithri's family shifted to Thanjavur in 1959, my grandfather was brought to stay with my uncle Padmanaban in the Salai Road house. Since my uncle's family was expanding as well, my uncle and aunty told my mother, "Akka now that Kittu is settled in Calicut why can't he care for his grandfather?" My mother did not give an immediate reply. She discussed the matter with her father and decided that I should not be burdened in a far-off place. My mother decided to rent a house near her school and look after my grandfather. Even though my uncles were not happy seeing their sister suffer because of my insane grandfather, they finally agreed since there was no other alternative. So, my mother rented a house in Subramaniapuram near her colleague Polly who also owned the house. My grandfather and my uncle's families visited my mother frequently.

Visit to Trichy during Summer Holidays in 1969

During the summer vacation in 1969, for 3 months we went to Trichy and stayed in June's house. But we visited my mother frequently and sometimes stayed there for a few days. In that house, Shyamala started to walk. We were thinking of buying a plot to construct a house so that my mother could live in that house with my paternal grandfather. In those times, we did not have bank loans for house construction and we also did not have enough money. Seeing our plight Dr. Thomas agreed to pay all the money for the house. The estimated cost was Rs. 60,000. My mother had inherited a pair of diamond earrings from her step-mother, Daisy, and she was willing to sell it to buy the plot.

We started looking for a plot in the holidays but could not finalise anything.

First birthday and First tonsure of Shyamala - July 1969

We started preparations for celebrating Shyamala's first birthday on July 3, 1969. We had a grand birthday followed by a nice lunch consisting of Biryani prepared by a famous cook Ismail. There were at least 50 guests to grace the occasion.

The next day, we proceeded to Lord Murugan Temple in Palani for the auspicious first tonsure for Shyamala. Then we left for Calicut.

Tonsure is the practice of cutting or shaving some or all of the hair on the scalp, as a sign of religious devotion or humility. The term originates from the Latin word tōnsūra (meaning "clipping" or "shearing") and referred to a specific practice in medieval Catholicism. In modern day India, it is routinely practiced by people of many religions with various beliefs. The first tonsure of a child is done generally around the first birthday. Some say that past birth history may be stored in the hair and it may affect life in this birth. Some believe that the dirt might have been accumulated in scalp while the baby was in uterus and during birth. Complete head shave cleans the scalp by removal of hairs and layer of dead cells. Some others say that it is a respect shown towards God by sacrificing their beauty (Hindus believe tonsure as ugliness).

Birth of Ramesh, my Sister's Third Son - August 1, 1969

My sister gave birth to her third son Ramesh on August 1, 1969.

Purchase of Plot and Booking of Cooking Gas Indane

After we reached Calicut we heard that my mother had purchased a plot of land 60 feet x 40 feet in her name in Mannarpuram and I drew the plan of the house and made a model with chart paper.

In Calicut, Krishnaswamy was the only faculty using Indane gas since 1970, when it was introduced in India for the first time.

*Indian Oil Corporation pioneered the launch of **LPG (Liquefied Petroleum Gas)** in India in the middle of the 1960's and transformed the lives of millions of people with the introduction of the cooking fuel. LPG led to improvement in the health of women in rural areas by replacing smoky and unhealthy chullahs with Indane. It is today a fuel synonymous with safety, reliability and convenience. Indane is today one of the largest packed LPG brands in the world with 92 million people using it in India. LPG is a blend of Butane and Propane readily liquefied under moderate pressure.*

He asked whether we were interested. Even though I did not have any idea about it, June readily agreed. I went with Krishnasamy and booked the gas cylinder. At that time, there was no distributor in Calicut and the gas cylinder used to come from Erode and we had to pick it up from the agent in Calicut. Then, we had to bring the cylinders in his car. From March 1970, we had cooking gas. In the whole campus, out of about 100 families, three of us had refrigerators, two had cars and a land line telephone.

Visit to Trichy during Summer Holidays in 1970

We came to Trichy in the summer vacation of 1970. We made arrangements to put up a fence and dig a well in our plot. When the jobs were completed we performed a *pooja* (worship) in the plot. Then, we submitted our plan for approval. Our vacations were coming to an end and after celebrating the second birthday of Shyamala, we left for Calicut happily thinking that we would have our own house soon. But **destiny** acted differently.

Snake incident

The Calicut campus had a lot of snakes, both poisonous and non-poisonous.

Once, when June opened the bathroom door she saw a snake coming towards her and we called snake catchers to kill it. They asked us to apply some pesticides so that the snakes would not enter the house.

Lecturer, Regional Engineering College (REC), Calicut, Kerala - August 10, 1970 to July 10, 1974

When a member of faculty left for higher studies, I was promoted to Lecturer from August 10, 1970. Kerala governments are quick compared to other governments in implementing some of the welfare schemes. There was no government funding for research at that time and as the college was new no consultancy services were initiated. So, the faculty had to concentrate on teaching only.

I was allotted E-2 quarters which was a 2-bedroom house with one study room and plinth area more than F-3 type. We moved to the new house in August 1970 and June decorated the hall with linoleum.

The house was at a lower elevation than the road. Usually in Kerala, natural topography is conserved as much as possible. There was a pathway connecting the road and the house which was decorated with white stones and hydrangea flowers on either side by June. This was appreciated by everyone in the campus.

Death of Uncle Thomas and "Our Own House" Dream - August 15, 1970

We received a shocking trunk call from Trichy on August 15 that Thomas had passed away due to a heart attack. We took a taxi and rushed to Trichy and reached on time for viewing the remains which were kept in the Seventh Day Adventist Church. He was buried in St. John's Church, near Trichy junction. After attending the third day memorial service, we left for Calicut but this time with grief, since our hope of having our own house had been shattered.

It took some time for us to come out of our grief. I told you earlier about my mother's close friend Baby aunty. Her husband Krishnaraj was about to retire from Golden Rock Workshop and they had started looking for a house since they had to vacate the Railway quarters after his retirement. Baby aunty approached my mother and said, "Dharma, Kittu is in Calicut so far away. Why don't you ask Kittu to sell the plot to us so that we could build our house before retirement?" My mother and most of our family members are very kind with a sacrificing nature. When my mother told us about this, June and I decided to say "yes" and with some difficulty asked my mother to sell the plot and take the plot money. Baby aunty's family constructed the house and they started to live there. Even after 20 years, whenever Baby aunty saw us she used to say, "Kittu and June because of you only we happily live in that house. Thank you so much."

After all, our dream house had been useful to my mother's close friend.

Tributes to my Uncle Thomas

Thomas uncle was my Godfather who respected me and took care of me like his own son. He was a very straightforward man and very good in his profession as a medical doctor. He was a sports lover. He was instrumental in promoting both football and tennis in Trichy. He is one of the reasons behind the fame of the Amirtharaj brothers.

Death of my Grandfather Arumugam- March 1, 1971

Within eight months of the demise of Thomas, we got the shocking news of the sudden passing away of my grandfather Arumugam due to a heart attack on March 1, 1971. So, within a short span I lost the two men who played a major role in shaping my life. But this time, we received the news late and we could reach my uncle Govindarajan's house only by 7 p.m.

And by that time, they had cremated him. We were very unfortunate in not paying our last respects to him. Most of our relatives were angry with us for coming late even though it was not our fault. But we had to remain silent. After completing the usual ceremonies connected with the death including a trip to Rameshwaram, we left for Calicut.

Tributes to my Grandfather Arumugam

My grandfather Arumugam was my first Godfather after the death of my father. He educated me and cared for me. He overcame the shock of the sudden early death of his son-in-law (also his sister's son) and permitted his daughter to complete her teacher training and work as teacher. In those times, widows were expected to stay at home. He believed in good education. For the benefit of his motherless children, he invited his friend Dr. Daisy to become a part of the family.

I fondly remember the days when we had lunch together every school day. Every night he had pooris (made of wheat and fried) for dinner. I used to stand beside him in anticipation and he would happily give one to me. Even though he did not like movies, he sent me to a movie on my 15th birthday in 1958.

He had been a teacher, a mentor, and a profound example of what it means to truly be a Man. He would never show his emotions. He was a leader among his family and friends. Since he was staying with his eldest son, Govindarajan, he took good care of all his grandchildren. He would lovingly spread the bedding on the floor at night and put it away in the morning.

He chose the groom, Ramaiyan, for my sister and one cannot find a more honest man than Ramaiyan. He ensured that his two fatherless grandchildren could settle well in life.

When my mother had a hysterectomy, he took care of her during her stay at Christian Medical College Hospital, Vellore and during her recuperation at home.

I have learned that to be a man, one must be committed to solid principles and standards. He must be dedicated to family, God and his country. He must focus his energies on causes he finds worthy. He must be a man of constant faith and courageous behaviour – all these qualities were possessed by my grandfather.

Two major blows within a year which was a repeat of 1946 when my father, my paternal grandmother and my nana all died within a year.

Birth of Premalatha (Pappi) - April 19, 1971

My sister gave birth to her fourth child, this time a girl, on April 19, 1971. She was named Premalatha and her nick name is Pappi.

June's Sister Eugenia's Marriage - May 29, 1971

June's sister Eugenia (Dinky) got married on May 29, 1971 to Darrel Nigli, who was working as chargeman in the Golden Rock Workshop of Indian Railways, Trichy and she started her life in the Railway quarters, Golden Rock, Trichy.

Death of my Grandfather Rathinaswamy (Hari) - December 10,1973

I told you earlier that my mother was staying with my paternal grandfather in a separate house. Somehow, she managed to work and take care of her father-in-law. In the beginning of 1973, my grandfather got a sore on his foot and his feet were always swollen but he managed his illness very well. Without getting bedridden with sickness he passed away on December 10, 1973. June had gone to Trichy for Christmas and I had gone to Ernakulam to participate in a bridge tournament at the Lotus Club. As usual, I missed his funeral and June was there with my mother in this hour of crisis. My sister's family had also moved to Trichy in June 1973 when my brother-in-law was promoted as Manager in the Trichy Municipal office. They also helped my mother to complete all the rituals.

Tributes to my Grandfather Hari

Rathinaswamy was a Station Master in the Railways and he married my grandfather Arumugam's sister, Gangamirtham. He was known for his calmness and kindness. He was doing well but suddenly he became insane. It was believed that someone might have done black magic on him. When his son (my father) became sick, his condition worsened and he was relieved from duty. After the death of my father, he lost his wife as well. My grandfather Arumugam had kept him in a small house next to my paternal aunt, Savithri's, house. He used to take his meals at our home. His insanity condition was severe in the beginning and subsided slowly. His English was excellent. He could read, write and speak it perfectly. He would read the English newspaper daily and apply for jobs.

He never troubled anyone. I feel sorry for him as he suffered from insanity for almost 30 years. He had no money at all and had very few belongings.

At least he was lucky not to be deserted. He was safe in the hands of Arumugam, my mother, my two uncles and aunties.

Personal Life

The social life in Calicut was enjoyable. A new building was constructed for the Officer's Club in which we could play indoor games. Every year we used to conduct tournaments for the faculty and their spouses. I used to win lot of prizes. Once, in the football match I scored a goal and my Head of the Department Dr. Subramanian congratulated me by saying that my goal was like that scored by the great football legend Pele. All my friends got married, Ramasamy to Chellam, Isaac to Leela, and Chandrasekar to Thangam. They were fond of Shyamala. June used to play shuttle daily. Two or three families would get together from time to time, hire taxis and go to Calicut city to watch Tamil movies and have dinner. Sometimes we enjoyed the food from the canteen owned by Vijayan. On some Sundays, some of my colleagues played rummy the whole day and drank toddy. One of our students Kalyana Sundaram was a cricketer and he played for the Ranji Trophy. The famous case of Rajan which shook the entire country during the emergency in 1976 was connected with our college. Rajan joined REC in 1971 as a student. It was alleged that he died as a result of torture in police custody. Once, I accompanied the students on an educational tour to Parambikulam Aliyar Project in Palakkad district, Kerala.

June had good friends like Meenakshi and Shyamala, both of whom were faculty members.

Vijay Amirtharaj's Visit

There was a tennis tournament organised by the Cosmopolitan Club, Calicut in 1972 and Vijay Amirtharaj, who was an upcoming tennis star, visited our house, had lunch, and enjoyed music played on the calypso.

Snake incident

The second incident took place when we found a snake in the pile of bed sheets and pillows. Again, we called snake catchers to kill it.

Shyamala's School

When Shyamala completed 3 years of age, she was admitted to the Malayalam medium nursery school situated in the campus. Kanchana used to take her to school and back. We wanted our daughter to study in English medium so that it would be easy for her later in college where courses are taught in English. It was believed in those days that a good education was provided by Christian institutions. When she completed 5 years, we wanted to admit her to an English medium school. We learned from our friends about St. Joseph's Anglo-Indian Convent in Calicut city. The word was that it was difficult to get admission into it.

St. Joseph's Anglo-Indian Convent had its beginning in 1862 and in 1906 the school came under the code of regulations for European in schools. From August 1923, the management of the school came under the governing body of the Apostolic Carmel Education Society of Kozhikode under the Society's Act of 1860.

Anyway, June and I decided to try our luck. When we went to the school in May 1973, the principal, Mother Superior Rosy Panikkal was kind enough to interview Shyamala and was impressed with her answers and personality. She admitted her to the school and also accepted our request for accommodation in the boarding. After purchasing everything required, we put her in the boarding school with a heavy heart. She cried when we left her for the first time to live with unknown people. We visited her every weekend and would eagerly wait for the next weekend to come. It was a hard decision to make. We wanted the best for Shyamala. As parents, we made a choice and we hoped it was not the wrong one. Somehow, she became used to the boarding school life and everyone loved her including Mother Superior.

For their Annual Day function, Shyamala welcomed the DSP, who was the chief guest, by garlanding him.

Robbery incident

With Shyamala away, every weekday, I went to the club in the evening and June played her shuttle game in the ladies' club. She used to come back to the house by 7 p.m., and I used to come by 8.30 p.m. One day on reaching home early I found June sitting on the steps leading to the house with a worried look which I could easily spot. She told me, "See Athan, some thief has entered the house through the tile roof." Generally, in Kerala, because of the weather all the houses had tiled roof with false ceiling in the bed rooms. When both of us entered the house, we saw that 2 tiles had been removed above the common toilet. Then we started to check everything. Our almirah was locked and we had our jewels inside the locker. Everything was safe. After a thorough search, we found out that only my undergarments were stolen. But entering a house and robbing was a big crime though from the loss point of view it was nothing to bother about. We complained to the Estate Officer immediately and as per his suggestion gave a complaint to the police station. Within 3 or 4 days we came to know that a labourer who used to clean our garden regularly was involved in the robbery. I told him, "Why did you do this just to rob my undergarments. If you had asked I would have given them free of cost." I thought of leaving it at that stage but college authorities thought otherwise. They asked me to hand him over to the police and we did so and the police took custody of him. Before we could leave, the police said that if called, I had to come to court to give my statement.

Actually, when I was in REC Trichy, in 1975, two years after the incident, I was called to Calicut and I gave my statement which no one questioned. Later I heard that he was imprisoned for 6 months. I was paid TA and DA for the trip.

Tooth incident

Another incident happened when Shyamala was in the boarding school. I had a toothache and went to a dentist in Calicut. He said the tooth was in a bad shape and had to be extracted. Then, after coming home, I ate prawn fry and suddenly by 9.30 p.m., my gum started to bleed. Even after 15 minutes it didn't stop and we went to the REC campus doctor's house. He was a retired person and he was kind enough to take us to the campus hospital and attend to my gum. He tried his level best but the bleeding continued until 3 a.m. Isaac and his wife were also with us. By 8 a.m., we went to the dentist in the college car and he put sutures in the gum and only then did the bleeding stop completely.

Mother's Stay with my Sister

In the meantime, my brother-in-law was promoted to the post of Manager in Trichy Municipality in June 1973 and my sister's family took accommodation in the official residence in Thillainagar. After the death of my grandfather Rathinaswamy, my mother vacated the house in Subramaniapuram and decided to stay with my sister's family. Even then, my mother frequently visited her brothers and their families.

Decision to leave REC Calicut

As we had to travel frequently to Trichy for different occasions like Diwali, Christmas, Birthdays, New Year etc., we decided to apply for a teaching position at REC Trichy in 1974. At that time Prof. P.S. Manisundaram was the Principal and no one could get a position without his consent even if the person was well qualified. For this we required a very high recommendation. We knew T. M. Narayanaswamy Pillai (TMN) who was a retired Vice Chancellor of Annamalai University whose recommendation would be valued by Manisundaram. With his kind blessing, I got an appointment in REC Trichy as Lecturer.

I had to give 3 months' notice for my resignation or pay 3 months' salary as penalty at REC, Calicut. I was not bold enough to ask for 3 months' time to join REC Trichy and so I decided to pay 3 months' salary. I arranged a lorry to move our things from Calicut to Trichy and as usual allowed June to pack and send the things since I went earlier to Trichy to join duty. My colleagues and Ramu helped June in packing and loading the lorry. June came alone with Shyamala in the train and I went to Erode to bring them by taxi. I went a little late to the station making June and Shyamala suffer a bit but anyway all of us reached Trichy safely. As soon as I joined as Lecturer on July 11, 1974 at REC Trichy, they allotted me the staff quarters No. 11, 7th street. We unloaded the things from the lorry at the allotted house. But we did not take up residence because it was the Tamil month of Adi. We waited till the month was over and we started our life in the house in the last week of August 1974. Till then we lived with aunt Amelia.

You were born in Andhra Pradesh, studied in Tamil Nadu for your UG degree and in Karnataka for your PG degree, and then spent the first part of your professional life in Kerala. What were your feelings when you came back to Trichy where both of you were brought up?

After spending 14 years away from Trichy, (incidentally it coincides with 14 years of exile in a forest by Lord Rama in the epic Ramayana) I came back to the place where I spent the first 17 years of my life.

Definitely a happy one for both of us since it was our native place. Both of us grew up there. We met each other and got married in Trichy. All our relatives and friends were in Trichy.

Trichy is famous for worship places of all religions, Cauvery and Coleroon Rivers, Uyyakondan Canal in the heart of the city, oldest Grand Anicut, RockFort, Hamampasanth mango, and tasty restaurants. Trichy is a typical countryside place, calm, quiet and serene. Standing on the RockFort and surveying the picturesque landscape caressed by a soft breeze, one discovers oneself perfectly at peace with Him and the world.

Native place is where our story begins. It is the place where the person is born and raised. Since the dawn of time people work at their native place and become famous at their native place. In the success of a person a native place plays a vital role.

First and foremost, the native place builds the foundation for education, culture, discipline, etc. He or she becomes acquainted with the available resources, growing business, occupations of the people, modes of travel and other necessary things to become successful. Furthermore, native place helps in maintaining the native identity and apart from this, a person uses his or her education and experience to give back to others. It helps the masses to become responsible towards their native society.

Did you become successful in your native place?

Yes. I became successful in my profession and sports. I contributed to the social upliftment and success of people associated with me. Of course, I had a few personal failures also.

Around me

Let us go through the major events, which took place, during this period.

India

Politics

Indian National Congress Split, 1969 - Indian National Congress split in 1969, due to differences between Indira Gandhi and the syndicate members of the party. Indira Gandhi set up a rival organization, which came to be known as Congress (R) - R for

Requisitionists. The Syndicate dominated Congress came to be known as Congress (O) - O for Organization.

Nationalisation of Banks, 1969 - Politics outdid economics in 1969 when Prime Minister Indira Gandhi nationalised 14 banks.

First Rajdhani Express, 1969 - The first Rajdhani Express was introduced in 1969 between Howrah and New Delhi and was the first fully air-conditioned train providing breakfast, lunch, dinner, coffee and snacks.

V.V. Giri as President - Dr. V.V. Giri became the 4th President of India on August 24, 1969 after acting President Mohammed Hidayatullah.

Birth of Himachal Pradesh, 1971 - Himachal Pradesh, India's 18th state, came into being on January 25, 1971.

Vth General Elections, 1971 - In order to consolidate her position after the split in the Congress, Indira Gandhi dissolved the Lok Sabha on December 27, 1970 and called elections in March 1971 one year ahead of time. The opposition parties - Cong (O), Jan Sangh, Swatantra and the Samyukta Socialist Party (SSP) formed the Grand Alliance. In the general elections held during March 1-10 to elect the fifth Lok Sabha, Indira Gandhi registered a massive victory. INC(R) won 352 seats, INC(O) 16, BJS 22, CPI 22, CPI(M) 25 and DMK 23. The total seats were 520. Indira Gandhi continued as Prime Minster.

Birth of Manipur State, 1972 - Manipur state in north eastern India was created on January 21, 1972.

Renaming of Mysore State, 1973 - Originally known as the State of Mysore, it was renamed Karnataka on November 1, 1973.

Railway Strike, 1974 - This was a strike by workers of Indian Railways in 1974 led by George Fernandes, President of All India Railway Men's Federation. The 20 days strike from May 8-27, by 17 lakh workers is the largest known strike. It was held to demand a raise in pay scale which had remained stagnant over many years. The strike was brutally suppressed by Indira Gandhi's government with thousands being sent to jail and losing their jobs.

Natural Calamities

Cyclone in Orissa, 1971 - On October 27, a tropical depression formed in the Bay of Bengal. It tracked northward, steadily strengthening until it reached a peak of 115 mph winds. The cyclone struck Cuttack, Odisha, on October 29, 1971 and dissipated 2 days later. The storm surge and flooding caused 10,800 fatalities.

War

Indo-China Border Fight, 1967 - Second Sino-Indian War of 1967 happened during September 11 to October 10, 1967. From August 13, 1967, Chinese troops started digging trenches in Nathu La on the Sikkimese side. Indian troops observed that some were "clearly" on the Sikkimese side of the border, and pointed it out to the local Chinese commander. Since there was no positive response from the Chinese side, the Indian army started to stretch wires along the border which was resented by the Chinese army. This led to frequent clashes between the two armies. All hostilities ended on October 10.

Indo-Pakistan War and Birth of Bangladesh, 1971 - The Indo-Pakistani conflict was sparked by the Bangladesh Liberation War, a conflict between the traditionally dominant West Pakistanis and the majority East Pakistanis during December 1971. On the evening of December 3, Sunday, at about 5.40 p.m., the Pakistani Air Force (PAF) launched a pre-emptive strike known as Chengiz Khan on eleven airfields in north-western India, including Agra which is 480 kilometres from the border. The Indian Air Force responded with air strikes that very night. This marked the start of the Indo-Pakistani War of 1971. The Prime Minister, Indira Gandhi, launched a full-scale invasion. This involved Indian forces in a massive coordinated air, sea, and land assault. The main Indian objective on the Eastern front was to capture Dacca and on the western front to prevent Pakistan from entering Indian soil. There was no intention of conducting any major offensive into West Pakistan. The Instrument of Surrender of Pakistan Eastern Command stationed in East Pakistan was signed between the Lieutenant General Jagjit Singh Aurora, the GOC-in-C of Indian Eastern Command and Lieutenant General A.A.K. Niazi, Commander of the Pakistan Eastern Command, at the Ramna Race Course in Dhaka at 4.31 p.m., IST on December 16, 1971. With this, the war ended and Bangladesh became independent.

Indo-Bangladesh Treaty of Friendship, 1972 - The Indo-Bangladeshi Treaty of Friendship, Cooperation and Peace was a 25-year treaty signed on March 19, 1972 forging close bilateral relations between India and Bangladesh. The treaty was also known as Indira-Mujib Treaty, after the Prime Ministers Indira Gandhi and Sheikh Mujibur Rahman.

Indo-Pakistan Simla Agreement, 1972 - The Simla Agreement (or Shimla Agreement) was signed between India and Pakistan on July 2, 1972 in Simla, capital of Himachal Pradesh. The agreement was ratified by the Parliaments of both the nations in the same year. It conceived the steps to be taken for further normalization of mutual relations and it also laid down the principles that should govern their future relations.

First Nuclear Bomb Test, 1974 - Smiling Buddha (MEA designation: Pokhran-I) was the assigned code name of India's first successful nuclear bomb test on May 18, 1974. The bomb was detonated on the army base, Pokhran Test Range (PTR), Rajasthan by the Indian Army under the supervision of several key army officials. The Indian Ministry of External Affairs (MEA) claimed this was a "peaceful nuclear explosion".

Tamil Nadu

The Kilvenmani Massacre, 1968 - The Kilvenmani massacre was an incident in Kilvenmani village, Tamil Nadu on December 25, 1968 in which a group of around 44 people, the families of striking village agricultural labourers, were murdered by a gang led by their landlords. The incident helped to initiate large scale changes in the local rural economy, prompting a massive redistribution of land in the region.

Renaming of Madras State, 1969 - In 1969, Madras State was renamed Tamil Nadu, meaning "Tamil country".

Annadurai's Death, 1969 - On September 10, 1968 Annadurai travelled to New York for medical treatment. He was operated for cancer in the gullet at the Memorial Sloan–Kettering Cancer Center. He returned to Chennai in November and continued to address several official functions against medical advice. His health deteriorated further and he died on February 3, 1969. His cancer was attributed to his habit of chewing tobacco. His funeral had the highest number of attendees (15 million) as registered with The Guinness Book of Records. His remains were buried in the northern end of Marina Beach, now called Anna Memorial. V. R. Nedunchezhian became the interim Chief Minister after the death of Annadurai.

Karunanidhi Became Chief Minister, 1969 - After the death of Annadurai, the power tussle between M. Karunanidhi and V. R. Nedunchezhiyan started. Most of the elected MLAs of DMK, including Mathiazhagan, Nanjil Manoharan and the celluloid hero MGR favoured Karunanidhi. To pacify Nedunchezhiyan a new post called Party President was created for Karunanidhi and Nedunchezhiyan was given the post of General Secretary. MGR was appointed as the Treasurer. Karunanidhi was sworn in as Chief Minister on February 10, 1969.

Invocation to Tamil Goddess, 1970 - The song "Niraarum Kadal Udutha" from Manonmaniam was adapted as "Invocation to Goddess Tamil" and approved by the Government of Tamil Nadu as the official Tamil anthem in June 1970. The song was written by Manonmaniam Sundaram Pillai and the music was composed by M.S. Viswanathan.

Vth Assembly Elections, 1971 - The fifth Legislative Assembly elections of Tamil Nadu were held in March 1971, when Karunanidhi decided to dissolve the state Assembly and face the elections in alliance with Indira's Congress a year before the end of his term. DMK won 184 seats, CPI 9, Praja Socialistic Party 4, Indian Union Muslim League 2, Cong(O) 15, Swatantra 6 and independents 8. The total number of seats were 234. Karunanidhi became Chief Minister for the second time.

Formation of ADMK, 1972 - A political feud between M. G. Ramachandran and the party's president, M. Karunanidhi, had been ongoing since the death of Annadurai in 1969. Karunanidhi made several attempts to weaken MGR's position within the party. MGR retaliated with corruption charges and a call for a boycott of the party's General Council. DMK's General Council suspended MGR from the party stating that he had involved himself in anti-party activities. Inspired by support from the party's lower cadres and his fans, MGR launched his own party, Anna Dravida Munnetra Kazhagam (ADMK) named after Annadurai's nickname Anna on October 17, 1972.

Death of Rajaji, 1972 - Chakravarti Rajagopalachari who was known as Rajaji died at 5.44 p.m., on December 25, 1972 in Madras.

First Victory by ADMK in By-Elections, 1973 and 1974 - The party tasted victory for the first time by winning the Dindigul parliamentary by-elections held on May 20, 1973. The party's candidate K. Maya Thevar won the election by polling 2,60,000 votes followed by Cong(O) 1,20,000, DMK 93,000 and Cong(I) polling a mere 11,000 votes. K. Maya Thevar selected the symbol two leaves for the ADMK party in 1973 from the District Collector Mr. Syria (IAS). Barely two years after the party was formed, it grabbed the Coimbatore (West) Assembly constituency from the ruling DMK in the February 1974 by-elections.

World

Politics

Dong Biwu Became President of China, 1968 - Dong Biwu became President of China on October 31, 1968 after Liu Shaoqi.

Nixon became US President, 1969 &1973 - Richard Mihous Nixon, a Republican, became the 37th President of USA on January 20, 1969 after Lyndon B. Johnson. He continued as President, after his re-election, from January 20, 1973.

Edward Heath became Prime Minister of England, 1970 - Sir Edward Heath became the Prime Minister of England on June 19, 1970, after Harold Wilson.

Death of Nasser, 1970 - At the end of an emergency Arab League Summit on September 28, 1970, Nasser suffered a heart attack and died around 6 p.m.

Muhammad Anwar El Sadat became President of Egypt, 1970 - Muhammad Anwar El Sadat became the third President of Egypt, and began serving from October 15, 1970.

Founding of Greenpeace Organisation, 1971 - Greenpeace a non-governmental environmental organization with offices in forty countries was born in 1971. Its goal was to "ensure the ability of the Earth to nurture life in all its diversity".

Nixon's Visit to China, 1972 - President Richard Nixon was the first US President to visit People's Republic of China during February 21-28, 1972. It was an important step in formally stabilizing relations between the US and China.

Space Technology

Death of Yuri Gagarin, 1968 - On March 27, 1968, Yuri Gagarin, the first man in space, died when his MiG-15 fighter jet clashed with a Su-15 which was also flying a test. He was with his instructor Vladimir Seryogin on a routine training flight.

First Man on the Moon, 1969 - Apollo 11 was the space flight that landed the first humans - Americans Neil Armstrong and Buzz Aldrin, on the Moon, on July 20, 1969. Armstrong became the first man to step onto the lunar surface six hours later on July 21. He spent about two and a half hours outside the spacecraft, Aldrin slightly less, and together they collected 21.5 kg of lunar material for return to Earth. The third member of the mission, Michael Collins, piloted the command spacecraft alone in lunar orbit until Armstrong and Aldrin returned to it.

Music

Break Up of Beatles, 1970 - The Beatles broke up on April 10, 1970.

Science and Technology

Birth of Microprocessor Computer on a Chip, 1971 - The Intel 4004 is considered the first microprocessor, the first general-purpose computer on a chip. It was the joint effort of a Japanese company called the Nippon Calculating Machine Corporation (Busicom, after the name of its calculators) and Intel.

Birth of Cell Phones, 1973 - Martin "Marty" Cooper (born December 26, 1928) is an American engineer. While at Motorola, he conceived the first handheld mobile phone in 1973 and led the team that developed it and brought it to market in 1983. He is considered the "father of the cell phone" and is also cited as the first person in history to make a handheld cellular phone call in public.

Scandals

Watergate Scandal, 1972 - The Watergate scandal was a major political scandal in the United States as a result of the June 17, 1972 break-in at the Democratic National Committee (DNC) headquarters at the Watergate office complex in Washington, D.C., and the attempted cover-up by President Nixon's administration.

Munich Olympics Massacre, 1972 - The 1972 XX Summer Olympics were held in Munich, West Germany, from August 26 to September 11, 1972. The Munich massacre was an attack on eleven Israeli Olympic team members, who were taken hostage and killed, along with a German police officer, by the Palestinian group Black September. They demanded 234 prisoners jailed in Israel and the German-held founders of the Red Army Faction (Andreas and Ulrike Meinhof) be released. West Germany released them. Mossad responded to the release with Operation "Spring of Youth" and Operation "Wrath of God", tracking down and killing Palestinians suspected of involvement in the massacre.

War

The Christmas Bombings of North Vietnam, 1972 - Operation Linebacker II was a US Seventh Air Force and US Navy Task Force 77 aerial bombing campaign, conducted against targets in the Democratic Republic of Vietnam (North Vietnam) during the final period of US involvement in the Vietnam War from December 18 to 29, 1972. It was also called "The December Raids" and "The Christmas Bombings".

Paris Peace Accord, 1973 - The Paris Peace Accords, the agreement on 'Ending the War' and 'Restoring Peace' in Vietnam, was signed on January 27, 1973. The treaty included the governments of the Democratic Republic of Vietnam (North Vietnam), the Republic of Vietnam (South Vietnam), and the United States, as well as the Provisional Revolutionary Government (PRG) that represented indigenous South Vietnamese revolutionaries. It ended direct U.S. military combat and temporarily stopped the fighting between North and South Vietnam.

Ending of America's Direct Role in Vietnam War, 1973 - Gradual withdrawal of US ground forces began as part of "Vietnamization", which aimed to end American involvement in the war while transferring the task of fighting the Communists to the South Vietnamese. Based on the Paris Peace Accord, direct US military involvement ended on August 15, 1973. 58,220 US service members had died in the conflict, with a further 1,626 missing in action.

> **Fourth Arab-Israeli War, 1973 -** The Yom Kippur War, Ramadan War, or October War also known as the 1973 Arab–Israeli War, was fought by the coalition of Arab states led by Egypt and Syria against Israel from October 6 to 25, 1973. Even though the Arab coalition tasted success initially, they had to withdraw due to Israeli attacks. On October 22, a United Nations brokered ceasefire quickly unraveled, with each side blaming the other for the breach. Finally, a second ceasefire was imposed cooperatively on October 25 to end the war.

CHAPTER 7

Life in Trichy, Part I – July 1974 to June 1984

Abstract

Me

The details of my career at REC Trichy as Lecturer (1974-1984), Shyamala's admission to school (1974), ear boring ceremony (1976), puberty ceremony (1980), Shyamala learning Bharatanatyam (1976 to 1980), deaths of my father-in-law, Lionel and June's uncle John (1977), Kumararaj's stay at REC (1977-78), my mother's retirement (1980), my mother's 60th birthday (1982) and Amelia's own house (1984) are presented.

Around me

In India, the most important events were Fakhruddin Ali Ahmed becoming President (1974), 1st satellite in space (1975), birth of Sikkim state (1975), 2nd emergency (1975), death of Fakhruddin Ali Ahmed (1977), Jatti becoming acting President (1977), founding of Janata Party (1977), VIth general elections (1977), Sanjeeva Reddy becoming President (1977), Morarji Desai becoming Prime Minister (1977), crash of Air India flight 855 (1978), setting up Mandal Commission (1979), Moraraji's resignation (1979), Charan Singh becoming Prime Minister (1979), Charan Singh's resignation (1979), Morbi Dam failure (1979), VIIth general elections (1980), Indira Gandhi becoming Prime Minister (1980), formation of Bharatiya Janata Party (1980), death of Sanjay Gandhi (1980), founding of InfoSys (1981), founding of Maruti Suzuki (1982), Zail Singh becoming President of India (1982), Birth of Telugu Desam Party (1982), launching of INSAT-1A (1982), Integrated Guided Defence

Missile Project (1982-83), Ist Indian to travel in space (1984) and birth of Bahujan Samaj Party (1984).

In Tamil Nadu state, the most important events were death of Kamaraj (1975), dismissal of DMK government (1976), change of name from ADMK to AIADMK (1976), President's rule (1976-77), VIth assembly elections (1977), MGR becoming Chief Minister for first time (1977), dismissal of MGR government (1980), VIIth assembly elections (1980), MGR becoming Chief Minister for second time (1980), establishment of Bharathiar University and Bharadhidasan University (1982) and establishment of Salem Steel Plant (1982).

In the World, the most important events were US President Nixon's resignation (1974), founding of Microsoft Corporation (1975), Zhou De becoming President of China (1975), end of Vietnam war (1975), Apollo-soyuz mission (1975), Landing of Viking 1 and 2 on Mars (1976), reunification of Vietnam (1976), founding of Apple computers (1976), Hua Guofeng becoming Premier of China (1976), Soong Ching-ling becoming President of China (1976), Jimmy Carter becoming President of USA (1977), Camp David Accord for Egypt and Israel (1978), first test tube baby (1978), Ye Jianying becoming President of China (1978), Exit of Shah and entry of Khomini in Iran (1979), Iran hostage crisis (1979), Saddam Hussain becoming President of Iraq (1979), nuclear accident on three mile island (1979), Margaret Thatcher becoming Prime Minister of England (1979), Zhao Ziang becoming Premier of China (1980), Moscow Olympics and its boycott (1980), Nikolai Tikhonov becoming Premier of USSR (1980), Iraq-Iran War (1980), killing of John Lennon of Beatles (1980), end of Iran hostage crisis (1981), assassination of Anwar Sadat, President of Egypt (1981), Reagan as US President (1981), First known AIDS death (1981), death of Brezhnev, USSR (1982), Yuri Andropov becoming General Secretary, USSR, (1982), first American woman in space (1983), Li Xiannian becoming President of China (1983) and Chernenko becoming General Secretary of USSR (1984).

Me

So, after spending nearly seven years at REC Calicut, you went to Trichy. Please tell us about your life at REC Trichy.

Lecturer, Department of Civil Engineering, Regional Engineering College, Tiruchirappalli, Tamil Nadu - July7, 1974 to July 10, 1984

I joined as Lecturer in the Department of Civil Engineering on Monday, July 11, 1974.

Regional Engineering College (REC) was started in Trichy in May 1964. REC is located in a very big campus of around 900 acres in Thuvakkudi Village at a distance of 16 kilometres from the city of Trichy on the Trichy-Tanjavur highway NH 67

I occupied my family quarters at No. 11, 7th street along with June and Shyamala during the last week of August 1974. It was a two-bedroom house with a fenced compound and open spaces in the front and back. REC celebrated its golden jubilee in 2014. The first principal of the college, Manisundaram, was the chief guest.

Personal life

Shyamala's School Admission – July, 1974

We admitted Shyamala in the 1st standard in R.S. Krishnan Higher Secondary School (RSKHSS) situated in the Bharat Heavy Electricals Ltd., 4 kilometres away from REC. It was an English medium school and under the Central Board of Secondary Education (CBSE).

A High-Pressure Boiler manufacturing plant was set up by the **Bharat Heavy Electricals Limited** (BHEL), India's largest public-sector engineering company, in May 1965 in Trichy. This was followed by a Seamless Steel Plant and a Boiler Auxiliaries Plant. The three manufacturing units constitute the BHEL industrial complex in Trichy. It has a huge factory campus on one side of the Trichy-Tanjavur main road and a residential campus on the other side. R. S. Krishnan was an outstanding Mechanical Engineer and as the first Project Administrator of BHEL, he successfully built up the industrial complex for Trichy.

Shyamala's Birthdays

Within a year, all of us made our own circle of friends. Some of Shyamala's close friends were Jijo, Jubin and Kanchana. We celebrated Shyamala's birthdays every year till her 12th standard, inviting all her friends. Kembu studio, owned by Natarajan, was situated in Tiruverambur about 8 kilometres from REC. They covered all the functions at our home and later, Shyamala's wedding as well.

Shyamala's Ear Boring Ceremony

The ear boring ceremony for Shyamala was conducted in the year 1975 when she was 7 years old.

Ear lobe piercing, known as Karnvedh Sanskar, is considered an important ceremony in many Hindu traditions. An auspicious day *and time is chosen for performing the ear-piercing ceremony. Special pujas and prayer is done and the ceremony is done under sunlight. Earrings are then offered to the child. The ear piercing in some regions is performed by the Goldsmith and he uses gold needles to pierce the earlobe. Gold never rusts and this is the reason for using gold needles. Technically speaking, ear boring is a part of acupuncture treatment. The outer part of the ears have a lot of important acupuncture and acupressure points. The point where the ears of a baby are pierced is known for curing asthma.*

Purchase of First Two-Wheeler -1975

Aunty Amelia purchased a new Lambretta scooter for me in 1975 and after keeping it for nearly 9 years I sold it to Chellappa, uncle Padmanaban's son-in-law.

Shyamala Learning Bharatanatyam - 1976

June wanted Shyamala to learn Bharatanatyam and through BHEL Officers' Club, we located a dance master Natarajan, who came to our house three days in a week from June 1976 to June 1979 to teach Shyamala. She was doing fine and the only thing to be regretted was that we never arranged an arangetram performance (to perform first time in public).

My Father-in- Law Lionel's Hospitalization and Death - 1977

On June 24, 1977, we celebrated June's birthday in Amelia's house and my father-in-law was also present. Within a week, he returned from his work complaining of some pain in the lower back. He was admitted to Child Jesus Hospital close to our house, and after some analysis the doctor told us that he had to be operated upon. After the surgery, the doctor left for Bangalore and the post-operative care was poor. He was given just routine treatment. A month had passed and we could not find any improvement.

Throughout that one month, June used to cook and take food for her father by bus from REC to the hospital and back. Until then June had neither travelled alone nor in a local bus. As she had never stayed with her father and never had a relationship with him, this was an unexpected chance to serve her father and take care of him. She did so selflessly and with great love from the day he fell sick. After a month, the doctors told us to take him to Madurai. We took him to Madurai but there his condition became worse. June went to Madurai to see her father and in the end, he passed away on August 10, 1977, holding her hand. They brought him by taxi to his house in Railway quarters where we were all waiting. Throughout their trip they had heavy rains and in fact as we were taking the body from the taxi to the house, there was a heavy shower accompanied by heavy winds. Next day he was buried in the cemetery located at Marsingpet Road, Beemanagar, Trichy.

June's Uncle John's Death - 1977

Before we could overcome this grief, one of June's uncles, John, who was working in the Indian Army, drank heavily and died while lying on the grave of my father-in-law on August 23, 1977. We did not know the reason. After the post mortem, he was buried in the same cemetery at Marsingpet Road.

Tributes to Lionel and John

After serving in the Indian Army, Lionel joined the Indian Railways as a crane inspector. He married Rachel on June 23, 1948 and preferred to stay with Mabel, Rachel's aunty. He was a sincere and hardworking man. As secretary of the Railway Institute, he maintained the institute well with the support of his team. Christmas and New year were celebrated on a grand scale in the institute with dance, tambola and many party games. George Evas, close friend of Lionel, was the Master of ceremony in every function and he was a great singer and would mesmerize everyone by his singing. Lionel was heartbroken at the loss of his only son Rodney in 1968. Otherwise, he was a happy-go-lucky person. He was a good hockey player. He was unfortunate not to have lived with his children since they were brought up by Amelia.

John was serving in the Indian Army. He was Amelia's favourite brother. We did not know the reason for his death.

Storm and Floods - November, 1977

The 1977 Andhra Pradesh cyclone (JTWC designation 06B), also known as the 1977 Diviseema Cyclone was a devastating one that struck in the entire state of Andhra Pradesh and neighbouring states, including Tamil Nadu, on November 19, 1977. My sister lost some jewels, books and clothes because of the Uyagundan breach and Koraiyar breach. My sister-in-law was alone with Denys (2 months old) and Donella (4 years old) in their Railway Quarters and a tree fell on the house and ruined the tiled roof. Immediately, we rushed to their house and brought them to our house. In my house as well, a tree with star shaped sweet smelling white flowers was uprooted.

Kumararaj (Jijju) Stay in REC - 1977 to 78

Uncle Govindarajan's eldest son is Kumararaj. Govindarajan wanted him to become a doctor and ophthalmologist so that he could take care of the AG Eye Hospital established by Govindarajan in Trichy. Kumararaj was quite intelligent and fairly good in studies but playful. He was doing his 11th standard in Kendriya Vidyalaya School (Central School) in the Small Arms Factory in Trichy. Govindarajan thought that if Kumararaj stayed in my house he could concentrate more on his studies. We too thought that this arrangement would be a small help to my uncle who had educated me and conducted our marriage.

So Kumararaj spent the year 1976-77 in our house at REC. We were both able to help him in his studies. He cleared his 11th standard and then PUC from Jamal Mohammed College, Trichy, successfully. Then, uncle was trying for his admission into MBBS. After some unsuccessful attempts, he was called for an interview at Thanjavur Medical College which was very close to our REC campus.

Before going to the interview uncle and aunty came to our house and told June, "June, you also come with us. Let us see whether you will be a lucky mascot for us." June readily agreed and went with them. They were really lucky that time and Kumararaj got admission in MBBS in Thanjavur Medical College and both my uncle and aunty were greatly relieved. When he was doing MBBS, he used to come to REC often and both June and he would talk the whole night about his studies and other activities.

Later, Kumararaj completed the Diploma in Ophthalmology from Joseph Eye Hospital, Trichy. He took some special training in Japan and UK and he is a much sought-after ophthalmologist in Trichy and Chennai. He married Dr. Sherin of the same college, who also became an ophthalmologist and has two daughters named Roshini and Dharshini.

Club Day - JMC orchestra and Bharatanatyam Performance – April, 1978

Annual Club Day of the Officers' Club was held on April 30, 1978 in which a variety entertainment programme was organized. It included music by Jamal Mohammed College orchestra and Bharatanatyam performance by Shyamala, Rani and Devi (daughters of Padmanaban). The entire programme was appreciated by Manisundaram. I was the Secretary of the club.

Shyamala Attaining Puberty - 1980

When Shyamala was studying in VI standard, she attained puberty in aunty Amelia's house. Some Hindu families in South India celebrate the arrival of puberty with great pomp and show. We were not exceptions. We also celebrated the occasion in our home in REC campus with customary Nalungu. We invited close relatives and friends. Aunty Amelia did not attend but did her part in contributing money and other requirements by sending her representative, Kamalam.

Puberty is a significant milestone in a girl's journey through life. It indicates her journey from childhood into adulthood. In some Hindu families, a function is arranged in which close relatives and friends take part. The maternal uncle brings the oil for the herbal bath and the bath is given by the girl's mother and aunts. After the bath, the girl is dressed up with new clothes and made to sit in a chair on a stage or the floor. The maternal uncle garlands the girl and all others bless the girl by applying turmeric paste on the face, neck and hands. After finishing the main function, gifts are given to the girl by relatives and friends. The function ends with a grand lunch. The main reason is to announce that there is an eligible girl in the family. In the olden times with no matrimony sites and brokers this could have been the legitimate way to seek proposals for a daughter. It could also be 'construed' as a way of telling the girl that this is a natural phenomenon that need not be hushed up or put under the carpet. It also gives a morale booster to the girl that she gets all guidance and support for further steps in life. It could have promoted a deeper bonding of the girl with her family, relatives and friends and vice versa.

Mother's Retirement - 1980

When my mother reached 58 years of age, she retired from her post as Headmistress on November 1, 1980. My mother selflessly served her school as a teacher and as a Headmistress for 32 years. All of us attended her retirement function in which she was honoured for her service and praised for her achievements.

Purchase of First Car - 1980

Aunty Amelia purchased a second-hand fiat car for me in 1980 for Rs. 22000. I slowly learnt how to drive and got my driver's license. I had spent more than Rs. one lakh in maintaining that car and finally in 1995 after using it for 15 years I sold it for Rs. 20000 through Rangabashyam, son of Venugopal and owner of car maintenance workshop. The car was purchased by a driving school and I used to see it very often whenever we came to Trichy.

Shyamala Learning to Drive - 1981

Shyamala started to drive my fiat car from 1981 when she was studying in VIth standard.

My Mother Dharmambal's 60th Birthday - November 1, 1982

Every year during summer holidays we (at least 20 close relatives and friends) used to go to Petavaithalai about 20 kilometres from Trichy and stay in a PWD guest house for two days. There, we used to bathe in the river, play games, cook our own food and practically have a lot of fun. We decided to celebrate my mother's birthday at Pettavaithalai. It was celebrated in a grand style with at least 50 people participating in it.

Aunty Amelia's Own House – January, 1984

Aunty Amelia constructed her own house in Raja colony just opposite her house in Heber road. I prepared a plan for her and one of my part-time students cleared the plan quickly from the Town Planning Department.

Shyamala's Achievements

Shyamala excelled well in her academics, co-curricular and extra-curricular activities.

Academics

She was always among the top 5% in her class. She used to score a centum in mathematics. She received a proficiency certificate almost every year. She scored 72% in the tenth standard CBSE board examination in 1984.

Co-curricular

Shyamala had won prizes in debate and quiz events.

Extra-curricular

Shyamala had won prizes in fancy dress completion and chess. She was a cadet in the National Cadet Corps (NCC). She was selected to represent Tamil Nadu for the Republic Day Parade in Delhi but I spoiled her chance by refusing to send her. I regret it now. She acted in plays and was a good Bharatanatyam dancer.

June's Role

June had become friends with some ladies of the campus like Mrs. George Joseph, Saroja, Sulochana, Mrs. Janagaraj and others. She made a beautiful garden in the front open space. She was the one who took care of most of Shyamala's needs. By the time I woke up in the morning Shyamala would have left for school. But now I make sure that I am awake when my grandchildren go to school and college to say bye.

June managed the home very well all by herself. She mingled with great ease with all my family members. After we came to Trichy, my mother and my relatives had the opportunity of seeing June's talents at close quarters and they all started to like her and accept her.

Professional Life

The Department

When I joined REC on July 11, 1974, Prof. P. S. Manisundaram was the Principal. He had been the Principal from the inception of REC, Trichy. He took his Master's degree in Civil Engineering at Nova Scotia University, Canada in 1958.

Dr. Venkatasubramanian was the Head of the Department. There were three Divisions namely- Soil Mechanics and Transportation, headed by Venkatasubramanian, Structural Engineering headed by Dr. Shanmugam and Hydraulics headed by Prof. S. Nagaratnam. I was under Prof. S. Nagaratnam. Prof. Nagaratnam did his Master's degree from Iowa University, USA under Hunter Rouse who was an expert in Fluid Mechanics.

Part-Time BE Programme

REC also offered a part-time programme for people working in the Government and Private sector and holding diplomas. It was a seven-semester programme and classes were held in the evening from 6 to 9 p.m., Monday to Friday. I was given the course on Design and Drawing (RCC and steel) and I was surprised when I saw my classmate from St. Joseph's High School, Venkatesan, in my class. He was working as a Junior Engineer in PWD. Later, I took Hydrology, Irrigation engineering and Civil Engineering laboratory at different times.

Taking classes for part-time students helped us in many ways namely in getting data for our research from various government departments and getting favours from Municipality, RTO, Revenue, Town Planning and other offices. In fact, Br. Brito helped me to secure a ration card for my daughter in a matter of just two days. It also created good interaction between the field and academia. I took one course every semester until my retirement.

Assistance in University of Madras examinations

There was only one government university, i.e., University of Madras to which all the colleges in Science, Arts, Engineering, Medicine and Law were affiliated. The other was Annamalai University, which was a private one. It had its own programmes and no college in the state of Madras was affiliated to that. Nagaratnam was the Chief Superintendent of Examinations, University of Madras at REC centre. Naturally, I had to assist him.

In those days, the university paid Rs. 5 per hour for invigilators on 3 hours duty. We would get the remuneration only after 10 to 12 months completion of duty. Naturally, people were reluctant to do invigilation duty. I was finding it difficult to get people to invigilate. I wanted to resolve this situation. I suggested to Nagaratnam that we could ask the university to advance some money towards invigilation and other stationery expenses of conducting examinations and settlements could be made after completion of the same. Nagaratnam realized the importance of this and I drafted the proposal. It was signed by him and the Principal and sent to the university. To our surprise the university agreed and the same system is being continued by all the universities even now.

Assistance in Annual Group Photos

One of the important activities was clicking group photos of faculty and students at the end of each academic year. Ponniah studio, Trichy and Kembu studio, Tiruverambur were hired to carry out this activity. I was in charge of fixing the dates, organizing the event and passing the bills.

Assistance in Conferences

I assisted Chidambaram, Lecturer, Hydraulics Division, in the organization of a conference on Fluid Power. I assisted in another conference organized by the English department on Communication Skills.

Hydraulics Laboratory In-charge

In 1975, Chidambaram went on study leave to do his Ph.D. So, they gave me courses which were handled by him. I was made in-charge of Hydraulics lab and given a course on Irrigation Engineering.

Manisundaram became first Vice Chancellor of Bharathidasan University - 1982

Manisundaram was appointed as the first Vice Chancellor of Bharathidasan University, Trichy in 1982.

Nagaratnam became Principal, REC - 1982

Prof. Nagaratnam became the Principal and Dr. M. Shanmugam became the Head of the Department of Civil Engineering.

As a Lecturer, during the period 1974 to 1984, I was only involved with teaching courses. There was not much scope for carrying out sponsored research projects, due to lack of funds from the central government.

School Project Guide - 1983 to 1984

Boiler Plant Girls High School approached me to guide their students in making a working model for a National competition in 1983-84. I suggested a working model of a water power plant. They agreed and I started guiding them. One of the technicians in the Hydraulics laboratory, Xavier fitted the necessary pump and plumbing connections. They won the state level competition and were selected to represent Tamil Nadu state in the National competition. In the National competition, they won the first prize as well. The headmistress, Radha, and the whole school were happy. They thanked me. Radha was a very strict lady and she would not admit any students based on recommendations. But once she admitted a student from REC solely on the merit of my recommendation.

I consider the next phase of my life at REC Trichy as a golden period, as indicated by the astrologer Balan Nair based on my horoscope in 1983. Some of the good things that happened were my promotion, award of a research project, my daughter's marriage and becoming a grandfather. The saddest thing to happen was the passing away of my mother.

Happy to hear the great things, but very sad to hear about the tragedy.

Around me

Let us go through the major events during this period.

India

Politics

New President, 1974 - Fakhruddin Ali Ahmed became the fifth President of India on August 24, 1974 after V.V. Giri.

Birth of Sikkim State, 1975 - 97.55% of voters approved a referendum, held on April 14, 1975, on abolishing the monarchy in Sikkim. Thus, Sikkim became the 22nd state in India on May 15, 1975.

Emergency in June, 1975 - A State Emergency was proclaimed by Indira Gandhi on June 25, 1975 after the Supreme Court upheld the Allahabad High Court's order which stated that Indira Gandhi's election in 1971 against Raj Narain and others was null and void and unseated her from the Lok Sabha but allowed her to continue as Prime Minister.

Founding of Janata Party, 1977 - Jayaprakash Narayan founded the Janata party on January 23, 1977. The party was an amalgam of Indian political parties opposed to the State of Emergency imposed between 1975 and 1977 by Indira Gandhi.

Death of Fakhruddin Ali Ahmed, 1977 - Fakhruddin Ali Ahmed died on February 11, 1977 after he collapsed in his office while preparing to attend his daily Namaz. The cause was a heart attack. Basappa Danappa Jatti, the Vice President of India, became the acting President of India.

VIth General Elections, 1977 - VIth general elections for Lok Sabha were held during March 16-20, 1977. Janata Alliance secured 345 seats out of a total of 534 seats, Bharatya Lok Dal/Janata party won 295 seats, CPI(M) 22 and DMK 1. Congress Alliance secured

189 seats, Indian National Congress 153, ADMK 19 and CPI 7. Morarji Desai was chosen as the leader of the alliance in the newly formed parliament and became India's first non-Congress Prime Minister on March 24, 1977.

Sixth President of India, 1977 - Neelam Sanjeeva Reddy became sixth President of India on July 25, 1977 after Bassappa Danappa Jatti.

Mandal Commission, 1979 - The Mandal Commission was established in India in 1979 by the Janata Party government under Prime Minister Morarji Desai with a mandate to "identify the socially or educationally backward".

Resignation of Desai, 1979 - The loose coalition barely held on to a majority with only 295 seats in the Lok Sabha and never quite had a firm grip on power. Desai lost a trust vote in parliament and resigned on July 28, 1979. Charan Singh, who had retained some partners of the Janata alliance, was sworn in as Prime Minister on July 28, 1979. Charan Singh was forced to resign within 24 days in office and called for elections in January 1980.

VIIth General Elections, 1980 - General elections were held during January 3 and 6, 1980 for the 7th Lok Sabha. The fight among Janata Party leaders and the political instability in the country worked in favour of Indira Gandhi's Congress(I). The Congress(I) won 353 Lok Sabha seats out of 374 seats secured by its alliance. Janata party (secular) won 41 seats, CPI(M) 37, Janata party 31, DMK 16, CPI 10, AIADMK 2, Shironmani Akali Dal 1 and Shiv Sena 0. The total number of seats were 529. Indira Gandhi was sworn in as Prime minister on January 14, 1980.

Formation of Bharatiya Janata Party (BJP), 1980 - After three years in power, the Janata Party was dissolved in 1980 with the members of the Jana Sangh reconvening to form the Bharatiya Janata Party.

Death of Sanjay Gandhi, 1980 - Sanjay Gandhi, son of Indira Gandhi, died instantly from head wounds in an air crash on June 23, 1980 near Safdarjung Airport in New Delhi. He was flying a new aircraft of the Delhi Flying Club, and while performing an aerobatic manoeuver over his office lost control and crashed. The only passenger in the plane, Captain Subhash Saxena, was also killed.

Founding of Infosys, 1981 - Infosys was established by 7 engineers namely N. R. Narayana Murthy, Nandan Nilekani, S. Gopalakrishnan, S. D. Shubulal, K. Dinesh, N. S. Raghavan, and Ashok Arora and it was registered as Infosys Consultants Private Limited on July 2, 1981.

Founding of Maruti Suzuki, 1982 - This Indian automobile company is popularly known as Maruti, which used to be called Maruti Udyog Limited at the time of its inception. Maruti Udyog Limited was founded by the Government of India in 1981, only to merge with the Japanese automobile company Suzuki in October 1982. The first manufacturing factory of Maruti was established in Gurgaon, Haryana,

Birth of Telugu Desam Party, 1982 - Telugu Desam Party (TDP), a regional political party, was founded by N. T. Rama Rao on March 29, 1982 in Andhra Pradesh.

Zail Singh became President of India, 1982 - Giani Zail Singh became the seventh President of India on July 25, 1982 after Neelam Sanjeeva Reddy.

Birth of Bahujan Samaj Party (BSP), 1984 - The Bahujan Samaj Party (BSP) was founded by charismatic leader Kanshi Ram on April 14, 1984 (birthday of Ambedkar), who was succeeded by his protégée, Mayawati, in 2003. It was formed mainly to represent Bahujans (literally meaning "people in majority"), referring to people from the Scheduled Castes, Scheduled Tribes and Other Backward Castes (OBC) as well as minorities.

Space Technology

Aryabhatta, India's First Satellite in Space, 1975 - Aryabhatta was India's first satellite named after the 5th century Indian astronomer. It was built by the Indian Space Research Organisation (ISRO) and launched by the Soviet Union on April 19, 1975.

Launching of INSAT-1A, 1982 - INSAT-1A was an Indian communications satellite which formed part of the Indian National Satellite System. Launched in 1982, it was abandoned in September 1983.

The Integrated Guided Missile Development Programme (IGMDP), 1982-83 - The Integrated Guided Missile Development Programme (IGMDP) of the Indian Ministry of Defence was initiated for the research and development of a comprehensive range of missiles. The project started in 1982–83 under the leadership of A. P. J. Abdul Kalam.

First Indian to Travel in Space, 1984 - Squadron leader Rakesh Sharma, Hero of the Soviet Union, is a former Indian Air Force pilot who flew aboard Soyuz T-11, launched on April 3, 1984, as part of the Intercosmos programme. He was the first Indian to travel in space.

Accidents

Air India Flight 855 Crash, 1978 - Air India Flight 855, Boeing 747, was a scheduled passenger flight that crashed during the evening of New Year's Day 1978 about 3 kilometres off the coast of Bandra, Bombay. All 213 passengers and crew on board were killed.

The Morbi Dam Failure, 1979 - This was a dam-related flood disaster which occurred on August 11, 1979 in India. The Machchhu - 2 dam, situated on the Machchhu River burst, sending a wall of water through the town of Morbi in the Rajkot district of Gujarat. Estimates of the number of people killed varied from 1800 to 2500.

Tamil Nadu

Death of Kamaraj, 1975 - Kumaraswami Kamaraj died on October 2, 1975.

Dismissal of DMK Government, 1976 - During the second emergency on January 31, 1976, Karunanidhi's government was dismissed by the central government of Indira Gandhi citing corruption charges against Karunanidhi and President's rule was imposed on the state.

Change of Name from ADMK to AIADMK, 1976 - In 1976, during the emergency, there was a rumour that all regional parties would be banned by Indira Gandhi's central government. The ADMK was renamed as All India Anna DMK so that it could at least pretend to be a national party. In those days, the DMK, AIADMK and the Akali Dal were the only regional parties in the whole of India.

VIth Tamil Nadu Elections, 1977 - This election was a four-cornered contest. The AIADMK allied itself with the Communist Party of India (Marxist), while INC (I) and Communist Party of India (CPI) contested as allies. The DMK and Janata Party (JNP) contested the elections alone. The elections were held on June 10, 1977. AIADMK alliance won 144 seats (AIADMK 130, CPI(M) 12 and others 2); DMK 48; Congress alliance 32 (INC 27, CPI 5) and JNP-10. The total number of seats were 234.

M. G. Ramachandran became Chief Minister for the First Time, 1977 - MGR, leader of AIADMK was sworn in as Chief minister for the first time on June 30, 1977.

Dismissal of MGR Government, 1980 - After the success of their alliance with Indira Gandhi's Congress in the Lok Sabha elections held in 1980, Dravida Munnetra Kazhagam pressed the central government to dismiss the Tamil Nadu government using similar allegations used by MGR to dismiss DMK government in 1976. The AIADMK ministry and the Assembly were dismissed by the central government and President's rule was imposed from February 17, 1980.

VIIth Tamil Nadu Elections, 1980 - Despite their victory during the 1980 Lok Sabha polls, DMK and Indira Gandhi's Congress failed to win the Legislative Assembly election. AIADMK alliance won the election winning 162 seats out of 234 seats. AIADMK 129; CPI(M) 11; CPI 9; DMK 37 and INC 31.

M. G. Ramachandran became Chief Minister Second Time, 1980 - MGR was sworn in as Chief Minister for the second time on June 6, 1980.

Establishment of New Universities, 1982 - Bharathiar University in Coimbatore, named after the Tamil poet Subramania Bharathiar and Bharathidasan University in Trichy named after the great revolutionary Tamil Poet, Bharathidasan were started in 1982.

Establishment of Salem Steel Plant, 1982 - Salem Steel Plant, a special steels unit of Steel Authority of India Ltd, pioneered the supply of wider width stainless steel sheets / coils in India. It was inaugurated at Salem in Tamil Nadu in March 1982.

World

Politics

Nixon's Resignation, 1974 - Richard Milhous Nixon became the only US President to resign the office, as a result of the Watergate Scandal. Gerald Rudolph Ford Jr. became the thirty-eighth President of US.

Zhou De, President of China, 1975 - Zhou De became President of China on January 1, 1975 after Dong Biwu.

Hua Guofeng, Premier of China, 1976 - Hua Guofeng became Premier of China on February 2, 1976 after Zhou Enlai.

Reunification of North and South Vietnam, 1976 - After the end of the war on April 30, 1975, reunification occurred on July 2, 1976. The Provisional Revolutionary Government of the Republic of South Vietnam and North Vietnam merged to form the modern-day Vietnam or the Socialist Republic of Vietnam.

Soong Ching-ling became President of China, 1976 - Soong Ching-ling became President of China on July 6, 1976 after Zhou De.

Carter became US President, 1977 - James (Jimmy) Earl Carter, Jr. became the 39th president of the United States, from January 20, 1977 after Gerald Ford Jr.

Ye Jianying became President of China, 1978 - Ye Jianying became President of China on March 5, 1978 after Soong Ching-ling.

New Heads in Iran and Iraq, 1979 - Mohammad Reza Shah of the Pahlavi dynasty left Iran for exile on January 16, 1979 after being overthrown by the Iranian Revolution. Ayatollah Khomeini became Supreme Leader of the country in December 1979. Saddam Hussein Abd al-Majid al-Tikriti became the fifth President of Iraq, from July 16, 1979.

Thatcher became Prime Minister of UK, 1979 - Margaret Hilda Thatcher, leader of the Conservative Party from 1975, became the first woman Prime Minister of United Kingdom on May 4, 1979. She was a research chemist and a barrister.

Nikolai Tikhonov, Premier of USSR, 1980 - Nikolai Tikhonov became the Premier, USSR on October 13, 1980 after Alexei Kosygin.

Zhao Ziyang became Prime Minister of China, 1980 - Zhao Ziyang became Prime Minister of China on September 10, 1980 after Hua Guofeng.

Reagan became US President, 1981 - Ronald Reagan became the 40th president of the United States of America from January 1981 after Jimmy Carter.

Assassination of Anwar Sadat, President of Egypt, 1981 - Anwar Sadat, President of Egypt was assassinated during the annual Victory Parade held in Cairo on October 6, 1981.

Death of Brezhnev, 1982 - Leonid Ilyich Brezhnev was the General Secretary of the Central Committee (CC) of the Communist Party of the Soviet Union (CPSU), presiding over the country from October 14, 1964 until his death on November 10, 1982.

Yuri Andropov became General Secretary, USSR, 1982 - Yuri Andropov became the General Secretary of Communist Party of Soviet Union on November 12, 1982 after Brezhnev.

Li Xiannian became President of China, 1983 - Li Xiannian became the President of China on June 18, 1983 after Ye Jianying.

Chernenko became General Secretary, USSR, 1984 - Konstantin Chernenko became the General Secretary of Communist Party of Soviet Union on February 13, 1984 after Yuri Andropov.

Science and Technology

Birth of Microsoft, 1975 - Microsoft, a multinational computer technology corporation was established on April 4, 1975, when it was founded by Bill Gates and Paul Allen in Albuquerque. Its current best-selling products are the Microsoft Windows Operating system.

Apple Computer, 1976 - On April 1, 1976, Steve Jobs and Wozniak formed Apple Computer.

First Test Tube Baby, 1978 - Louise Joy Brown (born July 25, 1978) is an English woman known for being the first human to have been born after conception by in vitro fertilisation or IVF

Nuclear Accident in Three Mile Island, 1979 - The Three Mile Island accident was a partial nuclear meltdown that occurred on March 28, 1979, in reactor number 2 of Three Mile Island Nuclear Generating Station (TMI-2) in Dauphin County, Pennsylvania, United States.

First AIDS Death, 1981 - Nick Rock became the first known AIDS death in New York City on January 15, 1981.

War

End of Vietnam War, 1975 - Direct US military involvement ended on 15 August 1973. The capture of Saigon by the North Vietnamese Army on April 30, 1975 marked the end of the war which lasted for almost 20 years after its start on November 1, 1955.

Camp David Accords, 1978 - The Camp David Accords were signed by Egyptian President Anwar El Sadat and Israeli Prime Minister Menachem Begin on September 17, 1978, following twelve days of secret negotiations at Camp David. The two framework agreements were signed at the White House, and witnessed by United States President Jimmy Carter. Due to the agreement, Sadat and Begin received the shared 1978 Nobel Peace Prize.

Starting of Iran Hostage Crisis, 1979 - The Iran hostage crisis was a diplomatic crisis between Iran and the United States. Fifty-Two American diplomats and citizens were held hostage for 444 days (November 4, 1979, to January 20, 1981), after a group of Iranian students, belonging to the Muslim Student followers of the Imam's Line, who were supporting the Iranian Revolution, took over. It is alleged that this happened because of non-return of the overthrown Shah Mohammad Reza Pahlavi, from USA.

Starting of Iraq-Iran War, 1980 - On September 22, 1980, the military of Iraq invaded Iran, marking the beginning of the Iran-Iraq War. These events led the Iranian government to enter negotiations with the US using Algeria as mediator. The hostages were formally released into United States custody the day after the signing of the Algiers Accords, just minutes after the new American President, Ronald Reagan, was sworn into office.

Space Technology

Apollo and Soyuz Mission, 1975 - The Soyuz was launched just over seven hours prior to the launch of the Apollo CSM on July 15, 1975. Both crews conducted a variety of experiments over a two-day period.

Viking 1 and 2 Landing on Mars, 1976 - NASA's Viking Project found a place in history when it became the first US mission to land a spacecraft safely on the surface of Mars and return images of the surface.

First American Woman in Space, 1983 - Sally Kristen Ride was an American physicist and astronaut. Born in Los Angeles, she joined NASA in 1978 and became the first American woman in space in 1983.

Sports

Moscow Olympics and its Boycott, 1980 - Led by the US at the insistence of President Jimmy Carter, 66 countries boycotted the XXII Olympiad held in Moscow during July 19 to August 3, 1980 because of Soviet invasion of Afghanistan.

Music

Killing of John Lennon, 1980 - John Lennon, of the Beatles, was shot dead on December 8, 1980 in the Archway of the Dakota, his residence in New York City.

CHAPTER 8

Life in Trichy, Part II - July 1984 to September 1992

Abstract

Me

The details of my second promotion (1984), purchase of first TV (1984), stay of Chandrasekar, Donella and Denys at REC (1984-85), Chandrasekar eloping (1985), my mother's heart attack (1986), Shyamala's admission to college for UG (1986), death of my mother (1986), Shyamala's admission to PG (1989), death of June's mother (1989), Shyamala's admission to Ph.D. (1991), Pappi's marriage (1991), Shyamala's marriage (1992), birth of my granddaughter Amenda (1992) are presented.

Around me

In India, the major events were Operation Blue Star (1984), assassination of Indira Gandhi (1984), Rajiv Gandhi becoming Prime Minister (1984), Bhopal gas tragedy (1984), VIIIth general elections (1984), Rajiv Gandhi continuing as Prime Minister (1984), blow up of Air India flight 182 (1985), starting of Indira Gandhi National Open University (1985), Operation Black Thunder I (1986), birth of Arunachal Pradesh (1987), Sino-India skirmishes (1987), Goa becoming a state (1987), R. Venkatraman becoming VIIIth President (1987), Indian Peace Keeping Force in Sri Lanka (1987), test firing of Prithivi I (1988), Operation Black Thunder II (1988), judgment on Bhopal gas tragedy (1989), IXth general elections (1989), V. P. Singh becoming Prime Minister (1989), kidnapping of Rubhaya Sayeed (1989), IPKF withdrawal (1990), Andhra Pradesh cyclone (1990),

V. P. Singh's resignation (1990), Chandrashekar becoming Prime Minister (1990), resignation of Chandrashekar (1991), assassination of Rajiv Gandhi (1991), Xth general elections (1991), Narasimha Rao becoming Prime Minister (1991), visit of Chinese Premier (1991), S.D. Sharma becoming Xth President (1992), Jain hawala scandal (1991) and New Delhi becoming a state (1992).

In Tamil Nadu State, the major events were MGR's illness (1984), VIIIth assembly elections (1984), MGR becoming Chief Minister (1985), death of Baktavatsalam (1987), death of MGR (1987), Janaki becoming Chief Minister (1988), resignation of Janaki (1988), President's rule (1988-89), IXth Assembly elections (1989), Karunanidhi becoming Chief Minister again (1989), birth of Pattali Makkal Katchi (1989), establishment of Manonmanium Sundaranar University (1990), dismissal of DMK government (1991), President's rule (1991), Xth Assembly Elections (1991) and Jayalalithaa becoming Chief Minister (1991).

In the World, the major events were birth of Macintosh personal computer (1984), Carl Lewis and Los Angeles Olympics (1984), Reagan becoming President of US again (1985), Gorbachev becoming General Secretary of USSR (1985), Iran Contra affairs (1985-87), discovery of hole in Ozone layer (1985), Chernobyl nuclear power plant accident (1986), first use of DNA in a criminal case (1986), world population touching 5 billion (1987), Li Peng becoming Prime Minister of China (1987), ending of Iran-Iraq war (1988), Gorbachev becoming Head of USSR (1988), Ben Johnson and Seoul Olympics (1988), Benazir Bhutto becoming Prime Minister of Pakistan (1988), Anand becoming Chess Grand Master (1988), Yang Shangkun becoming President of China (1988), George Bush becoming President of USA (1989), breaking of Berlin Wall (1989), Unification of Germany (1990), Human Genome Project (1990), release of Nelson Mandela (1990), John Major becoming Prime Minister of England (1990), Persian Gulf War (1990-91), Madrid conference for Arab-Israel peace (1991), resignation of Gorbachev (1991), dissolution of USSR (1991), Yeltsin becoming President of Russian Federation (1991), Bush-Yeltsin meet (1992), South African gesture and Barcelona Olympics (1992) and focus on climate change (1988, 1992).

ME

You had completed 10 years as Lecturer at REC. What about your promotion to the next level as Assistant Professor?

Promotion to Assistant Professor - July 11, 1984

To remove stagnation in a post, the Board of Governors approved a new policy which allowed Lecturers with 10 years of service to be promoted to Assistant Professor. So, I was promoted as Assistant Professor with effect from July 11, 1984, since I had completed 10 years as Lecturer.

First TV on the Occasion of LA Olympics - July 28 to August 12, 1984

Even though television was introduced in India in 1959, national telecast and colour TV were introduced in 1982. As the 1984 Summer Olympics at Los Angeles, USA were fast approaching, the markets were flooded with television sets. As lovers of sports, we decided to buy a television set to watch the Olympics. When I went to the market to buy a colour TV, there was no colour TV and I had to settle for a black and white Crown TV. We set up the Antenna and the TV at home ourselves and were happy to see the opening ceremony of the Olympics live for the first time.

Award of a Research Project - 1984-1985

I was made the Principal Investigator of a research project on "Water Resources Management" during 1984-85 which gave ample scope to carry out a detailed research on water management related topics. I will explain later about it.

Ilango becoming Principal - 1990

After the retirement of Nagaratnam in 1990, Dr. B. Ilango took charge as the Principal, REC Trichy from July 1990. As Professor in the Electrical Engineering Department, College of Engineering, Guindy, he had taught me the Electrical Engineering course during the second year of my B.E. degree.

Sekar's Stay in our House -1984 to 85

My sister's eldest son Chandrasekar (Sekar) joined the Polytechnic in Kanadukathan (Karaikudi Taluk about 120 kilometres from Trichy) in July 1982. He stayed in a hostel and my brother-in-law Ramaiyan was not happy about this. He tried and succeeded in transferring him to Seshayee Institute of Technology in Kattur, Trichy in July 1983. So, my mother and my sister's mother-in-law rented a house in Subramaniapuram along with Sekar. During his study, he became a close friend of his classmate Prabhu and visited his house often. During such visits, he became friendly with Prabhu's sister, Nirmala, who was a physically challenged person with both legs affected by polio. She worked in the Golden Rock Railway Workshop, Trichy. This friendship turned into love. My mother got suspicious and consulted my sister. They asked June and me whether Sekar could stay with us in REC during his final year of study. We were contemplating what to do. At the same time, another problem cropped up.

Donella and Denys at our House - 1984 to 1985

My sister-in-law Dinky's husband, Darrel Nigli, was sent to Sri Lanka in 1983 on deputation from Golden Rock Railway Workshop.

*The **Golden Rock Railway Workshop** (officially Central Workshop, Golden Rock) situated in Ponmalai (Golden Rock), Tiruchirapalli in Tamil Nadu, is one of the three mechanical railway workshops serving the Southern Zone of the Indian Railways. This repair workshop is basically a "Mechanical Workshop" which comes under the control of the Mechanical Department of the Indian Railways. The other two mechanical workshops of Southern Railway are located in Perambur, Chennai. They are "Carriage Works, Perambur" and "Loco Works, Perambur". This central workshop was set up in 1897 by South Indian Railways at Nagapattinam and it was shifted to Tiruchirappalli in 1928 because of its strategic location.*

When Darrel found it difficult to stay alone in Sri Lanka, he wanted to take Dinky. They could not take their two daughters, Donella and Denys, and so Dinky asked June whether they could stay at our home for a year. They were also studying in RSKHSS.

June had to give an answer to her sister and I had to give an answer to mine. Finally, we agreed to let our nieces and nephew live with us. My mother agreed to stay with us to help June in the cooking. Somehow, seven of us managed to live in that small house for one year. Everything went on smoothly until a shocking incident happened.

Sekar Eloping - January, 1985

January 2, 1985 was a Wednesday and Sekar did not return from his college that evening. Later, we came to know that he had gone to Chennai with his girlfriend, Nirmala. The entire family was shocked over this and it created misunderstanding among us. When Sekar was located in a police station in Chennai, he refused to come home without the girl. My sister's family had to come back without him. Later, he married her and stayed with her family.

Return of Donella and Denys to their House - 1985

Donella and Denys went back to their home after the return of their parents in May 1985.

My Mother's Heart Attack - January, 1986

My mother had a heart attack on January 25, 1986 and she was admitted to JM hospital near my uncle Govindarajan's house. I had gone to Chennai for a bridge tournament and they tried to locate me but I had not given any contact details to them. June stayed in the hospital and took care of my mother day and night. She was helped by my sister and aunties. After completion of the tournament I reached the hospital and everyone rebuked me. I had to stand shamed, not having any courage to look into their faces.

In a week's time, my mother got better and she was discharged She continued to stay in uncle Govindarajan's house so that it would be easy to monitor her.

Shyamala's Admission in College for UG Degree - July, 1986

Shyamala passed her twelfth standard examination with flying colours by securing 93 % in the CBSE examination held in March 1986. Even though she was very good in mathematics, she left it in twelfth standard. I wanted her to do engineering but June wanted her to do medicine. Since Shyamala had left mathematics, she lost her eligibility for an engineering degree. She had to write an entrance examination for admission into medical degree. She took it lightly and did not write the exam to her real potential and she was in the waiting list. Both of us were disappointed but I think that one can shine in any area with hard work.

First, she got admission in B.Sc. Chemistry in Holy Cross College, Trichy and then she got admission in B.Sc. Nutrition and Dietetics in

Seethalakshmi Ramasami College, Trichy. She chose the second one, since it was an emerging area.

Shyamala getting Driving License - August, 1986

When Shyamala completed 18 years of age I took her to the Regional Transport Office to apply for a driving license. The person in charge of issuing application said that she did not look like she was 18 years old. At this Shyamala got angry and refused to apply. Then, I pleaded her not to take it seriously and on another day, we went and completed the formalities and she got the license successfully.

Death of My Mother Dharmambal - December 7, 1986

June, my mother and I went shopping on December 6, Saturday 1986 and we returned to uncle Govindarajan's house at about 1 p.m., to drop off my mother. As she got down from the car she asked June, "When will we meet again?" June replied, "We decided to take you tomorrow to REC. Have you forgotten?" Mother said, "Yes. I forgot." At that time we did not know it would be her last words to us. As we were going to the car June said, "Why, Athan, she forgot about tomorrow?" I said, "Maybe due to old age."

Next day, as usual I went to the City Club to play cards and returned unusually early and after taking lunch we were sitting and chatting. The landline phone started to ring and when June picked up the phone, Kumamaraj said, "Akka come soon. Athai got a severe heart attack." Then, we rushed in our car to uncle's house and we were told that she was taken to JM Hospital. We turned quickly to JM Hospital and we saw the doctors trying to revive her. But they could not bring her back. They declared that my mother was brought dead.

We brought her to uncle's house and laid her on a cot in the hall. Since she had already offered to donate her eyes my uncle made necessary arrangements for the donation. Within the next three hours, they completed all the procedures to harvest her eyes. Slowly, all the relatives and friends started coming.

June and Kumararaj were awake throughout the night and June slowly came to know the events before my mother breathed her last.

On that Sunday morning, there were some arguments and misunderstandings when my uncle Padmanaban's daughter Prahada came to the house. Prahada left the house with a worried face. Over this, my mother was slightly upset. But later, my mother served lunch for Kumararaj and his classmates and she lay down in one of the rooms on the ground floor.

There was another guest, Yasodha, who was sitting in front of my mother's bed. She noticed my mother's leg shaking slightly. Yasodha became worried and called out for my uncle. All came running down and attended to her but they could not revive her and they rushed her to the hospital.

After her heart attack in January in the same year, she had been taking medicines regularly but after about six months she told my sister that she had stopped taking the medicines as she got disgusted in life. Of course, neither my mother nor my sister shared this with us.

We fixed the funeral and cremation for the next day that was Monday. Until that time, I have never gone to any cremation site of Hindus. This was the first time and that too for my mother. I led the funeral procession with the firepot and my Savithri aunt's son Jayaseelan accompanied me. At the site, I performed the necessary rituals and lit the pyre.

We completed all the rituals of the 15th day ceremony. At the end of the first death anniversary according to the Thithi, the annual ceremony was also completed.

As soon as death occurs, those gathered will avoid unnecessary touching of the body, as it is seen as impure. Preparations for the **cremation ceremony** *begin immediately. The funeral should take place as soon as possible—traditionally, by the next dusk or dawn, whichever occurs first. A priest should be contacted to guide in the decision-making process and direct the family to a Hindu-friendly funeral home. Organ donation is acceptable for Hindus, as there are no Hindu laws prohibiting organ or tissue donation. Embalming is also acceptable in Hinduism.*

Traditionally, the body is washed by family members and close friends. For the ritual washing, the deceased's head should be facing southward. A lighted oil lamp as well as a picture of the deceased's favourite deity should be kept by the deceased's head. For the "abhisegam" (holy bath), the body is washed in a mixture of milk, yogurt, ghee (clarified butter), and honey or purified water. Those washing may recite mantras. Then the big toes should be tied together, the hands should be placed palm-to-palm in a position of prayer, and the body should be shrouded in a plain white sheet.

Hindus generally hold a brief wake before cremation. The body should be displayed in a simple, inexpensive casket. "Vibuthi" (ash) or "chandanam" (sandalwood) should be applied to the forehead of a man, and turmeric should be applied to the forehead of a woman. A garland of flowers should be placed around the neck, and holy basil should be placed in the casket. During the wake, family and friends gather around the casket and may recite hymns or mantras. At the end of the wake, before the body is removed for cremation, many Hindus place "pinda" (rice balls) near the casket or rice in the mouth. At the end of the wake, the casket is removed feet-first and brought to the place of the cremation. The body can be brought to the cremation ground in a vehicle or in a cart. Sometimes the body may be carried by 4 men from the house to the cremation place.

Traditionally, all Hindus—except babies, children, and saints are cremated.

If a vehicle, such as a hearse, is used for transportation, the eldest son (known as "karta") and another male family elder should accompany the casket. It is customary that only men attend the cremation.

The family builds a pyre and places the body on the pyre. The karta will circle the body three times, walking counter-clockwise so that the body stays on his left, and sprinkling holy water on the pyre. Then the karta will set the pyre on fire and those gathered will stay until the body is entirely burned. Upon returning home, all family members will bathe and change into fresh clothes. A photograph of the deceased will be prominently displayed, and a garland of flowers are placed on the photograph. A small worship is done and then the family and guests will gather for a meal. A priest may visit the family at home and purify the house with incense.

The day after the cremation, the karta will return to the crematory and collect the ashes. Traditionally, the ashes are immersed in the nearby rivers. A small worship is done that day. The cremation marks the beginning of the mourning period, which lasts for few days ranging from 10 to 30 days depending upon the community. During this time, the family of the deceased will stay at home and receive visitors.

Generally, Hindus believe that life and death are part of the concept of samsara, or rebirth. The ultimate goal for many Hindus is to become free from desire, thereby escaping samsara and attaining moksha, the transcendent state of salvation. Once moksha is attained, the soul will be absorbed into Brahman, the divine force and ultimate reality.

They also believe that even though the physical body dies, the individual soul has no beginning and no end. It may pass to another through reincarnation, depending on one's karma (the consequences of one's actions over lifetimes). If the soul has realized the true nature of reality, it may become one with the Brahman.

Hindus believe in a reincarnation cycle of birth, death and rebirth. Traditionally, when the soul departs the physical body at death, it needs to move to an astral plane to await its next reincarnation. This plane is said to be populated by the three preceding generations of the deceased individual. When the newly deceased enters the plane, the oldest preceding generation moves onto their rebirth. Immediately after death, the individual's soul is believed to linger around its living family and may cause them harm until the shraddha rites are performed, letting the soul move onto the astral plane.

On the 15th day from the date of death, a simple ceremony is conducted at home and the next day, early in the morning a ceremony is conducted at a riverside attended by men. This is the first (adya) funeral ceremony, so it is known as adya shraddha. It is called **ekothistam** or **karumathi** *in southern part of the country. A priest conducts the ceremony. The most important part is Pinda offering to both the recently deceased and other close ancestors. This ceremony may be done on 5th, or 7th, or 11th day depending on convenience. It is believed that this will liberate the soul for its ascent into heaven.*

The annual ceremony also known as **Varshikka Shradda.** *One year after death, an annual death ceremony will be held that is called "Thithi". Thithi literally means "Date". It is the most important ceremony to be done by a son for his dead father, mother and ancestors. Hindus believe that if the annual ceremony is not held properly, the soul will not reach heaven and not get nourishment. Further, the soul will be neglected in heaven or even worse the souls of the ancestors will be sent to hell. Such is the bondage on living decedent that he has to conduct the annual death ceremony (Thithi) without that his Pithrus (Fathers and forefathers) will be put into eternal punishments. It is the same ceremony as done on the 15th day. This ceremony is done year after year.*

Shantha aunty prepared a tribute memory booklet in Tamil. I also gave an interview on All India Radio, Trichy about the importance of eye donation. June and my sister shared her jewels and I inherited the savings of Rs. 10,000.

Tributes to My Mother Dharmambal

Mother at 10 to Her Two Brothers

My mother was the eldest child and she had two younger brothers, one 5 years younger to her and the other 10 years younger. Within 7 days of her younger brother's birth, her mother passed away. My mother had to perform two roles, one as a sister and the other as a mother. As a female, she had to do her share of some household chores. She missed her childhood happiness and also the teenage happiness. Along with these responsibilities, she somehow completed her school studies.

Marriage at Age 20

My grandfather wanted my mother to marry his sister's son, Subramanian. Without knowing this, Subramanian went to join the Army. But he came back without joining. **Destiny.** First my grandfather got angry but later he calmed down and got my mother married to him in the year 1942 when she was 20 years old. Subramanian's father was relieved of his post, prematurely as Station Master in the Railways, due to mental illness. As compensation, my father was given a job as clerk in the Railways.

Mother became Widow at Age 24

After their marriage, my parents lived in Erode and Jolarpettai. I was born on August 24, 1943 and my sister was born on July 3, 1945. As my father was working in the Good Shed where coal was stored, he somehow contracted TB in the beginning of 1945. But his treatment failed and he left us for his heavenly abode on April 22, 1946. My mother was 24, I was 2.5 years old and my sister was 9 months.

Mother took up Teaching Profession at Age 26

My grandfather was a strong-willed man and after completing one year of mourning and the first anniversary rituals, he took a bold step and asked my mother to enrol herself in the one-year teacher training programme. My mother also obeyed him and after completing the training she got a teaching job in an elementary school. My grandfather was relieved that my mother could stand on her own feet even if she lost the support of my grandfather or her two brothers. She worked in the school for 32 years and retired as Headmistress in 1980 at age 58.

My mother's Contribution to her Brothers

As my mother started taking care of her two brothers from a young age, she was very attached to them till her death. She took care of their studies, played a key role in their marriage and helped both the families in matters of daily life. She stayed with them alternately throughout her life.

Mother Disappointed by Her Son and First Grandson

As the only son, I disappointed her by marrying against her wish. But within a few months she reconciled and pardoned me. In the same way, she was disappointed by her first grandson when he eloped with a girl of his choice. But she did not live long enough to reconcile with him.

I wish I could take back every pain and worry that I ever caused my mother. I wish that I could just undo, all the moments that made her blue.

Special about Mothers

> *"But there's a story behind everything. How a picture got on a wall. How a scar got on your face. Sometimes the stories are simple, and sometimes they are hard and heartbreaking. But behind all your stories is always your mother's story, because hers is where yours begin."*
>
> **- Mitch Albom**

> *"A father may turn his back on his child, brothers and sisters may become inveterate enemies, husbands may desert their wives, wives their husbands. But a mother's love endures through all."*
>
> **- Washington Irving**

Yes, my mother endured through not only her children but also her brothers and their families.

I can understand that your mother lived a life full of sacrifices. I am very much moved. May her soul rest in peace.

It is alright. We can continue.

Death of Samikannu - December 24, 1986

Dr. Samikannu joined REC as Resident Doctor. He and his family lived next door in house No.12. He was a paediatrician. He had his own house in Kattur, which was at a distance of 10 kilometres from REC, in which his in-laws stayed. He had a private practice in Tiruverambur which was at a distance of 8 kilometres from REC.

His wife was Rajakkili and he had four daughters namely Subha, Bindu, Priya and Anitha. They were aged between 3 and 9 years.

June and Rajakkili became close friends and all their children would be at our home most of the times. They used to study in our house. Shyamala used to play with them nicely and our house was always filled with children and their noises. Once, I remember that all the children went to the washroom one by one to wipe their tears after we saw a Chinese movie on Doordharshan. I taught Bindu to play Chess. Things were going on smoothly until that fateful evening on December 24, 1986.

Samikannu was looking after his patients in Tiruverambur on that evening and he suddenly felt some chest pain. He immediately left on his scooter for his home. Within 10 minutes after he reached home, he collapsed and was declared dead when he was rushed to a nearby hospital. It was so sudden and sad. With great grief, he was cremated the next day and they completed all the rituals connected with death.

The kids were about 7 to 13 years of age. Samikannu had purchased 4 plots for the four girls in Kattur itself. Rajakkilli was in a fix. God came to their rescue. Nagaratnam, who was the Principal at that time, offered her a temporary job at REC as an Assistant in the college library. June and I advised her to take it up even though her family members were not very keen for it. But Rajakkili was wise enough and took the job. The children were continuing their studies in RSK Higher Secondary School. I was also coaching Subha. One day I was slightly harsh to Subha for not studying and June got angry and told me that I should not be harsh to a fatherless girl.

Rajakkili was made permanent in 1989 and she retired in October 2013.

Here, I should appreciate Rajakkili. With her salary and by selling those plots, she made Subha a doctor with Gynaecology specialization, Bindu a Computer Engineer, Priya a doctor with Dermatology and Cosmetology specialization and Anitha an Automobile Engineer.

Shyamala becoming a Graduate and Admission to Post Graduation - July 1989

Shyamala successfully obtained B.Sc. degree in Nutrition and Dietetics in July 1989. We decided that she should pursue M.Sc. in Nutrition and Dietetics from Avinashilingam Deemed University, which was earlier Avinashilingam Institute for Home Science and Higher Education for Women, Coimbatore. We attended the interview on July 15 and we were returning happily carrying the news that Shyamala got admission in Coimbatore. But destiny had something else for us.

Death of my Mother-in-law Rachel - July 15, 1989

When we reached aunt Amelia's house in Raja Colony at about 1 a.m., on July 16, we found the house locked. June and Amelia were supposed to be in the house.

At that time, the watchman on street duty, informed us that June's mother Rachel had died in the Nalwazhi Hospital house in the morning of July 15. Then, we rushed there and came to know that she had passed away in her sleep. But as soon as I entered June asked about the interview and was happy that Shyamala got admission. But I took it as a bad omen and suggested that Shyamala need not study in Coimbatore. June also agreed and Shyamala joined M.Sc. Biochemistry in Seethalakshmi Ramasami College, Trichy. Rachel was laid to rest, next to her husband's grave.

Tributes to Rachel

June's birth mother Rachel was the eldest child with two younger sisters and two younger brothers. She was born into the Morton family which had migrated to India during the colonial period. She was a Protestant and married Lionel Narcis who was a Catholic on June 23, 1948. Lionel was working in the Railways. She had some informal training as a nurse and she joined her sister Amelia in the Nalwazhi Hospital. She worked in the Nalwazhi Hospital helping her sister for almost 40 years. After her death in 1989, Amelia could not run the hospital and closed it. She gracefully let her 3 children be brought up by her sister Amelia so that they would grow in comfort. She was grieved by her only son's suicide in 1968. She lost her husband in 1977. June and I never did anything worthwhile for her, thinking that Amelia might not like it.

Shyamala becoming a Post-Graduate – July, 1991

Shyamala became a post-graduate in Biochemistry in July 1991 and received a gold medal for her performance.

Shyamala's Ph.D. Programme - August, 1991

When she was called for an interview to Christian Medical College (CMC), Vellore, we attended the interview and she got selected for the Ph.D. programme. We packed everything and went to Vellore by train and got down at 1 a.m. at the station and took a room in a lodge. We stayed three days in the lodge trying to search for her accommodation and finally we got accommodation for her in a ladies' hostel which was slightly far away from CMC. We saw that she was comfortable and left for Trichy.

Within two months of her stay in Vellore, she wrote a letter that she had met Alex, who was completing his Ph.D. under the same guide, and they liked each other and would like to get married. When we formally approved, Alex's mother and their relatives came to our quarters and after getting to know about both our families, we agreed to get them married.

The full name of Alex is Joseph Alex Anand Davis. He had his B.Sc. and MSc. in Bio-chemistry from PSG Arts College, a famous college in Coimbatore. We call him Alex and his mother calls him Anand. Alex's father, Ignatius Davis, was a Civil Engineer and he died in a road accident while on duty. Alex's mother, Emily Davis, was a school teacher. Alex had an elder brother, Prakash, who died of cancer in 2009. He has a younger sister, Dr. Anita, an Ophthalmologist in BHEL Hospital, Trichy and a younger brother Rajesh, diploma holder in Mechanical Engineering now successfully running a medical diagnostic centre. They are Christians and are settled in Podanur, Coimbatore.

Premalatha's (Pappi) Marriage - October 21, 1991

My sister's only daughter, Premalatha's (Pappi), marriage to Balasubramanian was conducted in Rajapalayam where my brother-in-law Ramaiyan was the Municipal Chairman. June went five days before the marriage and as usual played a key role in the marriage proceedings. Balasubramanian, a Chemical Engineer, is now the Joint President (Manufacturing) in India Cements at Thalavoy.

Shyamala's Marriage - February 10, 1992

The marriage of Alex and Shyamala was solemnized by Bishop Lawrence, maternal uncle of Alex in St. Mary's Cathedral, Melapudhur, Trichy on Monday, February 10, 1992 at 4.30 p.m. The reception was held in Hotel Arun near Central bus stand, Trichy on the same evening at 7.00 p.m. On the previous day, Sunday, we had the engagement ceremony in the Ladies Club hall near aunt Amelia's house in which we had both vegetarian and non-vegetarian food. On Friday, February 14, 1992, we all went to Podanur, where Alex's mother had arranged a reception. June and I left that evening for Madurai to play in a bridge tournament.

History repeats itself! I, as a Hindu, married a Roman Catholic in 1967 and 25 years later my daughter, a Hindu, married a Roman Catholic in 1992.

Silver wedding Anniversary- August 1992

We could not celebrate our 25th wedding anniversary on August 30, 1992 since my daughter Shyamala was suffering from pre-eclampsia due to high blood pressure and the ensuing child delivery,

Became a Grandfather, Birth of Amenda - September 16, 1992

Shyamala had to withdraw from her Ph.D. programme after she became pregnant. She had a high blood pressure problem and had a C-section in Shyamala Nursing Home, Trichy at 11.45 a.m., on Wednesday, September 16, 1992 and delivered a beautiful baby girl. Immediately, Dinky and I took the baby to the paediatrician Dr. Kingsley for a preliminary check-up since Dr. Hema David, paediatrician, belonging to Shyamala Nursing Home was on leave. We had to check her lungs since she was a meconium baby. Dr. Kingsley issued a certificate that the baby was normal and in pink of health.

The baby was named Amanda.

Amanda is a Latin female gerundive name meaning having to be loved, deserving to be loved, or worthy of love or loved very much by everyone. The name "Amanda" first appeared in 1212 on a birth record from Warwickshire, England, and five centuries later the name was popularized by poets and playwrights. In the United States, "Amanda" slowly became more prominent from the 1930's to the 1960's, ranking among the top 200 baby names.

Later, based on numerology Amanda was changed to Amenda.

After three months, we went to Vellore where Alex rented a house in Thottapalayam very close to CMC. We asked Kaliaperumal, working on my research project and his wife Tamilarasi, our domestic help to find someone for taking care of Amenda. Kaliaperumal arranged his brother's daughter Ramana who was about 15 years old and we took Ramana to Vellore as well. After some time, Alex shifted their house to Katpadi. By July 1993, Alex finished his Ph.D. and he had to search for a job. Then both shifted to my quarters in July 1993. Alex joined St. Joseph's college as Lecturer and Shyamala joined Ph.D. in Bharathidasan University, Trichy.

You became a father at age 25 and a grandfather at age 49. Can you compare the two feelings?

When I became a father, I was not by the side of my wife or my daughter to know the pain a mother undergoes during delivery and the pain the child endures while coming out. I was about 400 kilometres from both of them. But for my granddaughter I was very near my daughter and I knew all the pain she underwent and within a few minutes of the arrival of my granddaughter, I was able to see her.

Since, I had been brought up by my grandfather, I knew everything a grandfather had to do. June and I enjoyed being with Amenda because, for first few years of her life she lived mostly with us.

With these sweet memories let us go to part III of my life at REC. The saddest and shocking incident was my daughter's fire accident.

Oh my God!

In addition, there were the deaths of my uncle Govindarajan and his third son Chinnakutti. There were also happy events like the trip to US by Alex, Shyamala and Amenda, my trips to Jerusalem and Bangkok and the birth of my grandson Joshua in USA. There was my mild cardiology problem and my retirement from REC.

Oh! There was a mix of sad and happy events. Let me prepare myself to hear them.

> ### Around Me
> Let us go through the major events that took place during this period.

India

Politics

Operation Blue Star, 1984 - Operation Blue Star was an Indian military operation between June 3-8, 1984, ordered by Prime Minister Indira Gandhi to establish control over the Harmandir Sahib Complex in Amritsar, Punjab, and remove Jarnail Singh Bhindranwale and his armed followers from the complex buildings.

Assassination of Indira Gandhi, 1984 - At about 9.20 a.m., October 31,1984, Indira Gandhi was assassinated by two of her security guards in her garden on her way to be interviewed by British actor Peter Ustinov, who was filming a documentary for Irish television in the office next door. One of the security guards Beant Singh fired three rounds after she fell to the ground.

Rajiv Gandhi became Prime Minister, 1984 - Rajiv Gandhi was sworn in as Prime Minister on October 31, 1984 after his mother's death.

VIIIth General Elections, 1984 - This election during December 26 to 28, 1984, was won by the Indian National Congress of Rajiv Gandhi with 404 seats out of 533 seats. The Telugu Desam Party of N. T. Rama Rao from Andhra Pradesh won 30 seats and became the first regional party to become a national opposition party. CPI(M) won 22 seats, AIADMK 12, CPI 6, BJP 2 and DMK 2.

Rajiv Gandhi Continued as Prime Minister, 1984 - Rajiv Gandhi was sworn in as Prime Minister for second time on December 31, 1984.

Establishment of the Indira Gandhi National Open University, 1985 - The Indira Gandhi National Open University (IGNOU) was established in 1985 in New Delhi by the Central government of India.

Birth of Arunachal Pradesh State, 1987 - Arunachal Pradesh became a state (24th) on February 20, 1987.

Goa Became a State, 1987 - Goa became a state (25th) on May 30, 1987. Daman and Diu were separated from Goa and continued to be administered as the Union Territory of Daman and Diu.

R. Venkataraman, President of India, 1987 - Ramaswamy Venkataraman became the eighth President of India on July 25, 1987 after Zail Singh.

IXth General Elections, 1989 - General elections were held on November 22 and 26, 1989 for 9th Lok Sabha. INC won 197 seats, Janata Dal 143, BJP 85 and Left parties 45. The total number of seats were 534.

V. P. Singh Became Prime Minister, 1989 - With the support of BJP and CPI (M), Vishnu Pratap Singh of Janata Dal was sworn in as Prime minister on December 2, 1989 and Devi Lal as Deputy Prime Minister.

V. P. Singh Resigns as Prime Minister, 1990 - V. P. Singh lost the vote of confidence in Lok Sabha on November 7, 1990, due to withdrawal of support by the BJP and he resigned on the same day.

Chandrashekhar became Prime Minister, 1990 - With outside support of Congress led by Rajiv Gandhi, Chandrashekhar was sworn in as Prime Minister on November 10, 1990. He had the direct support of 64 MPs and outside support of Congress with 197 MPs.

Chandrashekhar Resigns as Prime Minister, 1991 - When the Budget session was on, Rajiv Gandhi withdrew the support for Chandrashekhar on March 6, 1991 with a reason that two police constables were spying on him. Chandrashekhar resigned on the same day. The President dissolved the Sabha but Chandrashekar was requested to continue till the new Prime Minister was elected. He continued till June 21, 1991.

Xth General Elections and Assassination of Rajiv Gandhi, 1991 - The general elections for the 10th Lok Sabha were planned to be held during May-June 1991. First phase of polling was completed on May 20 for 211 out of 542 seats. Rajiv Gandhi came to Sriperumbudhur, near Chennai, on May 21 for an election meeting to support Congress candidate Margatham Chandrasekar. As he was walking towards the dais, he was garlanded by many well-wishers including children. At 10.21 p.m., the assassin, Dhanu (Thenmozhi Rajaratnam), approached and greeted him. She bent down to touch his feet and detonated an RDX explosive laden belt tucked below her dress. Gandhi, his assassin, and 14 others were killed in the explosion. The attack was blamed on the Liberation Tigers of Tamil Eelam (LTTE), a militant organization from Sri Lanka. The remaining election was postponed until mid-June and voting took place on June 12 and June 15. Voting was the lowest ever with just 53 per cent of the electorate casting votes. The congress party did poorly in the pre-assassination constituencies and swept the post-assassination constituencies. INC won 244 seats, BJP 120, JD 69, CPI(M) 35, CPI 14, TDP 13 and AIADMK 11. The total number of seats were 545.

P. V. Narasimha Rao became Prime Minister, 1991 - Indian National Congress was the single largest party with 244 members. They formed the government with the outside support of left parties with 49 members. Pamulaparti Venkata Narasimha Rao (popularly known as P.V.) an Indian lawyer and politician was sworn in as the Prime Minister on June 21, 1991. This was politically significant as he was the first Prime Minister from non-Hindi speaking South India. He led an important administration, overseeing a major economic transformation and several home incidents affecting national security. He is referred to as the "Father of Indian Economic Reforms".

Visit of Chinese Premier to India (1991) and Visit of Indian Prime Minister to China (1993) - Premier Li Peng visited India in December 1991. Prime Minister Narasimha Rao visited China in September 1993. The Agreement on the Maintenance of Peace and Tranquillity along the Line of Actual Control (LAC) on the India - China Border Area was signed during this visit.

Shankar Dayal Sharma became the President of India, 1992 - Shankar Dayal Sharma became the ninth President of India on July 25, 1992 after R. Venkataraman.

New Delhi Became a State, 1992 - New Delhi, the capital of India, became a state in 1992 under the National Capital Territory Act. Under this system the elected Government is given wide powers except law and order that remain with the central government.

Scandal

Jain Hawala Scandal, 1991 - The Hawala scandal involved payments allegedly received by politicians through four hawala brokers, the Jain brothers. It was a US $18 million bribery scandal that implicated some of the country's leading politicians. The story was broken by two Delhi based journalists Ram Bahadur Rai and Rajesh Joshi from the Hindi daily, Jansatta. Vineet Narain, a journalist, filed a public interest litigation in the Supreme Court of India.

Terrorist Attacks

Blow up of Air India Flight 182, 1985 - On June 23, 1985, the Boeing 747-237B serving Air India Flight 182 operating on the Montreal, Canada–London, UK–Delhi, India route was destroyed by a bomb at an altitude of 31,000 feet. It crashed into the Atlantic Ocean while in Irish airspace. It was the first bombing of a 747 jumbo jet killing 329 people, including 268 Canadians, 27 Britons, and 24 Indians.

Kidnapping of Rubaiya Sayeed, 1989 - The first challenge for V. P. Singh's government was the 1989 kidnapping of Rubaiya Sayeed by members of the Jammu Kashmir Liberation Front, a Kashmiri Muslim militant organization, on December 8, 1989 in Jammu and Kashmir. Rubaiya was the daughter of Mufti Mohammad Sayeed, the Home minister of India. The kidnappers demanded the release of five of their terrorists in exchange for Rubaiya. The government accepted their demands and freed the jailed terrorists.

Accidents

Bhopal Gas Tragedy, 1984 - The Bhopal disaster or Bhopal gas tragedy was a gas leak incident in India, considered the world's worst industrial disaster. It occurred on the night of December 2-3, 1984 at the Union Carbide India Limited (UCIL), a pesticide plant in Bhopal, Madhya Pradesh. Over 500,000 people were exposed to methyl isocyanate (MIC) gas and other chemicals. The government of Madhya Pradesh confirmed a total of 3,787 deaths.

Judgement on Bhopal Gas Tragedy, 1989 - Ending a legal battle over compensation for victims the Indian Supreme Court ordered the Union Carbide Corporation to pay $470 million in damages for the toxic gas leak at Bhopal.

Others

Operation Black Thunder, 1986 - Operation Black Thunder is the name of two operations that took place in India in the late 1980's to flush out remaining Sikh activists from the Golden Temple using 'Black Cat' commandos of the National Security Guards. The Operation Black Thunder I took place on April 30, 1986. Operation Black Thunder II began on May 9, 1988 in Amritsar and ended with the surrender of the militants on May 18.

War

Sino-India Skirmish, 1987 - The 1987 Sino-Indian skirmish was the third military conflict between the Chinese People's Liberation Army and Indian Army at Sumdorong Chu Valley. At the end of 1986, India granted statehood to Arunachal Pradesh, which is an area claimed by China but administered by India. The Chinese government proceeded to protest. These led to some tensions in the border. After a few rounds of dialogue in 1993, the two countries signed an agreement to ensure peace along the LAC.

Indian Peace Keeping Force (IPKF) in Sri Lanka, 1987 - Indian Peace Keeping Force (IPKF) was the Indian military contingent performing a peace keeping operation in Sri Lanka between 1987 and 1990. It was formed under the mandate of the 1987 Indo-Sri Lankan Accord that aimed to end the Sri Lankan Civil War between militant Sri Lankan Tamil nationalists such as the Liberation Tigers of Tamil Eelam (LTTE) and the Sri Lankan military.

Withdrawal of IPKF from Sri Lanka, 1990 - The IPKF began withdrawing from Sri Lanka in 1989, following the election of the V. P. Singh government and on the request of the newly elected Sri Lankan President Ranasinghe Premadasa, the last IPKF contingents left Sri Lanka in March 1990.

Space Technology

Prithvi I Test Fired, 1988 - Prithvi I, a surface-to-surface missile was test fired on February 25, 1988 and inducted into the Indian Army in 1994 having a maximum warhead mounting capability of 1,000 kg, with a range of 150 kilometres.

Natural Calamities

Andhra Pradesh Cyclone, 1990 - The 1990 Andhra Pradesh Cyclone or Machilipatnam Cyclone on May 5 was the worst disaster to affect Southern India since the 1977 cyclone. Over 967 people were killed. Over 100,000 animals also died in the cyclone with the total cost of damages to crops estimated at over $600 million.

Tamil Nadu

MGR's Illness, 1984 - M.G. Ramachandran arrived at Apollo Hospital Chennai on October 6, 1984, gasping for breath. He had multiple health problems like diabetes and kidney malfunction. He suffered a stroke on October 16, 1984. On November 4, he was admitted to Downstate Medical Centre, Brooklyn, USA. On November 19, he received a kidney transplant from his niece Leelavathi. He returned to Chennai on February 4, 1985.

VIIIth Tamil Nadu Assembly Elections, 1984 - The eighth Legislative Assembly election was held on December 24, 1984, when MGR was in USA for treatment. Anna Dravida Munnetra Kazhagam (ADMK) in alliance with Indian National Congress (INC) won the elections winning 193 seats out of 234. AIADMK won 132 seats, INC 61 and DMK 24. The total number of seats were 234.

MGR Became Chief Minister for the Third Time, 1985 - M. G. Ramachandran was sworn in as Chief Minister, for the third time, on February 10, 1985 after his return from US,

Death of Baktavatsalam, 1987 - Minjur Kanakasabhapathi Baktavatsalam who served as the Chief Minister of Madras state from October 2, 1963 to March 6, 1967, died on January 31, 1987 at the age of 89.

Death of MGR, 1987 - MGR never fully recovered from his illness and died on December 24, 1987 at 3.30 a.m., in Chennai Apollo Hospital. He was almost 71. His death sparked off a frenzy of looting and rioting all over the state. The violence during the funeral left 29 people dead and 47 police personnel badly wounded.

Janaki Ramachandran became Chief Minister, 1988 - After the death of MGR, V. R. Nedunchezhian was acting Chief Minister from December 24, 1987 to January 7, 1988. Then MGR's wife Janaki Ramachandran took over as Chief Minister on January 7, 1988.

Resignation of Janaki and President's Rule, 1988-89 - AIADMK split into two factions, one led by Janaki and the other by J. Jayalalithaa. Even though Janaki won the vote of confidence, her government was dismissed by Rajiv Gandhi on January 30 citing the disruptions in the assembly and President's rule was imposed from January 30, 1988. P. C. Alexander IAS (Retd) became the Governor.

IXth Tamil Nadu Assembly Elections, 1989 - At the end of one year of President's rule, elections were held on January 21, 1989. DMK won 150 seats, CPI(M) 15, JNP 4, AIADMK(J) 27, CPI 3, INC 26 and AIADMK(Janaki) 2. The total number of seats were 234.

Karunanidhi became Chief Minister, 1989 - Karunanidhi was sworn in as Chief Minister for the third time on January 27, 1989 after a gap of 12 years.

Birth of Pattali Makkal Katchi (PMK), 1989 - Pattali Makkal Katchi was founded by Dr. Ramdoss on July 16, 1989. It came out of Vanniar Sangam.

Establishment of Manonmaniam Sundaranar University, 1990 - Manonmaniam Sundaranar University was hived off the Madurai Kamaraj University on September 7, 1990 to cater to the three southern-most districts of Tamil Nadu - Tirunelveli, Tuticorin and Kanyakumari with its main campus in Abishekapatti, Tirunelveli.

Dismissal of DMK Government and President's Rule, 1991 - On January 30, 1991, the DMK government was dismissed by Prime Minister Chandrashekhar using Article 356 of the Indian Constitution. President's rule was imposed on Tamil Nadu from January 30 in spite of Governor Sardar Surjit Singh Barnala's good report. The reason cited was the deterioration of law and order and the DMK's alleged closeness to the LTTE. President's rule lasted till June 24, 1991. Sardar Surjit Singh Barnala (till February 15, 1991) and Bhishma Narain Singh (till June 24, 1991) were the Governors.

Xth Tamil Nadu Assembly Elections, 1991 - The Xth Legislative Assembly election was held on June 24, 1991. The All India Anna Dravida Munnetra Kazhagam (AIADMK) – Indian National Congress (INC) alliance won the elections and AIADMK leader J. Jayalalithaa became the Chief Minister. AIADMK won 164 seats, INC 60 and DMK 2. The total number of seats were 234.

J. Jayalalithaa became Chief Minister, 1991 - J. Jayalalithaa was sworn in as Chief Minister of Tamil Nadu for the first time on June 24, 1991.

World

Politics

Reagan's Second Term as US President, 1985 - Ronald Reagan won the Presidential elections in 1984 and started his second term from January 20, 1985 as 40th President.

Gorbachev became General Secretary, 1985 - Mikhail Sergeyevich Gorbachev became the General Secretary of the Communist Party of the Soviet Union from March 1985 after the death of Konstantin Ustinovich Chernenko and became Head of USSR from 1988.

Li Peng became Prime Minister of China, 1987- Li Peng became the Prime Minister of China on November 24, 1987 after Zhao Ziyang.

Benazir became Prime Minister of Pakistan, 1988 - Benazir Bhutto became the first female Prime Minister of Pakistan on December 2, 1988.

Yang Shangkun became President of China, 1988- Yang Shangkun became the President of China on April 9, 1988 after Li Xiannian.

H. W. Bush became US President, 1989 - George Herbert Walker Bush, a Republican, became 41st President of the United States from January 20, 1989.

Unification of Germany, 1990 - East and West Germany unified as Germany on October 3, 1990 after breaking of the Berlin Wall on November 5, 1989.

Release of Nelson Mandela, 1990 - Nelson Mandela, leader of the movement to end South African Apartheid, was released from prison after 27 years on February 11, 1990.

John Major as Prime Minister of UK, 1990 - John Major became Prime Minister of England on November 28, 1990 after Margaret Thatcher.

Madrid Peace Conference, 1991 - The Madrid Conference held from October 30 to November 1, 1991 in Madrid was hosted by Spain and co-sponsored by the United States and the Soviet Union. It was an attempt by the international community to revive the Israeli–Palestinian peace process through negotiations involving Israel and the Palestinians and Arab countries, including Jordan, Lebanon and Syria.

Resignation of Gorbachev, 1991 - Mikhail Gorbachev announced his resignation as President of the Soviet Union on December 25, 1991.

Yeltsin became First President of Russian Federation, 1991 - Boris Nikolayevich Yeltsin, a Russian politician became the first President of the Russian Federation, from December 26, 1991.

Proclamation by Bush and Yeltsin - President Bush and President Boris N. Yeltsin of Russia proclaimed a new era of "friendship and partnership" as they declared a formal end to seven decades of rivalry and outlined general principles for relations between the United States and Russia.

Special Event

Dissolution of Soviet Union, December 26, 1991 -The dissolution of the Soviet Union was enacted on December 26, 1991, by declaration no. 142-H of Supreme Soviet of the Soviet Union. The declaration acknowledged the independence of the former Soviet Republics and created the Commonwealth of Independent States (CIS). On the previous day, Soviet President Mikhail Gorbachev, the eighth and last leader of the Soviet Union, resigned, declared his office extinct, and handed over its powers – including control of the Soviet nuclear missile launching codes to Russian President Boris Yeltsin. That evening at 7.32 p.m., the Soviet flag was lowered from the Kremlin for the last time and replaced with the pre-revolutionary Russian flag. The Soviet State was born in 1917.

Science and Discovery

Birth of Macintosh Computer, 1984 - Steve Jobs of Apple introduced the original Macintosh computer on January 24, 1984. This was the first mass-market personal computer featuring an integral graphical user interface and mouse.

Hole in the Ozone Layer, 1985 - UK scientist, Shanklin, was working at the British Antarctic Survey, along with colleagues Brian Gardiner and late Joe Farman and they announced that they had discovered a hole in the ozone layer in the atmosphere above Antarctica in 1985.

Use of DNA in Criminal Case, 1986 - DNA was first used in a criminal case in England in 1986. DNA samples collected from the men living and working within the neighbourhood of two rape and murder scenes resulted in two positive outcomes. The one man originally convicted was proved to be innocent and the guilty criminal was caught.

The Human Genome Project (HGP), 1990 - An international scientific research project with the goal of determining the sequence of chemical base pairs which make up human DNA and of identifying and mapping all of the genes of the human genome from both a physical and functional standpoint was started in 1990.

War

Ending of Iran-Iraq War, 1980 to 88 - Started by Iraq dictator Saddam Hussein in September 1980, the war was marked by indiscriminate ballistic-missile attacks, extensive use of chemical weapons and attacks on third-country oil tankers in the Persian Gulf. It ended on July 20, 1988 after Iran's acceptance of a cease-fire.

Invasion of Kuwait by Iraq, 1990 - Iraqi leader Saddam Hussein ordered the invasion and occupation of neighbouring Kuwait in early August 1990 and it ended on February 28, 1991 after a massive US led air offensive known as Operation Desert Storm.

Sports

Carl Lewis in History Books, 1984 - The 1984 Summer Olympics (XXIII) were held in Los Angeles, California, USA in 1984. Carl Lewis, USA, entered the history books by matching the Berlin 1936 achievement of fellow American Jesse Owens, winning gold medals in the same four events: 100m, 200m, 4x100m relay and long jump. The fastest man was Carl Lewis who clocked 9.99 seconds in 100 metres.

Ben Johnson Tested Positive, 1988 - The 1988 Summer Olympics (XXIV), were held from September 17 to October 2, 1988 in Seoul, South Korea. Canadian Ben Johnson set a world record in the 100m sprint (9.79 seconds), but tested positive for steroids. He was the first world famous athlete to be disqualified for using drugs. After his disqualification, Carl Lewis, was awarded the 100m gold (9.92 seconds).

South African Gesture, 1992 - The 1992 Summer Olympic Games were held in Barcelona, Catalonia, Spain during July 25 to August 9, 1992. With the dissolution of the Soviet Union, twelve of the fifteen new states formed a Unified Team and finished with 122 medals. In the last lap of the 10,000m final, Derartu Tulu of Ethiopia darted into the lead and went on to win. At the finishing line, she waited for her opponent Elana Meyer, a white South African. They set off hand in hand for a victory lap that symbolised hope for a new Africa. Lindford Christie of GBR was the fastest man with 9.96 seconds.

Viswanathan Anand became Chess Grandmaster, 1988 - In 1988, at age 18, Viswanathan Anand became India's first Grandmaster by winning the Shakti Finance International Chess Tournament held in Coimbatore, Tamil Nadu, India.

Scandals

The Iran-Contra Affair, 1985 to 86 - The Iran–Contra affair was a political scandal in the United States that occurred during the second term of the Reagan Administration. It involved the secret sale of arms to Iran to secure the release of several US hostages and to fund the Contras in Nicaragua. After several investigations, Reagan was found not guilty. The rest of those indicted or convicted were all pardoned in the final days of the Presidency of George H. W. Bush, who had been Vice-President at the time.

Accident

The Chernobyl Accident, 1986 - The Chernobyl accident occurred on April 26, 1986, at the Chernobyl nuclear power plant in Ukraine (then in Soviet Union). Large areas of Ukraine, Belarus, and Russia were badly contaminated, resulting in the evacuation and resettlement of roughly 200,000 people. About 60% of the radioactive fallout landed in Belarus.

Focus on Climate Change

IPCC, 1988 - The Intergovernmental Panel on Climate Change (IPCC) was created in 1988, under the auspices of the United Nations, to produce reports that support the United Nations Framework Convention on Climate Change (UNFCCC), the main international treaty on climate change. The IPCC first assessment report was completed in 1990, and served as the basis of the UNFCCC.

Earth Summit, 1992 - During June 3 to 14, 1992, the Earth Summit (United Nations Conference on Environment and Development or UNCED) met in Rio de Janeiro, Brazil, as a twenty-year follow-up to the United Nations Conference on the Human Environment (UNCHE, in Stockholm). The goal of the 120 heads of state, over ten thousand government delegates, and hundreds of officials from UN organizations was to refocus global attention on the planet's degradation. It was the largest gathering of heads of state in history. It entered into force on March 21, 1994. The UNFCCC objective is to stabilize greenhouse gas concentrations in the atmosphere at a level that would prevent dangerous anthropogenic interference with the climate system. The parties to the convention have to meet annually from 1995 in Conferences of the Parties (COP) to assess progress in dealing with climate change.

World Population

5 Billion, 1987 - The Day of Five Billion, July 11, 1987, was designated by the United Nations Population Fund as the approximate day on which world population reached five billion.

CHAPTER 9

Life in Trichy, Part III - October 1992 to June 2003

ABSTRACT

Me

The details of Amenda's baptism, Shyamala's Ph.D. programme (1993), Amelia's new apartment (1993), our new quarters (1994), death of Ramesh (1994), moped accident (1994), Selvam's marriage (1995), business venture by Alex (1995), Shyamala becoming Lecturer (1995), Shyamala's fire accident (1995), Alex and Shyamala as Lecturers (1996), deaths of Chinna Kutty and Govindarajan (1996), Donnella's marriage (1997), first contact with Jesus Calls (1997), purchase of Maruti Omni (1997), Shyamala and Alex in US (1998-2003), my cyst operation (2000), Amenda's visit to India (2001), birth of Joshua in USA (2001), Denys' marriage (2001), my cardiology problem (2003), return of Alex and Shyamala to India (2003), my retirement (2003) and my new job (2003) are presented.

Around me

In India, the major events were the Babri Masjid incident (1992), fodder scam coming to light (1992), Indo-China peace agreement (1993), founding of Delhi Metro Rail Corporation (1995), renaming Bombay as Mumbai (1995), XIth general elections (1996), Vajpayee as Prime Minister (1996), visit of Chinese Premier (1996), Deve Gowda as Prime Minister (1996), Gujral as Prime Minister (1997), K. R. Narayanan as President (1997), Sonia Gandhi becoming President, INC (1997), Netaji Open University (1997), birth of Rashtria Janata Dal (1997), death of Mother Teresa (1997), XIIth general elections

(1998), Vajpayee as Prime Minister (1998), nuclear bomb test (1998), parliament dissolution (1998), peace effort with Pakistan (1999), Kargil War (1999), XIIIth general elections (1999), Vajpayee as Prime Minister (1999), renaming Calcutta as Kolkata (2001), attack on Parliament (2001) and Abdul Kalam as President (2002).

In Tamil Nadu State, the major events were birth of Marumalarchi Dravida Munnetra Kazhagam (1994), XIth assembly elections (1996), Karunanidhi becoming Chief Minister (1996), Jayalalithaa cases (1996), XIIth assembly elections (2001), Jayalalithaa's acquittal and return as Chief Minister (2002).

In the World, the major events were Clinton becoming President of US (1993), Oslo I Accord (1993), Jiang Zemin becoming President of China (1993), Nelson Mandela becoming President of South Africa (1994), assassination of Rabin, Israel Prime Minister (1995), Taliban's government in Afghanistan (1996), cloning of sheep (1996), Clinton's second term (1997), Google search engine (1997), Tony Blair becoming Prime Minister of UK (1997), Rowling's first novel (1997), death of Princess Diana (1997), Kyoto Protocol (1997), Zhu Rongji becoming Prime Minister of China (1998), impeachment and acquittal of Clinton (1998-99), world population touching 6 billion (1999), Y2K problem (1999), Putin becoming President of Russia (2000), Camp David Summit (2000), G.W. Bush becoming US President (2001), September 11 attack (2001), Anthrax attack (2001), Space shuttle Columbia disaster (2003), Wen Jiabao becoming Prime Minister of China (2003), Hu Jintao becoming President of China (2003) and invasion of Iraq (2003).

ME

Where did you celebrate Amenda's Baptism and her first birthday?

Amenda's Baptism – November 1, 1992

Amenda was baptized in St. Mary's Cathedral, Melapudhur, Trichy on November 1, 1992 where her parents had their wedding. Alex's sister, Anita, and her husband, Raj, were her Godparents

Amenda's First Birthday - September 16, 1993

Amenda's first birthday was celebrated in a grand manner on September 16, 1993 in my quarters No.11, 7th street, where her mother celebrated 14 birthdays.

Amenda's First Tonsure

Amenda had her first tonsure in November 1993 in Vailankanni's Church, Nagapattinum.

Ilango's Service Interrupted by Ponnusamy - September, 1993

When Ponnusamy was the Education Minister of Tamil Nadu, he was also the Chairman, Board of Governors of REC, Trichy. Due to some alleged misunderstanding between Ponnusamy and Ilango, Ponnusamy terminated the services of Ilango using the new rule that appointment of REC Principals was for three years instead of five years. But he forgot that Ilango was appointed for a period of five years. Dr. C.R. Kandasamy, Professor, Department of Production Engineering, was made the Principal in charge.

Ilango fought the case in the High Court and won it. He re-joined in February 1994.

After Ilango completed his term of five years, Dr. K.L.P. Mishra, senior most Professor and Head of the Department of Electrical Engineering, served as Principal from July 1995, Dr. P. Aravindan from July 1997 and Dr. M. Arumugam from July 2000.

Shyamala's Ph.D. Programme - July 1993

Shyamala registered for her Ph.D. in August 1993 under Bharathidasan University. Her topic was on "Use of Fungi in biodegradation of Oil." When she required samples, I approached one of my old part time BE students who was an estate manager in BHEL and he helped her by providing the necessary samples for her experimental study. She was progressing well in her research.

Aunt Amelia Selling her House and Purchasing Flat - 1993

After the death of Rachel, Amelia found it difficult to run the hospital. She was in her sixties and was worried about her future. We offered that she could stay with us in REC and her own house could be rented out. But she never agreed. Amelia was used to living independently and she never liked to live with others. She decided to sell the house in 1993. She booked a flat in Warner Gems, Cantonment. I approached one of my old students who had a construction firm and he readily agreed to buy the house for Rs. ten lakh. We sold the house and Amelia shifted to Warner Gems flat in June 1993. She paid Rs. five lakh for the apartment and deposited Rs. two lakh in SBI, Rs. two lakh in Vasavi Chit funds, and Rs. one lakh in Grover investments as fixed deposits. Her intention was to live on the interest earned from the bank deposits.

Shifting to Assistant Professor Quarters – January, 1994

Some vacancies came up in Assistant Professor quarters and I applied for the same and was allotted residence at No. 1, Fifth street. The plinth area and the open space area in the front and back were more compared to the present quarters and there was one room, toilet and bath and open terrace on the first floor. Actually, we would have continued in the present quarters but the roof was damaged and so we decided to move. We had to make some alterations and repair in the civil works of the new quarters and finally we occupied the house in January 1994 on Pongal day.

But I must tell you one thing. On the first day when we decided to see the house, before making a decision, my fiat car refused to start initially and with great difficulty it started after some time. Again, it was an indication that changing the quarters was not welcome. But I ignored it.

Death of Ramesh - January 30, 1994

I participated in a bridge tournament in Madurai on January 29 and 30, 1994. My sister was in Madurai at that time after my brother-in-law's retirement as Municipal Commissioner on April 30, 1992. I had told my sister that I would visit her after the match. When the match was over, I was tired and called her telling that I would come next time. I did not know that my next time would be the next day. After talking to her, I left for Trichy with my teammates.

Early morning my phone rang to inform the most shocking news that my sister's youngest son Ramesh had died in a road accident. June and I immediately started by a taxi to Madurai. After completing the cremation, we returned on the same day to Trichy. Ramesh died on the same date and month (January 30) on which Mahatma Gandhi was assassinated in 1948. Even today, I think about it and feel guilty. If I had gone to their house that evening, perhaps he would not have gone out at that time to be hit by a van. **Destiny.** When my sister was in Trichy, Ramesh used to come to REC to celebrate Diwali along with my mother. He was affectionate, sociable and smart.

Moped Accident due to Dog Chase - 1994

I met with a minor accident one Sunday morning in 1994. I was going to Thuvakkudi to purchase something and suddenly a Pomeranian dog belonging to Principal Ilango started to charge me. I could have stopped the moped but instead I accelerated and it skidded near the main gate of the campus. I got slightly hurt but the dog ran off. When I came home June found that there was slight swelling in the left shoulder. Then we went to Dr. Vijayaraghavan, an orthopaedic surgeon and after an x-ray he told us that there was a hairline fracture in the collar bone along with a dislocation. The dislocation was rectified immediately and I was put on a sling for a week.

Selvaraj's Marriage - April 5, 1995

My sister's second son, Selvaraj, got married to Amudha from Dindukkal on April 5, 1995 in Madurai. June went three days before the marriage and played a key role in the marriage by helping my sister.

Alex Starting a Diagnostic Laboratory - 1995

When the contract with St Joseph's College was over, Alex decided to establish a diagnostic laboratory in Coimbatore. There was a small misunderstanding between him and Shyamala regarding choice of profession and settling down in life. However Alex went ahead with his plan.

Shyamala Clearing NET and becoming Lecturer - August, 1995

While Shyamala was doing her research, she took the JRF-NET exam in 1995 and the result came in June, 1995 and she got a good score as usual. She was determined to become a Lecturer forgetting about her Ph.D. degree. She secured a Lecturer post in Velammal College for Women in Erode.

Shyamala's Fire Aaccident - November 9, 1995

Beginning of Careers

I went with Shyamala for her interview at Velammal College for women in Erode. She got selected and was offered the post of Lecturer. We found an outhouse in the former MLA's house opposite the college. We learnt that they never rented the outhouse to anyone but when we approached them, they gave us the house for rent. June packed all the necessary things and sent them along with Kaliaperumal and Nelson who were working on my farm. My friend Ramasamy from REC Calicut, who was working as a Principal in a Polytechnic and who stayed on the outskirts of Erode, and his wife Chellam came for boiling milk connected to the house warming ceremony. For connectivity, the owners allowed us to use their landline. Alex also started to live with her and he would go to Coimbatore daily for running his lab. Amenda was with us and she started her nursery class from July 1995 in the REC English Medium School run in one of the quarters in front of our street. Ramana stayed with us to look after Amenda.

In July 1995, Alex's business career was gaining momentum, Shyamala started her teaching career and Amenda started her education. Everything was going on smoothly until November 9, 1995.

Fire Accident

The house owners had a wedding in their house on Friday, November 10, 1995, preceded by an engagement ceremony the previous evening. Shyamala wanted some jewels to be brought from Trichy to wear for the engagement and wedding. I brought the jewels on Saturday, November 4, 1995, gave it and left the same evening for Trichy. Shyamala came to the bus stop to send me off. I did not know that I would be seeing her normal figure for the last time. Twenty three years have passed but that bus stop scene is fresh in my vision.

On Thursday, November 9, 1995, we were sleeping in our quarters. At about 2 a.m., our door-bell rang. Wondering who it could be, I opened the door to see my co-brother Darrel standing there.

"What Darrel? What happened?"

He said, "Kittu, I got a phone call from Amelia that Shyamala was not well and admitted in a hospital at Erode." By this time June had also joined us. Our phone was not working for the past two days. I took my TVS 50 to Tiruverambur, 7 kilometres from our quarters to book a taxi and came back home asking the taxi to come at 4 a.m. June and I left our house by 4.30 a.m., along with Amenda and reached aunty Amelia's house. When I called the house owner in Erode they said that she had tried to take sleeping tablets and was in the hospital. Then, we left Trichy along with aunty and reached Erode by 12 noon. Alex was waiting outside and he gave us the correct information that she had met with a fire accident. We completely broke down and ran to see her. She was lying down and talked to us as though nothing had happened. The nurses told that she was talking throughout the night about biology, chemistry and medicine. Then they shifted her to a special room and the doctor said that they were treating her. I took a room in a lodge close to the hospital and on Sunday I left along with aunty and Amenda for Trichy leaving June and Alex to look after Shyamala.

After taking leave for a week, I left for Erode on Monday. We informed Dinky and Darrel and they came to help us. Ramasamy's wife volunteered to give lunch. I used to go by bus, take my lunch in their house and bring lunch for June, Shyamala and Alex. This continued till Thursday. We were not sure of the treatment and we wanted to move her to Trichy. The hospital authorities had no objection. I phoned my uncle Govindarajan about the fire accident and at first, he got angry for not telling him about it earlier, and then asked us to bring her. We settled the hospital and lodge bills and on Friday, November 17, at 2.00 p.m., we left in the ambulance belonging to the hospital. The whole hospital watched us take Shyamala and put her in the ambulance. June, Alex and I sat around her. It was the most painful journey which we ever made and somehow, we reached JM hospital in Trichy by 6.30 p.m. My uncle made all the necessary arrangements in the hospital. Immediately, she was carried to the special room and Dr. Bhaskar, a General Surgeon and Dr. Ramachandran, a Reconstruction Surgeon examined her and came out and told us, "You see the burn injury is very serious, almost 80% burns. We will try our best but success is not sure. It will take a lot of money. If you say yes we start the treatment now itself."

June started to sob and as a formality I consulted her and we told the doctors, "Please start the treatment."

Everything was normal till Monday morning. Suddenly, the doctors told us that she may not survive and asked us to inform everyone. That morning I had gone to REC to apply for further leave and to make a part withdrawal from my PF account and from the bank. By the time I returned to the hospital Shyamala's condition had improved and the doctors started the treatment again. **A miracle.**

Life at JM Hospital

In the initial week, many unusual things happened. When my sister came from Madurai her bus met with an accident and she got hurt in her face due to the broken glass pieces. Donella was bitten by a dog when she was coming to see her. Priya fell down from the bicycle. Luckily, nothing serious happened. When Prof. Patrick Gomez, St. Joseph's College was about to donate blood for her in the Seahorse Hospital, there was an electrical fire and again nothing serious happened. Rani, Mohan, Kumar (relatives), Prabakar, Saravanan (my friends) Patrick Gomez (Alex's collaegue), Immanuvel, Lakshminarayanan, Nehru and Murali (Alex's students from St.Joseph's college) donated blood.

Within a week everything was streamlined. Breakfast for June, Alex and me came from uncle Govindarajan's house. For Shyamala the complete diet came from aunty Amelia's house. Amenda stayed with aunty Amelia. Priya and Chellappa gave us morning coffee and dinner. Alex and I had lunch in Mohanraj's house and brought lunch for June. Mohanraj was married to Rani, uncle Padmanaban's daughter. The lunch was prepared by Mohanraj himself and he used to serve us himself. I travelled up and down for various things on my TVS 50. June and Alex stayed in the hospital throughout by sleeping inside the room. June's sister, Dinky, would also stay during the nights and return home to cook and care for her family. This arrangement went on for almost two months. In between, Shyamala's friend, Kanchana, and her mother used to give us dinner. I never used to enter the room and I never allowed anyone else to enter the room either in order to prevent infection. I used to correct my examination papers by sitting in front of the room.

The treatment was also tough. I have to mention about the anaesthetist, Dr. Vedamanickam, and his wife Dr. Rebecca who took great care along with Dr. Bhaskar and Dr. Ramachandran and a number of nurses and the ward boys. Above all I should thank Mother Mary, whose statue was in the front of the hospital, for the miracle. Every day in the morning, I prayed to her when entering the hospital and in the evening when leaving the hospital.

Shyamala was discharged on January 15 and we brought her to Amelia's house.

How do you remember all the names after more than 20 years?

How could I not? Each one of them is in my daily prayers. The doctors, nurses, ward boys, helpers, blood donors and all relatives and friends who provided hospitality for about two months.

The doctors and the hospital staff treated her with professionalism and kindness. They did five washings along with skin grafts. Every time she was taken from the room to the operation theatre in the stretcher, June, Alex and I used to follow the stretcher with a heavy heart and wait outside till the process was completed. It usually took 2 to 3 hours.

Similarly my relatives and friends provided hospitality with great kindness. They never missed a single day and were always on time. Whenever we required blood, they voluntarily donated.

Shyamala and Alex in PGP College, Namakkal - June, 1996

After recovering from the accident, Shyamala and Alex joined PGP Arts and Science College in Namakkal as Lecturers. We took a house in Namakkal and Amenda was admitted in LKG in the school run by the PGP Trust.

Death of Chinnakutty and Govindarajan - November 1996

My uncle Givindarajan's third son, Venkat Raj, who was paralysed by whooping cough, died on November 5, 1996 at the age of 33. Even though Venkat Raj, who was fondly called China Kutty, could not walk or talk, he showed his love to all of us through his laughter. He was fond of June, my mother, and me. My uncle did all the rituals for him.

Within 22 days of Venkatraj's death, my uncle Govidarajan suffered a heart attack and died on November 27. See, God's plan. God allowed him to do everything for his son Venkat Raj and then took him away.

Tributes to My Uncle Govindarajan

We considered him a very strict man. After his MA from Presidency College, he did his MBBS from Madras Medical College. Whenever he came down for vacation during his student days he used to buy some gifts for all of us. After successfully completing his MBBS, he took a job in Singapore. After working for one year he returned to India and got married on February 10, 1958 to Mangayarkarasi. He brought our first radio (National Echo) and first table fan (TDK) both from Singapore. The owner of the hospital in Singapore wanted to give his daughter in marriage to my uncle and the hospital along with a lot of wealth. But my uncle sacrificed everything for the sake of his widowed sister obeying his father's wish.

After his marriage, he completed a one year Diploma in Ophthalmology and became an Opthamologist. He joined government service as Civil Assistant Surgeon in June 1959 and was posted in Pudukkottai. His first son Kumararaj was born in 1960, second son Anandaraj in 1961 and third son Venkat Raj in 1963.

He was transferred to Trichy in June, 1964. He started a private consultation in Jaffershah Street, Trichy and later, another one in Karur. He became very popular in Karur. When he was transferred to Tirunelveli again in 1968, he resigned from his job and concentrated on private practice.

He slowly established A.G. Eye Hospital in Officers' Colony Puthur, Trichy and after some time he constructed his own house, the first for our family, in Arunanagar, Puthur, Trichy. He made his first son Kumararaj, an Opthamologist and he now manages the hospital.

He paid the full fees for five years of my engineering degree. He had helped a lot during my sister's marriage. He helped all the brothers and sisters of his wife Mangayarkarasi to come up in life. He also helped and guided his brother in times of need.

Govindarajan was a man full of modern ideas which he did not fail to implement when the opportunity came. He was instrumental in getting me married to an Anglo Indian in the self-respect style. He got his first son Kumararaj married to a Christian, Dr. Sherin, from the Andaman Islands and his second son Anandaraj to Ammu (Saratha) of another caste and both the marriages were conducted in the self-respect style. Anandaraj has a degree in law and is the Administrator in A.G. Eye Hospital. Ammu is a Ph.D. holder in Management. They have two sons Guhan and Sreekanth.

Govindarajan held high positions in the Medical Association. Along with Gnanadorai Michael, Dr. Iqbal and Dr. Rajasekaran, he had done yeoman service to the society.

Donella's Marriage - February, 1997

June's niece, Donella, married Richardo Parker (Ricky) on February 20, 1997 in Hyderabad.

Shyamala and Alex in KSR College, Tiruchengode - June, 1997

After one year, both of them moved to K.S. Rangasamy (KSR) College of Arts and Science in Tiruchengode in June 1997, Shyamala as Lecturer and Alex as Head of the Department. Amenda was admitted in UKG in Rajammal Rangasamy Matriculation Higher Secondary School run by the KSR group in the same campus. We took a house close to the school. But when we shifted from Namakkal, the house (ground floor) was not ready. We had to stay in the car shed for two days where we cooked and ate. Only for the night, we slept on the first floor where the owner of the house was staying. In fact, we spent June's 48th birthday in the car shed. After staying in the house for about a week, Shyamala complained that she was seeing a ghost in the house. We did not know whether to believe her or not.

My First Contact with Jesus Calls Prayer Tower, Chennai

I knew that Mr. D. G. S. Dinakaran was running a Jesus Calls Ministry at Chennai and they were conducting a 24-hour prayer service through phone. I thought of contacting them for the ghost problem. That was the first time I called them. When I told them about the ghost problem, a Prayer Warrior prayed over the phone itself. I did not tell this to anyone in the family. After 10 days, slowly, I asked my daughter whether the ghost was there or not and she told us that it was not there. Then, I shared my prayer request with Jesus Calls with them.

They got on well and completed one year successfully. All three would go on the TVS 50. They earned a good name from the management. Within a year, Alex was promoted to the post of Vice Principal of the college.

Passing away of Mohanraj - 1997

Mohanraj, who looked after us meticulously for more than two months when Shyamala was in JM hospital unexpectedly became sick and passed away on November 23, 1997 due to cardiomyopathy. His wife Rani worked hard after that and made her daughter Varsha a Chemical Engineer and she herself has obtained a Ph.D. degree in Psychology.

Purchase of Maruti Omni - December, 1997

After I sold my fiat car after using it for 15 years, June wanted to buy another car to travel up and down to Tiruchengode. I purchased an 8 seater Maruti Omni availing a car loan of Rs. 2 lakh from the college. It was grey in colour. They deducted only Rs.1000 per month for the principal and interest. We made a lot of trips to Tiruchengode.

Opportunity for Shyamala's Family to go to USA - 1998

In the beginning of their second year, Alex got an offer for post-doctoral fellowship in Burnham Institute, California, USA in August 1998.

Alex Leaving for USA

After making all the necessary arrangements including selling his laboratory to his brother Rajesh, Alex left for USA and started working as a post-doctoral research fellow.

Kula Deivam Pooja – November, 1998

Shyamala completed the syllabus and other formalities at the college. She even organized a big conference there in which many took part and then vacated the house in Tiruchengode and we packed everything in the Omni and went to Trichy in November 1998. Shyamala's house owner tried to dodge the advance money and Shyamala fought with him until he gave back the advance. Poorni (James' daughter) and her daughter Selvi (same age as Amenda) also came in the car along with Shyamala, Amenda, June and me.

Since Shyamala was going abroad for the first time, we were told to worship our Kula Deivam before she left. Kula Deivam means family deity. It took some time for me to locate our Kula Deivam. It is in a village near Ariyalur town which is about 75 kilometres from Trichy. As November was the monsoon season in Tamil Nadu, we had great difficulty in reaching the temple due to bad roads. June, my sister Vasantha, Shyamala, Amenda, Ramana and I went and successfully completed the pooja. Nagaraj is the pandit of the temple.

Shyamala and Amenda Leaving for USA - December 1998

When we were getting ready to leave Trichy for Chennai to take the flight, there was unprecedented rains for a few days. Shyamala's friend Kanchana's father who was ill had to be brought on a cot from Vayaloor road to our neighbour's house in Gems Apartment because of the flood. Just two days prior to our travel the rain subsided and we left in a tempo traveller for Chennai. After seeing uncle Padmanaban and aunty Shantha in Chennai, we reached the airport. There was some crying associated with such parting and finally Shyamala and Amenda (5 years old) disappeared from our sight into the airport. There were no mobile phones at that time to communicate the progress inside the airport. We waited till the departure time of the flight and after confirming at the counter regarding the departure we left for Trichy from the airport with a heavy heart.

Shyamala's Life in USA - 1998 to 2003

Shyamala and Alex stayed in San Diego, California. In their words San Diego was a beautiful place filled with beaches. It has the world-famous San Diego Zoo, Legoland and Sea World. They visited all the places. Life for Shyamala, Alex and Amenda was full of fun and outings. They made a lot of friends. Weekends were filled with Church events and extracurricular activities for Amenda. Joshua could not enjoy all that his birth place had to offer as they left San Diego when he was one and a half years old.

Amenda's Credentials

Academics - Doyle Elementary School (Public) -1999 to 2001

Amenda studied grades I to III in Doyle elementary school. She was very good in academics. At the end of each academic year, she got consistent comments such as outstanding student, positive role model, pleasure to have in the class, sets a good example to others.

Academics - Spreckels Elementary School (Public) -2002, 2003

Amenda studied grades IV to V in Spreckels Elementary School. She excelled in academics.

She bagged a lot of awards as superstar of the week, outstanding student. She was appreciated very much for her book reports and Mrs. Wong still has copies of her book reports. She used to read books way above her grade level. She won prizes in invention showcase and reading railroad.

Sports

Amenda had a flair for sports. She became interested in soccer, basketball, gymnastics, and swimming. She joined the Mesa Soccer league and was selected as All Star to represent her team. She diligently used to swim every day. She also enjoyed playing basketball and performing gymnastic feats.

Music - Violin

Amenda started to learn violin in the IVth grade from James Preston. She purchased her own violin which she uses till now.

She performed in the Choral Honour Concert, organized by the Department of Visual and Performing Arts, San Diego City Schools, held in the College Avenue Baptist Church on March 16, 2002 and March 22, 2003.

She next performed in the All District Elementary Schools Instrumental Honour Concert held in Point Loma Nazarene University, Brown chapel on March 25, 2003.

Cyst Surgery - April, 2000

I was getting ready to go to Manila as Chairperson for an international conference on Sustainable Humane Cities during April 10-12, 2000, but a cyst in my back just 3 centimetres below my neck started giving trouble and when I consulted Dr. Bhaskar, he recommended that it had to be operated upon immediately. So, on April 18, 2000, after going to all my favourite temples I got admitted in JM hospital at about 11 a.m., and the cyst was removed by 2.30 p.m. I stayed a day for observation and got discharged the next day.

Death of James - March 22, 2001

James, brother of Amelia died on March 22, 2001 in Trichy. He was buried in St. John's Church Cemetry next to Mabel's grave.

Amenda's Visit to India - July to September, 2001

When Shyamala said that they were sending Amenda to Trichy from USA alone during her vacation from July to August 2001, we were happy but at the same time worried since she had not even completed nine years of age and was coming alone.

We all (June, Dinky, Darrel, Ahilan and I) went by Tempo Traveller to receive her at the airport. After verifying that we were her grandparents, the airline authorities handed over Amenda to us. Then we travelled back to Trichy. After spending some time in Trichy, June and I took her to her first teacher in the REC school, then to Namakkal and Tiruchengode Churches. We also went to Podanur to meet her paternal grandmother. We visited Black Thunder in Mettupalayam, Velankanni Church, Poondi Matha Church and Infant Jesus Church. We celebrated her birthday in advance in Trichy.

When her holidays were over we took her to Chennai and after ascertaining that her aircraft had departed, we left for Trichy. We were tracking her flight through the internet and we breathed a sigh of relief only when we heard from Shyamala that Amenda had reached them.

Birth of Joshua in USA - October 26, 2001

When Shyamala conceived for the first time in USA, she had a miscarriage. But she was lucky the second time. When she was admitted to the hospital on Friday 26, 2001 (San Diego time) at about 10 p.m., for delivery, Alex phoned us and asked us to pray for a safe delivery. The time was 10 a.m., in Trichy on Saturday 27, 2001. As Chairman Transport, I called one of my drivers and went to Srirangam Temple to pray to Lord Renganathar for a safe delivery. When I came out of the temple, June phoned and told me that Shyamala had delivered a boy baby and both were fine. He was christened as Joshua, meaning Saviour or Deliverer.

Denys's Marriage - September 30, 2001

Dinky's second daughter Denys got married to Kumaran on September 30, 2001 in Dubai. Only Dinky attended the marriage.

Discussions regarding Post Retirement -September, 2002

By September 2002, my wife started to worry about my retirement in August 2003 and asked me, "Athan, what we are going to do after your retirement? We don't have any house of our own. You know my foster mother will not even invite us to be with her. We have not opted for pension also. We do not have enough bank balance. We have already withdrawn money from PF account two times. How much you think we will get at retirement? How long that money will last us? You have been so careless in wasting money by going for bridge tournaments and playing rummy in the clubs. Even now you are not serious. I am really worried."

I had no answer to all her questions. I was quiet. She shook me and said "Come on, answer me now!"

I said, "June, as such I do not have any answer. But I can tell you that God shuts one door and opens another. Don't worry. So long who guided us? God and only God through various human beings. Will not the same God help us? I can think of working in self-financing colleges."

"You always tell this about God. Ok. I do believe. But If you did not get any job, what to do?"

"June, when you believe, you should believe completely. No ifs and buts."

Sorry to interrupt. Your wife mentioned wasting money in bridge tournaments and in rummy. Can you elaborate on these?

Sure. Actually, both cannot be treated equally. I will deal later with bridge tournaments in another section but I tell you about the rummy.

There are several games you can play using playing cards like rummy, 56, 304, whist, poker, memory, cricket and bridge. Most of the games are played for stakes, that is money. Rummy is one of the popular games played at home and clubs for stakes. When I was about six or seven years old, I used to see my uncle Padmanaban playing rummy with one of our relatives and I learnt the game. Then occasionally I started to play with boys of my age under the supervision of elders. This is how rummy came into my life. Then, it stopped on its own, until my marriage with June.

My foster uncle Thomas was a member of Union Club, Trichy and he made me a member so that I could play tennis and other card games. Whenever we came from Calicut I used to go to the club but I used to return early with uncle. No problem.

Then, when we shifted to REC Trichy, we used to visit aunty Amelia's house almost every weekend and on such visits occasionally I started to go alone (since Thomas had died) to the club for playing rummy and I used to return on time to the house. Neither my wife nor my aunty had any problem because everything was within limits.

On request from one of my friends who used to play bridge with me, I became member of City Club, Trichy which was more popular than Union Club.

Again, occasionally I started to go to City Club to play bridge or rummy. But the only difference was that I started to come late at night and sometimes the next morning. Naturally June did not like this and fought with me. On some days, she would not open the door and make me wait in the garden. I would plead with her that I would not repeat the same and then she would open the door but I would repeat it the next time, maybe after 10 or 15 days.

I have controlled so many things in my life but I could not control my habit of coming late to the house from the club. When I entered the club, I would say to myself, "I should go early to the house today." But, I would not. It is the devil's work.

Then I started to play in Chennai clubs whenever I visited Chennai for some official or private work. You won't believe one thing. I played knowing fully well the consequences. On an average, the loss or gain would be about few thousands ranging from Rs. 10,000 to 15,000 per year.

This habit finally came to an end in the year 2007, just before we left Tamil Nadu for Gurgaon. For the last eleven years, the thought of going to the club to play rummy has never come to my mind.

My Cardiology Problem - January, 2003

On Sunday January 5, 2003, I went to worship Namakkal Anjaneyar for the New Year along with Anitha, youngest daughter of Dr. Samikkannu. I went to Samayapuram Mariamman Temple on Friday, January 10, 2003. An unusual thing happened. As I worshipped Amman and turned, a man, who seemed to be going to Sabarimalai, fell at my feet and touched my feet with both his hands. I was taken back and afterwards he got up and walked off. On Saturday, January 18, June made onion bhajji, which was my favourite, and I ate a lot of them. During the night, I felt some uneasiness and I thought it was some gas trouble. I took gelusil and after some time I fell asleep. Next day was Sunday and it went off well. But again, I got the same feeling in the night and struggled to get sleep. Around 4.30 a.m., on Monday morning of January 20, 2003, we decided to go to BHEL hospital, thinking that private hospitals in Trichy may complicate the matters just to pull out money. I called Rajan, who was the night duty driver for the college ambulance and June and I went to the BHEL hospital. After the initial check-up, they put it as mild heart attack and I was admitted in the ICU. My wife was very upset. This, we never expected. Heart attack is a very costly and deadly disease. They started the medication immediately after doing the ECG. June was alone and somehow, she gathered courage and informed aunty Amelia, Anandaraj and her sister Dinky, who had gone to Hyderabad to see her daughter, Donella. By 10 a.m., all my colleagues including the Principal, Dr. Arumugam, Anandraj and my bridge friends came to see me and to console June. Anandaraj gave Rs. 10,000 to June and Alagappan offered Rs.10,000 but June said it was not required at that time. Later, I returned Anandraj's money. An advantage with the BHEL hospital was that we did not need to pay any advance money either for the treatment or for medicines. The cardiologist was a very nice doctor and I was well looked after. On the first night when I was admitted, June stayed awake in our Maruti Omni the whole night alone out in the open. I do not know how worried she might have been being all alone. By Tuesday evening Dinky and Darrel came back from Hyderabad and June was slightly relieved to see her sister. Aunty Amelia came after I was discharged from the hospital. Slowly, I began to recover and they shifted me to the special room. On Friday, after four days in the ICU, tread mill and other tests were conducted and they did not find any serious issue. They told us that medication, diet and walking should be enough. I was discharged on Monday after a week's treatment. As advised I took one month's medical leave. During the medical leave, Arumugam, Principal, asked me not to give up the charge of Chairman, Transport so that I could use the college vehicle. You won't believe me if I say that the total charges from BHEL were only Rs. 12,000 to be paid in two instalments which was deducted from my salary.

After a month, I showed my reports to another cardiologist, Dr. Murali (a close friend of my bridge friend Viswanathan), of Srirangam just for a second opinion and he also confirmed the findings of the BHEL hospital.

June earnestly followed the dietary advice for me and we started to walk daily for 30 minutes. Once our REC hospital doctor Ganapathi told me that I was very strict with the diet and I could relax a bit.

When I came to Chennai, I did a complete check-up and my medication was changed.

When I shifted to Gurgaon, Dr. Jitendar Gupta changed one or two medicines and I am continuing with them.

Shyamala's Decision to Come Back to India

Alex was trying to get green card in US. When George W. Bush (Jr.), became President of US, he introduced stringent rules for getting green card especially after the attack on Twin Towers. While they were trying, I got a mild heart attack. As a culmination of these events, Alex and Shyamala decided to come back to India in May 2003. Alex got an appointment in Orchid Chemicals & Pharmaceuticals Ltd, Chennai.

Choice of Contributory Provident Fund instead of Pension

There were two schemes of retirement benefits for the faculty of RECs. In Scheme one faculty could retire at the age of 58 and get pension as per the relevant state rules. In the other scheme faculty could retire at 60 and get contributory provident fund, calculated based on minimum contribution by the faculty towards their provident fund, instead of pension. When we were asked to exercise our option, a few of us worked out the pros and cons of the two schemes and we found that scheme two was more beneficial as per bank interest rate and the salary scale prevailing at that time. So, few of us numbering around 15, opted for scheme two. Later, due to increase in the scale of pay and decrease in bank rates for fixed deposits, scheme one became better but we were not allowed to change the option.

In the meantime, the government of India decided to convert all RECs into NITs directly controlled by central government without the financial and administrative control of the relevant state governments. Most of the state governments agreed except Tamil Nadu and West Bengal. After almost one to two years of delay, finally all RECs became NITs in July 2003.

Self-financing Engineering Colleges by Private Sector

The concept of allowing private engineering colleges to be run as self-financing colleges was approved by the Chief Minister of Tamil Nadu, M.G. Ramachandran, in 1985-86 for two reasons. One was to produce more engineers and the other was to curb the Tamil Nadu money going to Karnataka where privatisation of engineering colleges had started earlier.

Looking for a Faculty Position after Retirement

Self-financing engineering colleges created good openings for the retired faculty of IITs, NITs, government engineering colleges and even from public sector units. Since I was pushed to a stage where I had to work after my retirement, I started to apply in December 2002 itself to a few selected self-financing engineering colleges.

Good News about my Job

Within 10 days of my discharge from the hospital, I got a phone call from Mr. Subramanian, Secretary, Meenakshi Ammal Trust, Chennai. He told me, "Sir, with respect to your application for a faculty position, we are happy to offer you an appointment as Professor and Head of the Department of Civil Engineering at Arulmighu Meenakshi Amman College of Engineering, near Kanchipuram. The consolidated salary per month will be Rs. 25,000 and we will provide you a rent free and electricity free air-conditioned 3 bedroom accommodation in the campus. We would like you to join in the second week of June, when the college reopens for the academic year 2003-2004. Please think and confirm within a week."

June and I became very happy and decided to accept. We thought God had opened another door. Not only another good job with campus accommodation but as Professor and Head of the department which I could not get at REC, Trichy.

Why did you decide to retire 3 months earlier than your actual date of retirement?

We were hesitant to ask for time to join in September 2003 thinking that they might cancel our appointment. As usual it was the only offer I got out of many applications. We phoned to the secretary to inform him that we accepted the offer and we would like a written offer letter. Within a week, the offer letter was received and we decided to submit my resignation letter on March 1, 2003, so that I could be relieved on June 1, fulfilling the condition that three months' notice needs to be given. Dr. K. A. Kuppuswamy, who was the Head of the Department, was reluctant to relieve me and tried to delay but finally signed and sent the paper by June 5, 2003. A notification was issued by the Registrar that my resignation had been accepted and I would be relieved on June 4, 2003.

Astrologer Shelvi's Forecast - January and February 2003

I have to tell you something about astrologer Shelvi's forecast in Kumudam Bakthi (a monthly Tamil magazine) for my rasi Rishaba. All those born in Rishaba Rasi should think twice before taking voluntary retirement. This, he wrote in the month of January and February. At that time, we never thought it would have a great impact for me.

REC Trichy also became NIT in July 2003. They took one important decision that all those who were under CPF scheme and who were in service when REC became NIT will come under Pension scheme. Since I was not in service at the time of REC becoming NIT, I lost the chance of getting a pension. I gave a representation in 2005, to consider me for pension and it was rejected because I did not fulfil the required condition. See, how correct Shelvi's forecast was for me.

Visit to AMACE - April, 2003

The Secretary of Meenakshi Ammal Trust had invited us to visit the college campus before joining. So, we went in April 2003 during Easter holidays. On Saturday April 19, June and I visited the office of Meenakshi Ammal Trust in KK Nagar, Chennai at about 9.30 a.m. We were waiting in one of the rooms and around 10 a.m., someone came to me and asked, "Shall we go?" I was taken aback and after looking at my watch I said, "We will go after 10.30 a.m., since it is Raghu Kalam from 9.00 to 10.30 a.m. He said okay and left the room. Slowly I went out and asked someone about the person who met us and he told us, "Sir, he is the owner and Chairman of the trust." I was surprised because he was very simple and straight forward. We left the office at 10.35 a.m., in a white ambassador. The chairman sat in the front with the driver and June and I sat at the back. It was quite a long journey of about 2 hours covering a distance of about 80 kilometres. The college was about 15 kilometres from Kanchipuram town in a village called Vadama Vandal. The chairman took us to the Principal, Ramachandran, who then took us to the hostel mess for lunch. It was reasonably good. After the lunch, Ramachandran took us to see the quarters which were at the entrance of the college and then to the Civil Engineering department and other departments. The quarters were a flat type in which there were nine houses, 3 on each floor. It was really very posh and modern.

After spending about two and a half hours, we left the college at about 3.00 p.m., and in the car the chairman turned around and asked, "Sir, do you like the college and the quarters?" I said "Yes. We like both." Then he continued, "When you would join?" I said, "I have to see for an auspicious date to join which may be in the second week of June." He said "That is fine for us. The college will reopen in the third week of June." There was no further conversation till we reached Chennai around 5.30 p.m. Then we took an auto to reach my uncle's home at Mandaiveli.

Arrival of Shyamala and Family in Chennai - May, 2003

Shyamala, Alex, Amenda and Joshua reached Chennai on May 2. We booked a furnished guest house in Triplicane for Rs. 20,000 per month. Aunty Amelia, Dinky and Darrel stayed for a few days in the guest house. Donella also came with her son Ryan and spent a few days. We had to do three things - to get Person of Indian Origin (PIO) card for Joshua, search for a house for Shyamala and a school for Amenda. We decided to search in Adyar area for the house and school.

PIO Card for Joshua

Since Joshua is an American citizen we had to get a Person of Indian Origin (PIO) card for him which would permit him to stay in India up to 16 years of age. Alex and Shyamala went to the Bureau of Immigration, Chennai and obtained the card for Joshua.

School for Amenda

When Shyamala and Alex went for admission in St. Patrick's School, Gandhi Nagar, Adyar the Principal told them that there was no seat and they should look elsewhere for a school. Then, I suggested to take a recommendation letter from Alex's uncle, Bishop Lawrence. Alex did so and went for the second time to meet the principal along with the recommendation letter. Amenda was given admission immediately in VIth standard.

In India, in most places, there is less value for merit but there is lot of value for recommendation and bribe.

House for Alex and Shyamala

Next, we started to look for a house close to the school and we were lucky to get a house on Gandhi Nagar main road. It was on the second floor for a rent of Rs. 7000 per month. By June 1, we shifted to the flat and started to settle in. Then, June and I left for Trichy to prepare for my retirement. Amenda started to go to school and Alex started to go to his work at Orchid Chemicals & Pharmaceuticals Ltd. Tamilarasi and Ramana's sister, Anjalai, helped Shyamala in the house work

My Retirement - June 4, 2003

As my retirement day was approaching, we started packing a few things, discarding some, and sharing the rest with Dinky, aunty Amelia, Kaliaperumal and others. We also packed a few things for Shyamala's house in Chennai. Starting from June 2, there were send-off parties by the college and departments of Civil Engineering and Transport. I handed over charge as Chairman Transport to Mr. Udayakumar.

On June 4, around 4 p.m., I was called to the Principal's chamber and Principal Arumugam handed over the retirement cheque consisting of my PF and CPF to me. After glancing at it, he asked me, "Why the amount is low?"

It was Rs. 8.69 lakh. Normally, a person in my position used to receive around Rs.12 to 14 lakh.

Before I could answer the Registrar interrupted and said, "This is after deduction of car loan (principal and interest) of around Rs. 2.00 lakh and two part-withdrawals from the PF. Therefore, it is low."

When I was born, I had nothing, when I got married I had nothing and when I retired I got something at least.

Then, I left the chamber bidding good-bye.

The next few days I got busy in surrendering my Indane gas connection, BSNL landline telephone connections and completing other formalities in the bank and post office. I fixed a lorry for transporting our household things from Trichy to Kanchipuram and I sent the lorry on Monday, June 9 along with Kaliaperumal and Nelson.

On Monday, June 9, we left REC Trichy at about 12.30 p.m., for Kanchipuram in my omni with Rajaratnam as the driver.

We reached Kanchipuram at about 8 p.m., and the lorry also arrived at the same time. We unloaded all the things into the quarters. We then left for Chennai asking Kaliaperumal, Tamilarasi and Nelson to be in the house. We reached Shyamala's house at about 10.30 p.m.

Normally, retirement is an emotional thing. Even though you were taking up another job, what were your feelings on the last day of your work?

You are right. Parting due to retirement is always sorrowful as William Shakespeare says in Romeo Juliet, "Parting is such sweet sorrow that I shall say goodnight till it be morrow."

I also felt sad to part with the place and the people I had been with for 29 long years.

But, I was not allowed to go through this sadness for long since anxiety for the new job took over.

I have heard lot of things about issues in retirement.

***Issues in Retirement** - Mixed feelings arise when one retires from his professional life which must have lasted for 30 to 40 years with long hours of work, commitments during weekends or sometimes over holidays. Feelings involved may be positive like relief or a sense of accomplishment. But most of the time it brings on the feeling of* *approaching doom, unproductivity, losing official identity and a fall in importance among family members.*

Retirees mostly feel alone as if no one cares. Usually the social circle comprises of work place friends whose visits slowly dwindle as time goes by.

So, what can new and soon-to-be retirees do about mental challenges? You have to come to terms with the fact that you're not alone, or what you're going through is some anomaly. Lots of people have shared similar situations with me. They all found comfort in being able to talk about it, and in helping others become aware of the challenges they may face.

I counsel that retirees don't have to be in a rush to change things. Adjusting to retirement takes time and practice. As you proceed through it you'll learn how to handle thoughts and feelings just as you did when you got married, had your first child, or purchased your first home. Take a moment to reflect on all the thoughts and feelings that came with those experiences, and how you learned to manage them over time.

It's also important to point out that you're in control and responsible for your feelings. If you want to change them, you have to do something different. Whether it's reaching out to family and friends instead of just hoping they'll call, signing up for a yoga or writing class, or re-branding yourself through volunteer opportunities, retirement requires you to be exactly what you have been trained to do: Be productive!

There is no doubt that many people will experience these mental challenges, as well as others, which makes it important not only to identify them, but to also share your story and solutions for overcoming them. It's all part of the ever-changing retirement puzzle that you'll surely figure out just as you have done with all the other things life has thrown at you. It's what makes life and retirement a journey instead.

God had designed that I should not experience the issues in retirement and I should continue teaching even after my regular retirement. **Destiny**

Maybe because there was delay in REC becoming NIT, maybe because you were not bold enough to ask for some more time till your actual date of retirement for joining your new assignment,

maybe because you did not manage your finances well to have saved more money, maybe because you were not serious in getting a house of your own, you were forced in to a situation where you had to work and earn in an entirely new place, did you feel that way?

Naturally, somewhere, sometimes I would have felt those things. But as you know I believe in God's design and I just overcome those feelings very easily.

But before you go further, you have to tell us about the golden period in your career from 1984 to 2003 at REC, Trichy.

Oh yes. That is the most important part.

Around Me

Let us go through the major events that took place during this period.

India

Politics

Babri Masjid Incident, 1992 - On December 6, 1992, a large crowd of Hindu Kar Sevaks destroyed the 16th century Babri Masjid in Ayodhya, Uttar Pradesh, in an attempt to reclaim the land known as Ram Janmabhoomi (birthplace of the Hindu God Rama).

Indo-China Peace Agreement, 1993 - On September 7, 1993 India and China signed an agreement to maintain peace and tranquillity along LAC in the India - China border areas.

Creation of Delhi Metro Rail Corporation, 1995 - The Delhi Metro Rail Corporation Ltd. (DMRC) was created on May 3, 1995 with E. Sreedharan as first Managing Director.

XIth General Elections, 1996 - Atal Bihari Vajpayee became the Prime Minister on May 15, 1996 after general elections were held on April 27, May 2 and 7, 1996 to elect the 11th Lok Sabha. The result was a hung parliament with BJP alliance getting 187 seats (BJP 161; Shiv Sena 15; Samanta party 8; Haryana Vikas Party 3), INC 140, National Front 79 (JD 46; SP 17; TDP 16) and Left Front 52 (CPI(M) 32; CPI 12; RSP 5; AIFB 3), TMC 20, DMK 17 and BSP 11.

Resignation of Vajpayee, 1996 - After failing to gather enough support, Vajpayee resigned on May 28, 1996.

Deve Gowda as Prime Minister, 1996 - With the support of the Indian National Congress, Deve Gowda of Janata Dal was sworn in as Prime Minister on June 1, 1996.

Visit of Chinese President, 1996 - Chinese President Jiang Zemin began his three-day visit, the first visit by a Chinese Head of State from November 28, 1996. Four agreements were signed for mutual cooperation.

Deve Gowda's Resignation and Gujral as Prime Minister, 1997 - Due to pressure from the INC, Deve Gowda resigned and I. K. Gujral was sworn in as Prime Minister on April 21, 1997.

Birth of Rashtriya Janata Dal, 1997 - The Rashtriya Janata Dal based in Bihar was founded in 1997 by Lalu Prasad Yadav.

K. R. Narayanan became President, 1997 - Kocheril Raman Narayanan was sworn in as the tenth President of India on July 25, 1997.

Resignation of Gujral, 1997 - Over the difference of opinion in the Jain Commission interim report in which DMK was criticized (later given clean chit) Gujral resigned on November 28, 1997.

Sonia Gandhi became President, INC, 1997 - Sonia Gandhi, wife of Rajiv Gandhi, was elected as the President of Indian National Congress party on March 14, 1997.

Netaji Open University, 1997 - Netaji Subhas Open University (NSOU), for distance education, was established in 1997 to commemorate his birth centenary in Kolkata.

XIIth General Elections, 1998 - Atal Bihari Vajpayee became Prime Minister for second time on March 18, 1998 after the general elections were held on February 16, 22, and 28, 1998 to elect the 12th Lok Sabha. No party or alliance was able to create a strong majority. NDA won 254 seats (BJP 182; AIADMK 18; Samata Party 12; Biju Janata Dal 9; Shironmani Akali Dal 8; Shiv Sena 6; WBTMC 7; PMK 4; MDMK 3; Lok Shakthi 3), INC 141, United Front 64 (CPI(M) 32; CPI 9; JD 6; DMK 5; TMC 3; RSP 5).

Nuclear Bomb Test, 1998 - Pokhran-II (Operation Shakti) was the series of five nuclear bomb test explosions conducted at the Indian Army's Pokhran Test Range in May 1998. It was the second Indian nuclear test.

Parliament Dissolved, 1999 - President K. R. Narayanan dissolved the Parliament on April 17, 1999, after the BJP coalition government led by Prime Minister Vajpayee failed to win a confidence vote in the Lok Sabha falling short by a single vote due to withdrawal of AIADMK.

XIIIth General Elections, 1999 - Atal Bihari Vajpayee was sworn in as Prime Minister for the third time on October 13, 1999 after the elections were held from September 5 to October 3, 1999 to elect the 13th Lok Sabha. NDA won 270 seats (BJP 182; JD(united) 21; Shiv Sena 15; DMK 12; Biju JD 10; Nationalist TMC 8; PMK 5; INLD 5; MDMK 4; J&KNC 4; Shironmani AD 2; RLD 2), TDP 29, INC 114 and AIADMK 10.

Vajpayee's Visit to Japan, 2001 - A joint declaration for bilateral cooperation was signed by Prime Ministers Atal Vajpayee, and Koizumi, at Tokyo during December 7-11, 2001.

Abdul Kalam became President, 2002 - A. P. J. Abdul Kalam became eleventh President of India on July 25, 2002.

Renaming of Cities

In November 1995, the Shiv Sena party, presiding the coalition government in Maharashtra renamed **Bombay as Mumbai** after the Hindu goddess Mumbadevi, the city's patron deity. **Calcutta** officially became **Kolkata**, reverting to its pre-colonial name on January 1, 2001.

Scams

Fodder Scam - Lalu Prasad Yadav, Chief Minister of Bihar and Jagannath Mishra, former Chief Minister were implicated in the Fodder Scam that involved the embezzlement of about Rs. 9.4 billion from the government treasury. It came to light in 1992.

War

Peace Effort with Pakistan, 1999 - A cross border bus service was inaugurated on February 19, 1999 connecting Delhi with the city of Lahore, Pakistan via the border transit post at Wagah. The Lahore Declaration, a bilateral agreement and governance treaty between India and Pakistan, was signed by Prime Minister Nawaz Sharif and Prime Minister Vajpayee on February 21, 1999, at the conclusion of a historic summit in Lahore.

The Kargil War, 1999 - The Kargil War was an armed conflict between India and Pakistan between May and July 1999 in the Kargil district of Kashmir and along the Line of Control (LoC). The cause was the infiltration of Pakistani soldiers and Kashmiri militants into positions on the Indian side of the LoC.

Attack by Terrorists

On December 13, 2001, 9 terrorists, belonging to Lashkar-e-Taiba (Let) and Jaish-e-Mohammed infiltrated the Parliament House in a car with a fake identity sticker and attacked the parliament with AK47 rifles, grenade launchers, pistols and grenades. The attack led to the deaths of five terrorists, six police personnel, two Parliament Security Service personnel and a gardener and led to increased tensions between India and Pakistan.

Mob Killings

Graham Stuart Staines, an Australian Christian missionary along with his two sons Philip (aged 10) and Timothy (aged 6), was burnt to death by a gang while sleeping in their station wagon at Manoharpur village, Keonjhar district, Odisha, India on January 23, 1999. It was alleged that he forcibly converted Hindus into Christianity.

Bombings and Death Toll

257 were killed in a series of 13 car bomb explosions in Mumbai on March 12, 1993. 33 people were killed in The Brahmaputra Mail bombing on December 30, 1996 and 58 in the 12 bomb attacks in 11 places, all within a 12 kilometres radius in Coimbatore on February 14, 1998. Beant Singh the Chief Minister of Punjab was assassinated on August 31, 1995 in Chandigarh in a car bombing.

Natural Calamities

10,000 people were killed in the Latur earthquake, measuring 6.2 on the Richter scale in Maharashtra on September 30, 1993. 1077 were killed in the cyclone in Andhra Pradesh on November 6, 1996.

Accidents

400 people were killed in a fire accident in a school function in Mandi Dabwali, Haryana on December 23, 1995. 250 pilgrims

were killed in Amarnath tragedy in Jammu and Kashmir on August 21, 1996 due to unusual snowfall and 349 killed in mid-air collision involving Saudi Arabian Airlines and Kazakhstan Airlines on November 12, 1996 near Delhi.

Death of Mother Teresa - September 5, 1997

After several years of deteriorating health, with heart, lung and kidney problems, Mother Teresa died on September 5, 1997, at the age of 87. Nirmala Joshi, M.C. (Sister Nirmala), a Catholic Religious Sister succeeded as the Head of Missionaries of Charity and expanded the movement overseas.

Tamil Nadu

Birth of MDMK, 1994 - Marumalarchi Dravida Munnetra Kazhagam (MDMK), a political party was formed by V. Gopalsamy (Vaiko) in 1994 after he was forced out of DMK.

XIth Tamil Nadu Elections, 1996 - Karunanidi became Chief Minister of Tamil Nadu on May 13, 1996 after the eleventh Legislative Assembly elections on May 2, 1996. DMK and Tamil Manila Congress (split from INC over differences with AIADMK) won 212 out of 234 seats. DMK won 173 seats, TMC 39, CPI 8 and AIADMK 4.

Jayalalithaa's Cases, 1996 - On July 11, 1996, Janata Party leader Dr. Subramanian Swamy filed a complaint in court accusing Jayalalithaa of amassing wealth (Disproportionate Assets-DA) worth Rs. 66.65 crore disproportionate to her known sources of income during 1991 to 1996. On December 7, 1996, she was arrested. In April, 1997, the DMK Government set up three special courts to try 47 corruption cases against Jayalalithaa, her former cabinet colleagues and others and prosecution launched against Jayalalithaa, her close friend Sasikala and two others in a Chennai Court in DA case. She was charge sheeted in DA case. In 1999, she was discharged in coal import deal case by Special Court and upheld by Madras High Court. On February 2, 2000, Special Court convicted her in Pleasant Stay Hotel case related to permission granted for construction allegedly flouting rules. In October 2000, a Special Court in Chennai convicted Jayalalithaa in TANSI land deal case. Trial on DA case was progressing.

XIIth **Tamil Nadu Elections, 2001** - In the twelfth legislative assembly election held on May 10, 2001, AIADMK alliance won 196 out of 234 seats. (AIADMK 132; TMC 23; PMK 20; INC 7; CPI(M) 6; CPI 5), DMK 31, BJP 4. Jayalalithaa was sworn in as Chief Minister of Tamil Nadu for the second time on May 14, 2001. Due to the Supreme Court's verdict, she had to step down and O. Panneerselvam was sworn in as Chief Minister on September 21, 2001. On December 4, 2001, Madras High Court acquitted Jayalalithaa in the TANSI case and Pleasant Stay Hotel case. On February 21, 2002, Jayalalithaa was elected to Assembly in a by poll election from Andipatti constituency. She was sworn in as Chief Minister on March 2, 2002. On a petition by DMK, Supreme Court transferred the trial in the DA case to Bengaluru on November 18, 2003.

World

Politics

Bill Clinton became President of US, 1993 - William Jefferson "Bill" Clinton of Democratic Party was sworn in as the 42nd President of United States on January 20, 1993.

Jiang Zemin became President of China, 1993 - Jiang Zemin became President of China on March 27, 1993 after Yang Shangkun.

Nelson Mandela became President of South Africa, 1994 - The African National Congress (ANC) gained control of the National Parliament with 63 percent of the vote. Nelson Mandela became the first black President of South Africa on May 9, 1994.

The Taliban's Government in Afghanistan, 1996 - The Taliban, a Muslim fundamentalist group, took control of Kabul and Afghanistan's government in 1996.

Bill Clinton became President Second Time, 1997 - Bill Clinton became President for the second time on January 20, 1997.

Tony Blair became Prime Minister of UK, 1997 - Tony Blair became PM of UK on May 2, 1997 after John Major.

Zhu Rongji became Prime Minister of China (1998) - Zhu Rongji became Prime Minister of China on March 17, 1998) after Li Peng.

Putin became President of Russia, 2000 - Vladimir Putin became President of Russia on May 7, 2000 after Yeltsin.

George W. Bush Became President of USA, 2001 - George W. Bush, son of former president George H. W. Bush (1989-93), became the 44th President of USA on January 20, 2001. He was a Republican.

Wen Jiabao became Prime Minister of China, 2003 - Wen Jiabao became Prime Minister of China on March 16, 2003 after Zhu Rongji.

Hu Jintao became President of China, 2003- Hu Jintao became President of China, on March 15, 2003 after Jiang Zemin.

Science and Technology

Cloning of Sheep Dolly, 1996 – Dolly, a female domestic sheep, was the first mammal cloned from an adult somatic cell, using the process of nuclear transfer by Sir Ian Wilmut, Keith Campbell and colleagues at the Roslin Institute, University of Edinburgh, Scotland, and the biotechnology company PPL Therapeutics, near Edinburgh. She was born on July 5, 1996 and died from a progressive lung disease on 14 February 2003.

Google Search Launched, 1997 - Google Search, Google Web Search or Google, owned by Google Inc. was first launched on September 15, 1997. It is the most-used search engine on the World Wide Web, handling more than three billion searches each day.

Death

Assassination of Yitzhak Rabin, Israeli PM, 1995 - The assassination of Yitzhak Rabin took place on November 4, 1995 at 9.30 p.m., at the end of a rally in support of the Oslo Accords at Kings of Israel Square in Tel Aviv. The assassin, an Israeli ultra nationalist named Yigal Amir, radically opposed Rabin's peace initiative and the signing of the Oslo Accords.

Princess Diana in Car accident, 1997 - On August 31, 1997, Diana, Princess of Wales died as a result of injuries sustained in a car crash in the Pont de l'Alma road tunnel in Paris, France.

Others

J.K. Rowling's First Novel, 1997 - J. K. Rowling, a British novelist published her first novel *Harry Potter and the Philosopher's Stone* in 1997.

Climate Change

Signing of Kyoto Protocol on Climate Change, 1997 - The Kyoto Protocol extends the 1992 UNFCCC that commits State Parties to reduce greenhouse gases emissions, based on the premise that global warming exists and man-made CO_2 emissions have caused it. The Kyoto Protocol was adopted in Kyoto, Japan, on December 11, 1997 and entered into force on February 16, 2005.

Scandal

Impeachment and Acquittal of Bill Clinton, 1998-99 - The incidents connected with Paul Jones's law suit against Clinton and Clinton's affair with Monica Lewinsky led to the impeachment by the House of Representatives on two charges, one of perjury and one of obstruction of justice, on December 19, 1998. He was subsequently acquitted by the Senate on February 12, 1999. Two other impeachment articles – a second perjury charge and a charge of abuse of power failed in the House.

World Population Reaches 6 Billion, 1999 - The United Nations Population Fund designated October 12, 1999 as the approximate day on which the world population reached six billion.

Y2K problem, 1999 - Y2K bug, Year 2000 bug or Millennium Bug, in the coding of computerized systems was projected to create havoc in computers and computer networks around the world at the beginning of the year 2000. After international alarm, feverish preparations and programming corrections, few major failures occurred in the transition from December 31, 1999, to January 1, 2000.

War

Signing of the Oslo 1 Accord, 1993 - The Oslo I Accord, 1993 was the first face-to-face agreement between the governments of Israel and the Palestine Liberation Organization (PLO). In the Letters of Mutual Recognition, the PLO acknowledged the state of Israel and pledged to reject violence, and Israel recognized the PLO as the representative of the Palestinian people and as partner in negotiations. Yasser Arafat was allowed to return to the Occupied Palestinian Territories. In 1995, the Oslo I Accord was followed by Oslo II. Neither promised Palestinian statehood.

Camp David Summit involving US, Israel and Palestine, 2000 - The 2000 Camp David Summit at Camp David was between United States President Bill Clinton, Israeli Prime Minister Ehud Barak and Palestinian Authority Chairman Yasser Arafat. It occurred between July 11-25, 2000 to end the Israeli–Palestinian conflict but concluded without an agreement.

Invasion of Iraq, 2003 - The 2003 invasion of Iraq lasted from March 20 to May 1, 2003 and initiated the Iraq War, dubbed Operation Iraqi Freedom by US. The mission was to disarm Iraq of weapons of mass destruction, to end Saddam Hussein's support for terrorism, and to free the Iraqi people. Around 1,60,000 combined force of troops from the US, UK, Australia and Poland invaded Iraq and deposed the Ba'athist government of Saddam Hussein.

Worst Terrorist Attack Ever, 2001

The September 11 Attacks on USA, 2001 - The September 11 attacks (9/11 attacks) were four coordinated terrorist attacks by the Islamic terrorist group Al-Qaeda on the US on the morning of Tuesday, September 11, 2001. Four passenger airliners which departed from airports on the U.S. East Coast bound for California were hijacked by 19 Al-Qaeda terrorists. American Airlines Flight 11 and United Airlines Flight 175 were crashed into the North and South towers, respectively of the World Trade Centre complex in New York City. Within an hour and 42 minutes, both 110 storey towers collapsed, with debris and the resulting fires causing partial or complete collapse of all other buildings in the World Trade Centre complex, including the 47 storey 7 World Trade Centre Tower, as well as significant damage to ten other large surrounding structures. American Airlines Flight 77 was crashed into the Pentagon (headquarters of the United States Department of Defence), Arlington County, Virginia, leading to a partial collapse in the Pentagon's western side. United Airlines Flight 93, initially was steered toward Washington, D.C., but crashed into a field near Shanksville, Pennsylvania, after its passengers tried to overcome the hijackers. In total, the attacks claimed the lives of 2,996 people (including the 19 hijackers). It was the deadliest incident for fire fighters and law enforcement officers in the history of the United States, with 343 and 72 killed respectively.

The Anthrax Attacks in USA, 2001 - The 2001 anthrax attacks, or Amerithrax (FBI case name) occurred within US over the course of several weeks beginning on September 18, 2001, one week after the September 11 attacks. Letters containing anthrax spores were mailed to several news media offices and two Democratic US Senators, killing five people and infecting 17 others.

Accidents

The Space Shuttle Columbia Disaster, 2003 - The disaster occurred on February 1, 2003, when Columbia disintegrated over Texas and Louisiana as it re-entered Earth's atmosphere, killing all seven crew members including Kalpana Chawla.

CHAPTER 10

Research and Administration - July 1984 to June 2003

Abstract

Me

The details about my teaching career, research projects, administrative experience as Chairman of Transport Committee, NSS Officer, Secretary/Treasurer of Officer's Club, Member, Board of Governors and President of Temple Committee are presented.

So far you have shared your personal life while you were in REC Trichy during July 1974 to June 2003 and your professional life from 1974 to 1984. What about your professional life from 1984 to 2003?

I would like to divide my professional life into three parts namely teaching, research and administration.

Teaching - 1974 to 2003

I taught Civil Engineering courses for full-time and part-time UG and PG students. Some of the major courses taught by me were Irrigation and Hydraulic Structures, Design and Drawing of Public Health and Irrigation Structures, Hydrology, Construction Management, Basic Civil Engineering, Hydraulics Laboratory, and Civil Engineering Laboratory.

I was in charge of Hydraulics Laboratory for a long time and Environmental Engineering Laboratory for three years. I compiled notes for Design and Drawing of Environmental and Irrigation Structures and for Hydraulics Laboratory and Civil Engineering Laboratory.

I was Member of Board of Studies and involved in the revision of syllabus at regular intervals.

Chief Coordinator for Development of PG Programme in Water Resources Engineering and Management, 1993-94 and Programme In-Charge until Retirement in 2003

Some of the engineers in the Water Resources Organization, Government of Tamil Nadu passed a resolution in their general body meeting that REC should start a part-time PG programme in Water Resources Engineering for the benefit of the practicing engineers.

Principal, Dr. Ilango, asked me to be the Chief Coordinator for designing the new programme. I started the work earnestly. I studied similar programmes in IITs and College of Engineering, Guindy and I designed the curriculum such that it was not highly mathematical but more practical oriented. It was approved by the Bharathidasan University and the AICTE. It was the only part-time PG programme to be approved by the AICTE in all of India.

The programme was reasonably popular and successful.

Research - 1984 to 2003

As I told you earlier, the government awarded grants from 1980 for carrying out research.

I carried out the following five R & D projects during this period

Sponsored by Government of India and World Bank

1. "Water Resources Management Project" sponsored by Ministry of Human Resources Development (MHRD) for a capital grant of 14.5 lakh and a recurring grant of Rs. 7 lakh from April 1985 to March 1992 for which I was the sole investigator and coordinator.
2. "Water Management Studies for Paddy using Non-ponding and Treated Sewage Effluent Irrigation" sponsored by AICTE for an amount of Rs. 4 lakh from April 1997 to March 2000 for which I was the sole investigator and coordinator.
3. "Exploitation and Assessment of New Water Sources from Small Catchments" sponsored by Rajiv Gandhi National Drinking Water Mission, Ministry of Rural Development for an amount of Rs. 2.31 lakh from April 1996 to March 1998 for which I was the coordinator and co-investigator along with Dr. K. A. Kuppuswamy and Dr. V. Chandramouli.

4. "Water management studies for Agniar River Basin" sponsored by World Bank for an amount of Rs.10 lakh from August 2000 to February 2002 for which I was the coordinator and co-investigator along with Dr. K. A. Kuppuswamy and Dr. V. Jothiprakash.
5. "Development of Interactive Software for Reservoir Simulation" sponsored by the World Bank for an amount of Rs. 3.52 lakh from May 2002 to December 2002 for which I was the co-investigator along with Dr. V. Jothiprakash.

1. Water Resources Management Project

Background

Dr. Chidambaram, Assistant Professor Hydraulics applied to the Ministry of Human Resources Development (MHRD) to fund a Water Resources Management Project in 1981-82 but unfortunately, he passed away before the funding came. When a funding of Rs.10 lakh was received in 1983, Nagaratnam, Principal, used up Rs. 6 lakh for purchase of computers and he allotted remaining Rs. 4 lakh for the project. When he asked both Dr. Kuppusamy and Dr. Palanichamy to implement the project they refused giving some lame excuses. Finally, I was approached and I agreed to execute the project. **Destiny**

I prepared a plan of action and submitted it to Nagaratnam but he did not approve it. He pushed away the file in a disrespectful way. He knew I did not like it. I did not meet for him at least a month. On another occasion when Prof. Krishnan and I were talking with him regarding maintenance of attendance of students, he praised me in front of others to compensate for the earlier incident. He asked me to re-submit the same plan and approved it.

Proposed study

After going through lot of literature, I came to the conclusion that water management was the need of the hour because the water resources potential remains the same for a country where as the demand for domestic, industrial and irrigation uses go on increasing. I had decided to undertake the following areas of study.

Demonstrate and Propagate
- The use of sprinkler and drip irrigation for increasing yield per unit of water for certain crops

- New methods of irrigation for the paddy crop (one of the largest consumer of water) to conserve water
- Use of solar voltaic system to conserve electrical energy
- Adoption of scientific farming to increase the yield
- Use of computers for simulation studies

Establishment of Demonstration cum Research Farm

I wanted to create a demonstration cum research farm in the campus. I went to Tamil Nadu Agricultural University, Coimbatore, Centre for Water Resources Management, Anna University and Indian Agricultural Research Institute, New Delhi to collect first-hand information about their research farms. Then I made a plan for my farm. An area of five acres was selected on the eastern side of the campus very near the oxidation pond which was used to treat the sewage of the campus. The treated sewage effluent was directed to a tank in a neighbouring village, Valavanthankottai. The entire study area was fenced with barbed wire and a gate was put up at the entrance. With the help of a consultant, I located a bore well near the entrance and installed a submersible pump in the well. The pump yielded good quality water throughout the year. The yield was so much that after sometime it was used to supply water to the hostels.

Next an office and a store room were created. Sprinkler and drip irrigation equipment were purchased. Open channels for irrigation and a floor for thrashing paddy were constructed.

A meteorological station was set up at the centre of the farm which had Simon's rain gauge, evaporimeter, wind anemometer, sunshine recorder, thermometers and solar pyranometer. Weather data was recorded daily.

After a year, the farm was extended by another five acres which was exclusively used for orchard crops irrigated by drip system using solar photovoltaic pumping.

After another year, soil water crop clinic with a glass house was created to test the soil, water, and crops.

Research Studies and Results

Experiments were conducted on the use of sprinkler and drip irrigation for vegetables and groundnut for 5 years (April 1987 to March 1992). The yield per unit of water was found to be more with less water consumption compared to the control irrigated by conventional surface irrigation.

Use of a new type of irrigation called non-ponding irrigation, based on moisture content, gave us encouraging results so that yield per unit of water could be increased.

Use of treated sewage effluent irrigation for paddy also increased yield per unit of water and at the same time conserved natural water.

So, a separate project was submitted to AICTE for funding to carry out further detailed studies and it was approved.

Use of solar voltaic system for irrigation to conserve electrical energy was successful.

Under this study a photovoltaic system was purchased and installed in the farm and it was used to irrigate the orchard crops by drip irrigation. A demonstration was performed in an open exhibition in Trichy for bringing awareness to the farmers.

Establishment of soil-crop-water clinic to test the soil, water and crop for their quality was set up. It also had a glass house in which crops could be grown under controlled conditions. We also used modern technology like computers in developing software and model studies.

Under this a moisture meter was designed by the final year students of Electrical Engineering which can be used by the farmers to measure the soil moisture based on which irrigation can be given.

A software program was written by Dr. Moses Shanthakumar and me to predict the yield of paddy under water stress.

To disseminate the results of the above experiments, the following were organized.

Seminars/Workshops/Training Programmes Organized- Coordinated by me

1. State Level Seminar on "Water Conservation"- June 26, 1991

A one day state level seminar was conducted on June 26, 1991 on "Water Conservation" to propagate the awareness about sprinkler and drip irrigation. The seminar was co-sponsored by Tamil Nadu Water Supply and Drainage Board (TWAD), State Bank of India (SBI), Southern Petrochemical Industries Corporation (SPIC), The Institution of Engineers, Pasumai Finance and Industries, Chennai. I spoke on Sprinkler and Drip Irrigation. It was attended by 50 farmers.

2. Training Programme on "Advanced Techniques in Water Management"- December 27, 1991

A one day training programme was organized on December 27, 1991 to gain first-hand knowledge about advanced techniques like micro computer applications, remote sensing and simulation studies in Water Resources Management. The resource persons were faculty were from IIT Madras, Anna University, Chennai, Bharathidasan University, Trichy and REC, Trichy.

Periodic Annual Reports

1st Review Meeting - 1988

I presented a video report in the first review meeting on August 19, 1988 at IIT Delhi and the project was appreciated. A further grant of Rs. 3 lakh was sanctioned for 1989-90.

2nd Review Meeting - 1990

I presented a report in the second review meeting held on August 23-24, 1990 at IIT Delhi. Further grant of Rs. 7.5 lakh was sanctioned for the year 1990-91.

3rd Review Meeting - 1992

I presented the final report of the project in the last review meeting held during October 12-14, 1992.

This was the only project which received a recurring grant of Rs. 7 lakh.

Papers published

Twelve papers were published in National conferences.

As a result of trial studies on Paddy, a paper on "Effect of Sewage Effluent Irrigation on Paddy" was published in the North American Water and Environment Congress held during June 22-28, 1996.

Impact of the project

The project earned a good name all over India. Dr. Pundarikanthan, my teacher at College of Engineering, Guindy in my IIIrd year of study became the Director, Centre for Water Resources at College of Engineering, Guindy. He visited the farm once and appreciated the research work. When he went back he asked his students to visit the farm. Principal Nagaratnam would bring any important visitor from the State or Central government or foreign dignitaries to visit the farm. The farm was the pride of REC.

2. Water Management Studies for Paddy Using Non - Ponding Irrigation and Sewage Effluent Irrigation - 1997to 2000

The result of trial studies and publication of paper motivated me to write a proposal to carry out extensive study in this area and I submitted the proposal to AICTE for a research grant in the academic year 1996-97.

I was very happy to see the letter of acceptance. An amount of Rs. 4 lakh was sanctioned for three years from 1997 to 2000.

Broad objective 1: To find the effect of non-ponding irrigation on paddy with respect to its yield and other parameters.

Area of Study

Non-ponding irrigation means that irrigation is given to the crop depending upon the moisture content during the non-critical period. The farmer's practice is to keep the field under the submerged condition with water standing to a certain depth throughout the crop period. This way water used is more and yield per unit of water is less.

Experiments were conducted by using non-ponding irrigation during the non-critical period. The experiments were done for two varieties of crops for two seasons and for three years.

Broad objective 2: To find the effect of treated sewage effluent irrigation on paddy with respect to its yield and other parameters.

Area of Study

In order to conserve the declining supply of natural water, I had to think of an alternate source of water for the hungry paddy crop. I learnt that municipalities used treated sewage effluent for growing grass and some fodder crops. I thought of extending this to paddy.

Treated sewage effluent was available in our campus from the oxidation pond. We collected the water samples and tested it and found it fit to be used for irrigation.

Experiments were conducted by applying sewage effluent irrigation to the crop after its transplantation throughout the crop period. In the nursery, natural water irrigation was given.

Control experiment

In the control experiment, irrigation was given with natural water using submergence method.

Quality of Paddy

The quality of paddy obtained from both the experiments was tested by Paddy Processing Centre, Tanjavur and found to satisfy the minimum standards.

Results

The results showed that there was about 20% more yield for the crop irrigated with sewage effluent irrigation compared to control and about 20% less yield in non-ponding irrigation compared to control but there was conservation of 75% of natural water in non-ponding irrigation compared to the control.

National seminar on "Applications of Treated Sewage Effluent Irrigation" - March 23, 1998

To disseminate the knowledge on sewage effluent irrigation, a National seminar on "Applications of Treated Sewage Effluent Irrigation" was organized, by me, on March 23, 1998. Various researchers shared their successful experiences in using treated sewage effluent irrigation for various crops.

Papers Published

Twelve papers were published in national conferences and two in international conferences.

Presentation in Review Meeting - November 2-3, 1999

The progress and results of the research were presented in the review meeting held at IIT Madras on November 2-3, 1999.

Award by AICTE

An evaluation report was received from AICTE dated November, 1999 and I am sharing the same.

"The AICTE funded projects under different schemes sanctioned in 1996-97 have been reviewed by a Project Evaluation Committee at its meeting held on November 2-3, 1999 at IIT, Madras.

With regard to the project sanctioned to you namely, Water Management Studies for Paddy using Sewage Effluent Irrigation and

Non-ponding Irrigation, I am happy to inform you that the Monitoring Committee has placed on record its appreciation for carrying out the project exemplarily well. A certificate of merit after approval by competent authority will be issued in due course."

National Seminar on "Water harvesting"- June 25-26, 1993

Dr. Muthukumaran, the Vice Chancellor of Bharathidasan University, asked me to organize a National Seminar on Water Harvesting. He added that water harvesting is the need of the hour and no one had organized a seminar on this topic. He wanted the seminar to be organized during the third week of June 1993 for two days.

I prepared a complete proposal and set the date for June 25-26, 1993. The seminar covered three areas - water harvesting in hilly areas, plains and rooftops. The recommendations included the need to remove authorized and unauthorized encroachments in tanks and ponds, inclusion of water harvesting in school curriculum, motivation of public through print and electronic media, allocation of funds for augmentation of surface water during monsoon and enforcement of mandatory rooftop water harvesting.

Some of the notable attendees were Dr. S. Muthukumaran, Dr. B. Ilango, Principal, REC, Prof. V. Mahalingam, Director of Technical Education, Government of Tamil Nadu, and Prof. C. N. Balasubramanian, Director, Irrigation Management Training Institute, Trichy.

Impact of the Seminar

The seminar created a huge impact on academicians, NGOs, general public government and print media all over India. Ramanarasu of the Hindu wrote an article on this seminar which was published throughout India. The recommendations sent to government agencies at the centre and state and MS Swaminathan Research Foundation were acknowledged.

Kumudam, a weekly magazine in Tamil published pamphlets about water harvesting which were circulated as a compliment along with the copy of Kumudam. Various governments took steps to make rain water harvesting especially rooftop harvesting mandatory for all households.

3. "Exploitation and Assessment of New Water Sources from Small Catchments"- 1996 to 98

I presented the project proposal to the Ministry of Rural Development in New Delhi on February 16, 1996. I came to Delhi by flight from

Chennai by 10 a.m., for my presentation at 3.30 p.m. It was peak winter and I started to shiver. I went to Connaught Place market and purchased a sweater. The proposal was accepted and an amount of Rs. 2.31 lakh was sanctioned. The majority of research was carried out by Dr. V. Chandramouli. At the end of the project I played a major role in the preparation of the final report for submission to the ministry.

4. "Water Management Studies for Agniar River Basin"- 2000 to 2002

Institute for Water Studies, Taramani, Chennai was the coordinator between World Bank and the Tamil Nadu government.

When project proposals under various thrust areas were invited, Dr. Jothiprakash and I decided to apply.

Dr. Jothiprakash studied B.E. Civil Engineering in Arulmighu Meenakshi Amman College of Engineering (AMACE), Kanchipuram, M.E. in Irrigation Water Management in Centre for Water Resources, College of Engineering, Guindy and took his Ph.D. from IIT Madras under Dr. S. Mohan. I knew Dr. Mohan through my water resources management project. When Dr. Jothiprakash informed him that he was going to join REC Trichy, Dr. Mohan advised him to collaborate with me to carry out research. Accordingly, from day 1, Dr. Jothiprakash joined my research team and we wrote a proposal for the World Bank.

The proposal was shortlisted and both of us went to Institute for Water Studies to present the project before the Research Advisory Committee in April 2000. My classmate Vaithilingam was the Chief Engineer.

The project was approved in May 2000 for an amount of Rs. 10 lakh for a period of 2 years from August 2000 to February 2002. We employed Research Assistants and purchased a computer and other peripherals and set up an office in the Department of Civil Engineering. We had to undergo a very complex time bound schedule. The inception report was presented in September 2002. Two interim reports were presented in April 2001 and October 2001 respectively. The draft final report was presented in February 2002 and the same was approved with certain suggestions. The final report was submitted in June 2002.

Appreciation

When the draft final report was presented, the Research Advisory Committee appreciated the project and said that it was one of the best projects that had been carried out.

Workshop Organized

A state level workshop was organized for Irrigation Engineers of Water Resources Organisation, Government of Tamil Nadu to disseminate the findings of the project on May 29, 2002.

Outcome

One of the recommendations of the project regarding interlinking of rivers in Tamil Nadu was taken up for implementation.

5. "Development of Interactive Software for Reservoir Simulation"- 2002 to 2003

Dr. Jothiprakash and I presented the project proposal in April 2001. It was sanctioned in April 2002 for an amount of Rs. 3.52 lakh. The inception report was submitted in August 2002. The interim report was submitted in November 2002 and final report in December 2002.

The user-friendly software had been designed by Dr. Jothiprakash with specific reference to Agniar river basin. However, it could be replicated and used in real time applications for other river basins too.

Workshop Organized

A state level workshop was organized on the "Use of the Software to the Irrigation Engineers of Tamil Nadu" during December 16-20, 2002.

Have you visited any foreign country in connection with these project works?

I have visited Jerusalem and Bangkok.

Visit to Jerusalem

I accidently received a brochure of an international conference on "Environmental Challenges for the Next Millennium" to be held in Jerusalem during June 1999. **Destiny!** The name Jerusalem made me write a paper on "Curriculum for Environmental Education". The paper was accepted and my Principal Aravindan was kind enough to sponsor me out of my project funds. I visited Jerusalem during June, 1999 and presented my paper. I visited Palestine and saw the birth place of Jesus. I saw the place of crucifixion and resurrection of Jesus in Jerusalem. I visited all the holy places.

On the last day, a dinner was hosted by the organisers. There were about 10 people at my table. As the dinner was coming to an end, a lady in her late twenties approached me and asked, "Are you from Tamil Nadu, India?" I said "Yes." Then, she introduced herself as Juliet from Australia. She was a Civil Engineer with a Ph.D. in Environmental Engineering. She said that she liked my presentation and had visited Chennai. We exchanged our email ids and left the venue.

At that time, I never thought that I would meet her again and play a small role in her life. I will discuss about this later.

Touching the Soil of My Birthplace, Cuddappa - June, 1999

During the last two days of my stay in Jerusalem, I developed toothache and somehow managed with combiflam, pain killer. After landing in Bombay, I visited a dentist and got temporary relief. I could not eat much in the train to Chennai and was continuously sleeping in my upper berth. Suddenly I heard the name Cuddappa and I got up with a startle. The train was standing in Cuddappa station. I got down from the train and touched the soil of my birth place. See, God's plan.

Your first visit to a foreign country was a holy land and your second visit was to a city known for night life - contrasting styles. Please talk about Bangkok.

Visit to Bangkok

An international conference on "Civil and Environmental Engineering" was organized by Asian Institute of Technology, Bangkok during November 8-12, 1999. My abstract and full paper was accepted. This time the Principal said that they would advance money for the trip and I would have to repay in monthly instalments. The budget was around Rs. 50,000.

I left with Ahilan (Project Assistant) by Pallavan Express for Chennai on Saturday. After visiting important temples and churches, we went to writer Balakumaran's house at about 10 p.m. He was about to go out to purchase a few things on Diwali eve but cancelled his plan and took us to his house on the first floor. He briefed me about the historical connection between Tamil Nadu and Thailand and gave me the address of his friend in Bangkok in case I needed any help. He also gave me a photo of 'Visiri Samiyar' and Diwali eve prasadam.

Ahilan saw me off at the Chennai airport that night and I reached Bangkok airport at about 7.30 a.m. I took a taxi and reached the hotel.

I presented my paper on "GIS and Simulation for a Study of the Grand Anicut Canal Irrigation System in India". I visited the Department of Civil Engineering at AIT. I went on a sight-seeing trip and saw some beautiful Buddhist Temples.

I found an Indian restaurant and ate nice lunch every day.

Administrative Years

Chairman, Transport Committee - 1996 to 2003

REC, Trichy, had a Transport Committee to take care of the transport vehicles. A senior faculty would be nominated by the Principal as the Chairman of the Transport Committee. It had representatives from faculty, non- teaching staff and students.

When Dr. K. L. P. Mishra became the Principal Prof. M. Narayana Rao was the Chairman. When the Principal had difficulty in getting the official car allotted for him, he was not happy with Narayana Rao. He called me in the last week of March 1996, explained everything, and requested me to take up the post of Chairman.

Until then I had never used any college vehicle and I knew I would have to tackle the transport staff, students, faculty and non-teaching staff. After thinking for some time, I decided to say no to the Principal. When I entered his chamber, he leaned forward with anxiety almost willing me to say yes. In order not to disappoint him, I changed my mind and said I would take charge for one semester. He was very happy and immediately called his secretary to prepare the order. I took charge as Chairman Transport from April 1, 1996.

When I took over, there were two ambassador cars (both petrol), two matador vans, one trekker and three buses. I called for a meeting of the transport staff and received their problems. Then I collected all the details about the running of the department from the office junior superintendent and I found out there was no proper office. First thing I did was to set up an office room on the ground floor of the Department of Civil Engineering. I designed my own system for vehicle allotment, fuelling and mileage testing, repair and maintenance. Two types of irregularities happen namely cheating during re-fuel and repair. I also found out that there was no driver for night duty and in case of an emergency the same driver who had day duty had to work during the night as well. I appointed two drivers on temporary basis and I allotted night duty by turns. Mileage tests were conducted for all the vehicles. The vehicles were fuelled to full tank every time to calculate the mileage. I introduced vehicle allotment slips based on the requests from the customer and availability of vehicles. Except the Principal's car no vehicle could leave the garage without my permission. Every day after they returned from their trips in the night, the drivers had to inform me so that I could sleep peacefully.

At the end of the semester I asked Mishra to relieve me but he said "Krishnamoorthi, please continue for one more semester."

In 1997, a committee from National Board of Accreditation came to REC for the first time for accrediting our programmes. I coordinated the transport arrangements for them including hiring taxis from outside.

One day Mishra told me, "See Krishnamoorthi, there is a driver, Varadarajan, an ex-serviceman, who drinks and comes to work. Please take care of him."

Next day I called Varadarajan and counselled him for a long time and told him to park the trekker in my car shed every day. This was on trial for 15 days and he stopped drinking and coming to work. He was a very respectful driver. Unfortunately, he passed in a two wheeler road accident in front of the quarter's gate three years back.

Mishra used his vehicle only for official purposes and very rarely used it for personal needs. His wife never used the college vehicle. When Mishra retired in 1997, he requested me for a vehicle to get dropped at the railway station saying he would pay the charges. Of course, I gave the vehicle happily but did not charge him. Some of the faculty became jealous because Mishra would sanction any advance I requested but for others he would approve only after it was forwarded by the Registrar.

Dr. P. Aravindan joined as Principal in June 1997 and I did not ask him to relieve me from the Transport Committee. We got along very well. Also, I was able to bring more welfare measures for the drivers and conductors, purchase new vehicles and air condition the cars with the kind approval of Aravindan. I also introduced allowance for drivers for their school trips and revised their pay scales. I purchased a new bus, ambulance, maruti omni, trekker and eicher for hostel use. I made the Transport Department important and the staff was given their due recognitions.

After the retirement of Aravindan, Dr. M. Arumugam, Professor Electrical Engineering Department whom I knew very well became the Principal. I had served for almost four years by that time and introduced a rule that no faculty could be Chairman for more than three years. So, I was relieved reluctantly by the Principal in June 2001 and Dr. K. Sankaranarayanasamy of Mechanical Engineering was appointed as the Chairman. But he could not continue for even one semester. He was followed by Dr. Ponnambalam who also failed. I was sent SOS by Arumugam through Dr. Sivan and again, I became the chairman from February 2002 till my date of retirement, on June 4, 2003.

I should also mention Boopathi of Highhway Auto Garage and his father for their kind help in understanding the complexities of the transport sector. I should thank all the transport staff for their full cooperation. They did not put me in difficulty even for a single day. Chinnaiyan, Raju, Palaniandi, Vijayan, Varadarajan, Rajan, Mariappan, Rajaratnam, Kaliaperumal and Balamurugan (office) need special mention.

June also helped me a lot in attending phone calls and allotting the vehicles in my absence.

Treasurer/Secretary, Officer's Club - 1990 to 1995

The highlight of my association with the Officer's Club was the organization of "Talent Time" in which the faulty, their children and the students gave scintillating performances in orchestra, dance and classical singing on January 26, 1993. My daughter, Shyamala, was the choreographer and I used to take the children of the campus to the hostel for rehearsals. It was an unforgettable event at REC, talked about even today. The second one was a marathon event in which the students and children took part.

We conducted sports events every year giving away attractive prizes. Children's Day celebrations were something everyone looked forward to.

National Service Scheme (NSS) Officer - 1993 to 1995

*The **National Service Scheme** (**NSS**) is an Indian government-sponsored public service program conducted by the Ministry of Youth Affairs and Sports of the Government of India. Popularly known as NSS, the scheme was launched in Gandhiji's Centenary year, 1969. Aimed* *at developing student's personality through community service, NSS is a voluntary association of young people in Colleges, Universities and at +2 level working for a campus-community linkage.*

As an officer of NSS for two years during 1993-95, I organised events in villages involving village people, students, staff and their children.

In charge of Important Functions

I was responsible for conducting important functions held in the college. In one such function R.M. Veerappan, Education minister of Tamil Nadu and Chairman of Board of Governors of REC was the chief guest. It was in the year 1992. Dr. Ilango, Principal at that time, asked me to conduct the event in a grand manner. I organised everything and gave a rehearsal in the afternoon. He was satisfied. The function was conducted very well and the next day he congratulated me and said "Thank you, Krishnamoorthi!" The minister complimented the conduct of the function and was happy to sanction welfare schemes for the college. June used to pack the mementos to be given to the chief guests in innovative ways which always noticed and appreciated.

Dr. M. Shanmugam voluntarily retired in 2000 as Professor and Head of the Department. He donated Rs. 25,000 as fixed deposit and wanted a gold medal to be awarded to the first rank holder in Civil Engineering every year from the interest earned. I was a member of the committee formed to frame the guidelines to be followed in selecting the deserving student. I was in charge of making the gold medal every year till my retirement. June used to wrap it beautifully.

President, Temple Committee - 2000 to 2003

When the Vinayaga Temple in REC was short of funds, they requested me to become the President to improve the bank balance. I hesitated at first, but after giving it a thought, I took charge from January 1, 2000. Within a week, I received an invitation from BHEL to attend Lord Krishna and Radha's marriage function. While at the function, someone came and sat next to me. He started to talk with me and that is how God introduced a very spiritual man, Ramasubramanian, of BHEL to me. I have benefitted so much from him. **God's design.**

Ramasubramanian introduced me to various temples including Rajarareswari Temple in Small Arms Factory. I used to take his aged mother in the REC vehicle to this temple. During construction of Santhoshi Matha Temple in the BHEL campus he involved me in all the important activities. I offered my wedding ring to be placed under one Deity after getting permission from June.

As chairman, I started giving prasadams on special occasions, improved the Hundi collection and received charity from different people including Manisundaram. I also fixed a notice board to display the events of the temple. On the day of Gujarat earthquake on January 26, 2001, we were counting the money in the Hundi and a small part of collection was given as relief fund. I raised the bank balance to a reasonably high level.

Member, Board of Governors - 2000 to 2002

As a senior faculty, I served as Member, Board of Governors for 2 years. I worked hard to give promotions to senior faculty who had no Ph.D. but had carried out R&D projects. The Chairman Prof. Anbalagan, Education Minister, was sympathetic and tried to implement the scheme. But the Education Secretary prevented him from approving it in 2000. Dr. Thambi Durai became the chairman in 2001 when the government changed. He asked for time to study the proposal but that time never came.

CHAPTER 11

Game of Contract Bridge - 1966 to 2018

ABSTRACT

Me

The details of my record in various tournaments are presented.

Starting of Bridge

When I was doing my M.E. at IISc Bangalore, Zahoor Ahmed taught me a new game called "bridge". It was easy to learn and I took a special interest in the game. I participated in my first tournament held at Bowring Institute, a famous club in Bangalore.

What is the game?

Bridge is an intellectual game executed with playing cards. It is a subject by itself. There are textbooks and journals related to bridge. It involves systems, techniques, and mathematics. It is played worldwide. It is also a part of the Olympics. By playing bridge people can improve their acumen, memory, focus, wit and patience. A few people have submitted Ph.D. thesis on this game.

Four people and a pack of 52 cards are required to play a game. Tournaments are conducted in four events. They are Swiss League, team of four Progressive Duplicate, Master Pair and Individual. In the first two the best team is judged, in the master pair the best pair and in the individual the best individual is judged.

In REC, Calicut I started to partner with Ramasamy. Some of the other players were Krishnasamy, Ramakrishnan, Isaac, Chandrasekar, Babu, Prasad and Lakshminarayanan. In the first tournament we played, organised by Lotus Club, Cochin , we did not win any prize.

Next, we played in the Nationals held in Bangalore in 1970. We didn't get any prize. It was a great experience to see all the top-ranking players of India. There we admired Ruby Roy of West Bengal.

After Ramasamy got married, our families went to Ooty and played in a tournament in 1972. I was the winner in the individual event and was awarded a silver lamp. The lamp is in my pooja room and I still use it.

The South Zone Bridge Tournament was planned in Cochin in October 1972. Tamil Nadu State Bridge Association decided to form a team by selecting three best pairs in Tamil Nadu. Preliminaries consisted of selecting one pair from each district. Ramasamy and I decided to take part from Coimbatore district since Ramasamy belonged to that district. We came first and we were invited to play in the final selection in Chennai consisting of 12 best pairs from Tamil Nadu. The Butler method was used for scoring. It was conducted for two days. Each pair had to play 12 boards with every other pair. At the end of 11 rounds, Ramasamy and I came third and we were selected to represent Tamil Nadu in the South Zone tournament in October 1972 and in the Nationals in January 1973. We played fairly well in the South Zone tournament but could not get any prize. A small misunderstanding cropped up between us which we quickly resolved. But we could not go to the Nationals because of academic work.

We established contact with Cosmopolitan Club in Calicut. Mavoor Prabhu of Calicut Cosmopolitan Club was a bridge enthusiast and used to conduct friendly matches and tournaments.

Results during the Period 1966 to 1974

State Level Events

Names	Event	Conducted by	Date	Position
S. Krishnamoorthi	Individual	South Indian Bridge Association, Ooty, Tamil Nadu	1972	I
S. Krishnamoorthi T. N. Ramaswamy	Master Pairs	Officer's Club, Coimbatore, Tamil Nadu	1972	I
S. Krishnamoorthi P. Ramakrishnan	Master Pairs	Cosmopolitan Club, Coimbatore, Tamil Nadu	1973	II

When I joined REC Trichy in 1974, there was a hiatus as I could not find bridge players.

I became a member of City Club, Trichy and there I found a few players. We formed a team and started to practice. By this time, a couple at REC, Mrs. and Mr. Kalyanasundaram, started playing bridge. We came to know that BHEL conducted R. S. Krishnan Memorial Bridge Tournament every other year. We found few players in Srirangam Club and as bridge supporters started to promote Bridge in Trichy district. We took part in tournaments held at Trichy, Mettur, Neyveli, Coimbatore, Madurai, Tutucorin, Coonoor, Pudukkottai, Thanjavur, Chennai, Bangalore, Cochin and Trichur. I became the Secretary of Tiruchirappalli District Bridge Association (TDBA). We initiated Trichy District Bridge Championship and it was held every year. Annual tournaments by City Club and Srirangam Club, in the name of Thathachariar, were conducted. I knew Thathachariar through Thomas and both of them were promoters of tennis in Trichy. Thathachariar was also a lover of bridge. He owned mango orchards and Himampasanth variety of mango grown in his garden are famous all over the world.

The key players were Alagappan, Viswanathan, Marimuthu, Mrs. and Mr. Kalyanasundaram, Moses Santhakumar, Prabhakar, Rajendran, Jayaseelan, Gunasekar, Saravanan, Ramasamy, Rajagopal, Nambudripad, Perumal, Ganesan, Herbart and Rajmohan. I should mention Dr. Ram Prasad, a dentist in BHEL hospital, for his contributions to the development of bridge in Trichy.

We won many events in various tournaments held at different levels.

Results from 1974

District Level Tournaments

Names	Event	Conducted by	Date	Position
S. Krishnamoorthi S. Moses Santhakumar	Master Pairs	117, Infantry Battalion Trichy, Tamil Nadu	April 1992	I
S. Krishnamoorthi S. Moses Santhakumar C. Alagappan P. Marimuthu	Swiss League	Trichy District Bridge Association, Tamil Nadu	March 1993	I

S. Krishnamoorthi S. Moses Santhakumar P. Marimuthu Col. Nair	Swiss League	Trichy District Bridge Association, Tamil Nadu	February 1994	I
S. Krishnamoorthi P. Marimuthu T. M. Gunasekar T. M. Saravanan	Swiss League	Trichy District Bridge Association, Tamil Nadu	May 1995	I
S. Krishnamoorthi S. Moses Santhakumar	Master Pairs	Brigadier's Association, Trichy, Tamil Nadu	May 1995	I
S. Krishnamoorthi S. Moses Santhakumar T. M. Gunasekar T. M. Saravanan	Progressive Duplicate	Brigadier's Association, Trichy, Tamil Nadu	May 1995	I
S. Krishnamoorthi R. Prabhakar N. Kalyanasundaram Aparna Kalyanasundaram	Progressive Duplicate	117, Infantry Battalion, Trichy, Tamil Nadu	May 1995	I
S. Krishnamoorthi R. Prabhakar N. Kalyanasundaram Aparna Kalyanasundaram	Progressive Duplicate	117, Infantry Battalion, Trichy, Tamil Nadu	November 1995	1

Inter-District Level Tournaments

Inter-District tournaments were conducted only for three years from 1992 to 1994.

Names	Event	Conducted by	Date	Position
S. Krishnamoorthi S. Moses Santhakumar P. Marimuthu Col. Nair	Progressive Duplicate	Inter District Bridge Tournament, Gopichettipalayam, Tamil Nadu	March 1994	I

State Level Tournaments

In these tournaments, teams from other states like Karnataka, Kerala and Andhra Pradesh also participated.

Names	Event	Conducted by	Date	Prize
S. Krishnamoorthi S. Moses Santhakumar N. Kalyanasundaram S. Rajagopal T. N. Ramaswamy P. Marimuthu	Swiss League	Chemplast, Mettur, Tamil Nadu	November 1991	IV
S. Krishnamoorthi S. Moses Santhakumar T. N. Ramaswamy P. Marimuthu	Progressive Duplicate	Tamil Nadu State Championship, Madurai, Tamil Nadu	February 1992	I
S. Krishnamoorthi S. Moses Santhakumar	Master Pair	IIT Gymkhana Club, Chennai, Tamil Nadu	April 1992	I
S. Krishnamoorthi S. Moses Santhakumar T.N. Ramaswamy P. Marimuthu	Swiss League	Parisutham Nadar Memorial Tournament, Union Club, Tanjavur, Tamil Nadu	July 1992	IV
S. Krishnamoorthi P. Marimuthu S. Rajendran G. Jayaseelan S. M. Sekkilar	Swiss League	SPIC Tournament, Tuticorin, Tamil Nadu	July 1992	III
S. Krishnamoorthi P. Marimuthu N. Kalyanasundaram Aparna kalyanasundaram	Swiss League	Officer's Club, Pudukkottai, Tamil Nadu	August 1992	I
S.Krishnamoorthi C. Alagappan	Master Pairs	Officer's Club, Pudukkottai, Tamil Nadu	February 1993	II
S. Krishnamoorthi C. Alagappan	Master Pairs	LRDE Tournament, Bangalore, Karnataka	May 1993	VI
S. Krishnamoorthi R. Prabhakar V. Perumal T.M. Saravanan	Progressive Duplicate	LRDE Tournament Bangalore, Karnataka	May 1993	VI

Players	Event	Tournament	Date	Position
S. Krishnamoorthi S. Moses Santhakumar Rajagopal T. M. Gunasekar Col. Nair	Swiss League	Annual Tournament, City Club, Trichy, Tamil Nadu	October 1993	II
S. Krishnamoorthi C. Alagappan	Master Pairs	Invitation Tournament, Madurai, Tamil Nadu.	October 1993	I
S. Krishnamoorthi S. Moses Santhakumar P. Marimuthu S. Kathiresan	Progressive Duplicate	Annual Tournament, Lotus Club, Cochin	December 1993	II
S. Krishnamoorthi S. Moses Santhakumar	Master Pairs	TVS Tournament, Madurai, Tamil Nadu	January 1994	I
S. Krishnamoorthi S. Moses Santhakumar T.N. Ramaswamy P. Marimuthu N. Kalyanasundaram Aparna Kalyanasundaram	Swiss League	TVS Tournament, Madurai, Tamil Nadu	January 1994	III
S. Krishnamoorthi S. Moses Santhakumar T.N. Ramaswamy P. Marimuthu	Swiss League	ARJ Tournament, Coimbatore, Tamil Nadu	August 1994	VI
S. Krishnamoorthi S. Moses Santhakumar T.M. Gunasekar T.M. Saravanan	Swiss League	P.S. Reddy Tournament, Chennai Tamil Nadu	June 1995	IV
S. Krishnamoorthi S. Moses Santhakumar T.M. Gunasekar T.M. Saravanan	Progressive Duplicate	P.S. Reddy Tournament, Chennai Tamil Nadu	June 1995	III
S. Krishnamoorthi T.N. Ramaswamy	Master Pairs	Officer's Club, Pudukkottai, Tamil Nadu	October 1995	IV
S. Krishnamoorthi S. Moses Santhakumar T. M. Gunasekar T. M. Saravanan	Progressive Duplicate	Thatham Memorial Tournament, Trichy, Tamil Nadu	February 1996	I

Players	Event	Tournament	Date	Place
S. Krishnamoorthi T. M. Saravanan Herbert Balachander Narendra Prasad	Progressive Duplicate	K.J. Seetharaman Memorial Tournament, Chennai, Tamil Nadu	February 1996	IV
S. Krishnamoorthi S. Moses Santhakumar	Master Pairs	Chelliah Memorial Tournament, Chennai, Tamil Nadu	May 1996	V
S. Krishnamoorthi S. Moses Santhakumar T. N. Ramaswamy P. Marimuthu	Swiss League	P.S. Reddy Tournament, Chennai, Tamil Nadu	June 1996	II
S. Krishnamoorthi S. Moses Santhakumar S. Viswanathan T. M. Gunasekar T. M. Saravanan	Swiss League	Tamil Nadu State Championship, Chennai, Tamil Nadu	July 1996	III
S. Krishnamoorthi S. Moses Santhakumar S. Viswanathan T. M. Saravanan	Progressive Duplicate	Officer's Club, Pudukkottai, Tamil Nadu	September 1996	II
S. Krishnamoorthi S. Moses Santhakumar S. Viswanathan T.M. Gunasekar T.M. Saravanan	Swiss League	Annual Tournament, City Club, Trichy, Tamil Nadu	October 1996	II
S. Krishnamoorthi S. Moses Santhakumar P. Marimuthu V. Perumal	Swiss League	TDCL Tournament, Trichy, Tamil Nadu	June 1997	II
S. Krishnamoorthi S. Moses Santhakumar T. N. Ramaswamy P. Marimuthu T. M. Gunasekar T. M. Saravanan	Swiss League	P.S. Reddy Tournament, Chennai, Tamil Nadu	July 1997	I
S. Krishnamoorthi C. Alagappan S. Viswanathan T. M. Gunasekar T. M. Saravanan V. Perumal	Swiss League	Golden Jubilee Independence Cup, Chennai, Tamil Nadu	September 1997	III

Players	Event	Tournament	Date	Position
S. Krishnamoorthi C. Alagappan	Master Pairs	Annual Tournament City Club, Trichy, Tamil Nadu	December 1997	I
S. Krishnamoorthi C. Alagappan N. Kalyanasundaram Aparna Kalynasundaram V. Perumal	Swiss League	Annual Tournament City Club, Trichy, Tamil Nadu	December 1997	II
S. Krishnamoorthi V. Perumal	Master Pairs	Thatham Memorial Tournament, Srirangam Club, Trichy, Tamil Nadu	January 1998	I
S. Krishnamoorthi V. Perumal	Master Pairs	TDBA, Trichy, Tamil Nadu	July 1998	II
S. Krishnamoorthi S. Viswanathan N. Kalyanasundaram Aparna Kalyanasundaram	Swiss League	Thatham Memorial Tournament, Srirangam Club, Trichy, Tamil Nadu	December 1998	I
S. Krishnamoorthi S. Viswanathan N. Kalyanasundram Aparna Kalyanasundaram	Swiss League	Thatham Memorial Tournament, Srirangam Club, Trichy, Tamil Nadu	January 2000	I
S. Krishnamoorthi S. Viswanathan T. N. Ramaswamy Namboodripad	Swiss League	Kerala State Championship, Trichur, Kerala	October 2000	I
S. Krishnamoorthi C. Alagappan S. Viswanathan V. Perumal	Swiss League	S.K. Menon Memorial Tournament, Coonoor, Tamil Nadu	September 2001	III
S. Krishnamoorthi S. Viswanathan	Master Pairs	Annual Tournament City Club, Trichy, Tamil Nadu	August 2002	I

S. Krishnamoorthi C. Alagappan S. Viswanathan T. M. Gunasekar T. M. Saravanan	Swiss League	R.S.K. Memorial Tournament, BHEL Trichy, Tamil Nadu	September 2003	III
S. Krishnamoorthi S. S. Mani		Ramaratnam Memorial Tournament, Chennai, Tamil Nadu	March 2006	II

Tamil Nadu State Championship, Madurai Tamil Nadu – February, 1992

I won the first prize with Moses Shanthakumar, Ramasamy and Marimuthu as partners in the Progressive Duplicate in the Tamil Nadu State championship in Madurai during February 1992. We won this six days after Shyamala's wedding. This was the first time June came with me for a tournament.

ARJ Memorial Tournament, Coimbatore - August, 1992.

I lost in the tie to enter the finals of the Swiss League event in the ARJ Tournament held in Coimbatore in 1992. I cannot forget this tournament. Two days before the tournament my daughter, Shyamala, who was pregnant, had high BP and was admitted to a hospital in Vellore. When she became better I took her by train to Trichy where she was supposed to have the delivery. I reached at about 7 a.m., and immediately left Trichy by bus to Coimbatore for the tournament. I reached the venue of the tournament by 2 p.m., and the third round was about to start. As I was entering, some players told me, "Go soon. Your team is trailing. You have to pull up your team." Then, in the remaining four rounds we played well and brought the score up but lost in a tie.

Kerala State Championship - October, 2000

Along with Viswanathan, Ramasamy and Namboodripad as partners I won the Swiss League event of the Kerala State Bridge Championship in Trichur. Here, I have to tell you about God's design. For the Trichur tournament Viswanathan and I wanted our respective families to accompany us. So, June, Viswanathan, his wife, two daughters and I went by train. We got down and booked two rooms in a hotel and proceeded to Guruvayur Temple at about 5 a.m. We had a good dharshan and then came back to the hotel.

The tournament was for two days. There were four rounds on the first day and two rounds on the second day for the Swiss League event. We were at the second position on the first day and at the end of fifth round on the second day. Everyone started discussing the conditions for our team to come first at the end of round six. We would have to win our last round by a maximum of 25 points and the top team should not get more than 15 points in their last round. You won't believe it. Exactly the same thing happened. We finished our last round first and we got 25 points. The opposing team got only 15 points and we became the winner just by 1 point. It was surely Guruvayurappan's Gift to us. That was our first Swiss League win in a State championship.

Zonal Level Tournaments

Names	Event	Conducted by	Date	Position
S. Krishnamoorthi S. Moses Santhakumar T. N. Ramaswamy P. Marimuthu	Swiss League	South Zone Tournament, Cochin, Kerala	May 1992	IV

National Level Tournaments

Names	Event	Conducted by	Date	Position
S. Krishnamoorthi C. Alagappan	Master Pairs	All India Invitation Tournament, Chennai, Tamil Nadu	September 2002	IV

All India Invitation Tournament, Chennai, Tamil Nadu - September, 2002

I Won the fourth prize with Alagappan as partner in the Master Pair event of the Well Knit held in Chennai.

This was a beautiful tournament. They invited the top-ranking pairs from India covering all the states. There were 72 pairs and each pair had to play every pair 2 deals in 2 rounds. At the end of every round scores were displayed on a big screen. A total of 142 deals were played with 72 deals on the first day and 70 deals on the second day. At the end of the first day, we secured 11th position with a score of 1387.77 and at the end of second day we secured 2nd position with a score of 1414.44. Finally adding both the scores we secured 4th position with 2802.21.

I cherish this as one of my best tournaments.

International Level Tournaments

Names	Event	Conducted by	Date	Position
S. Krishnamoorthi C. Alagappan T. R. Krishnan S. R. C. Sekhar G. Rajagopal T. R. Rajagopal	Swiss League	Tamil Nadu vs. Sri Lanka, Tamil Nadu Bridge Association, Chennai, Tamil Nadu	October 2002	I

Tamil Nadu vs. Sri Lanka, International Tournament, Chennai, Tamil Nadu - October 2002

I won the first prize with Alagappan, S.R.C. Sekar, T. R. Krishnan, T. R. Rajagopal and G. Rajagopal as partners in the Swiss League event of the International Bridge tournament involving Tamil Nadu and Sri Lanka held in Chennai.

Three teams to represent Tamil Nadu were picked by the Tamil Nadu Bridge Association as Tamil Nadu A, B and C. Two teams were selected from Sri Lanka as Sri Lanka A and B.

I was in Tamil Nadu C. On the first two days, each team had to play a double round robin of 8 rounds. At the end of round robin, the top two teams would qualify for the finals to be played on the third day. On the first day, all of us finished 4 rounds and my team was in the last position with 52 victory points. On the second day, our score improved and at the end of 8 rounds we scored 123 victory points out of possible 200 points. Since there were odd number of teams each team would get one bye round on each day. We had the last round as bye.

Here I have to talk about God's design. In my eighth round I made a wrong bid. But that mistake turned out to be lucky for us as it brought a lot of points.

After finishing 8 rounds, I excused myself to go to my hotel for my regular prayer. I told one of my teammates to inform me about the result. I waited till 10 p.m., but no call came. I was too nervous to call and ask. Finally, I got a call that we had finished second and had entered the finals. My teammate further added that there was a tie between our team and another team of Tamil Nadu as both finished with 123 points. It took lot of time for the director to break the tie. Team A were awarded minus points because when they played with Sri Lanka B, they made a mistake of sitting in the same direction. So, we qualified. God's design again. Sri Lanka A finished the round robin with a top score of 130 victory points.

Next day, the finals were between Tamil Nadu C and Sri Lanka A. We had to play 4 rounds of 16 boards each to decide the winner. We played very well and led from the first round. At the end of 4 rounds we beat them by 109 to 55 International Match Points (IMPs), the difference being 54 IMPs.

It was the greatest moment of my bridge life. I had an International win against Sri Lanka.

World Level Tournaments

Here, I must tell you about Kribakaramurthy. Kribakaramurthy did his Engineering degree from IIT Madras and has been playing bridge since his college days. He is an expert international player. He is the CEO of Agsar Paints. He became the President of Bridge Federation of India in the year 2013. He made lot of efforts to conduct the World Bridge Championship in India for the first time. He successfully conducted the 42nd Bermuda Bowl in Chennai during September-October 2015. I went to Chennai to watch the league matches.

There were a few side events which were open to all. I played one pair event with Alagappan as partner. The scoring was as per victory points. We played 7 rounds and secured 82nd position out of about 250 pairs.

I had the complete satisfaction of playing in a World Cup Bridge event and I should thank Kribakaramurthy and his team.

Internet Tournaments

Now, I play different types of events on Bridge Base Online (BBO). I play at least one match every day.

Wow! Your professional life and bridge life grew together, I wonder how you managed it. I am sure your wife must have sacrificed her time with you for this to happen.

Actually, June neither encouraged nor discouraged me in my bridge life. But I feel sad now for leaving her alone most of the time when going for the tournaments.

Who are your favourite partners and players?

My favourite partners are Ramasamy, Moses Shanthakumar, Alagappan and Viswanathan. My other notable teammates are R. Prabhakar, T. M. Saravanan, T. M. Gunasekhar and P. Marimuthu (late). Among the world players, I like Bellodona of Italy, Zia Mohammed, Rodwell and Meckstroth of USA. In India, I like many like Ruby Roy, Shah, Nachiappan, Nagappan, Jagannathan, Sundarram, G. K.Sundaram, Venkatraman, Kribakaramurthy, Sridhar, Vasudevan, Srikrishnan, Prabhakar, Shivadasini, Venkatesh, Madukar Rao and Kushari.

After I started to play in Gurgaon and Delhi, I have won many first prizes in the Master Pair event by playing with Rakesh Agarwal, Mahender Chopra, Subash Mehta, Gen. Vijan, Rashmi, Capt. Marwaha, J. N. Pandey, Major Iyer, Ranjan Bhattacharya, Sham Sharma, S. S. Gupta and Madhu Kochar as partners. Others to be mentioned are Sunil Bhatia, Uma Relan, Mukesh Shivadasini, Anil Bharihoke, R. K. Garg, A. K. Sinha, Amarjeet, Kanwarjit Singh, Mangalam, S. D. Gupta, Rehan, Pinni, Richa and Anjali.

Faculty in the Bridge Education Program

I have been enrolled as a faculty to teach bridge in colleges, schools and clubs under the "Bridge Education Program" initiated by the Bridge Federation of India. Bridge has been recognised by the government of India as a mind sport.

CHAPTER - 12

Life in Kanchipuram - June 2003 to July 2007

ABSTRACT

Me

The details of my joining Arulmighu Meenakshi Amman College of Engineering AMACE (2003), my 60th birthday (2003), first time accreditation (2004), misunderstanding with Chairman (2004), Chief Superintendent of Examinations, Anna University (2005-07), winning design competition (2005), College Day function (2007), Shyamala's life in Chennai (2005-07), Shyamala and Alex leaving for Gurgaon (2005), Amenda's trips for violin examinations (2005-06) and Raja's marriage (2006) are presented here.

Around Me

In India, the major events were birth of Janata Dal (2003), 14th general elections (2004), Manmohan Singh becoming Prime Minister (2004), visit of Singh to USA (2005), Pondicherry name change (2006), visit of Bush to India (2006), birth of MNS party (2006), reopening of Nathu La pass (2006), agreement with Russia for fighter aircraft (2007), launch of 10th PSLV with 4 satellites (2007) and return of SRE-1 (2007).

In Tamil Nadu, the major events were the arrest of Jayendara Saraswathi (2004), Kumbakonam school fire (2004), tsunami (2004), killing of Veerappan (2004), birth of DMDK (2005), 13th Assembly elections (2006) and Karunanidhi as Chief Minister (2006).

In the World, the major events were ASEAN Business Summit (2003), CoP9 (2003), Spirit landing on Mars (2004), CoP10 (2004), death of Arafat (2004), Athens Olympiad (2004), Bush continuing as President (2005), Huygens landing on Titan (2005), CoP11 (2005), IPCC third assessment report (2005), execution of Saddam Hussein (2006), CoP12 (2006), launching of New Horizon (2006), Gordon Brown as Prime Minister of UK (2007) and China's anti-satellite missile test (2007).

ME

Wow! I am just wondering how you had managed to be very successful in teaching, research, administration and the game of bridge all at the same time in 29 years. Definitely, you are different from others.

After your retirement you joined AMACE. How was your life at AMACE?

Joining AMACE - June 11, 2003

I had told you earlier about my appointment as Professor and Head, Department of Civil engineering at AMACE and about my daughter Shyamala settling in Gandhinagar, Adyar, Chennai.

Kanchipuram *was known in early Tamil literature as Kachi or Kachipedu but was later Sanskritized to Kanchi or Kanchipuram. According to legend, the name Kanchi is derived from Ka referring to the Hindu God Brahma and anchi, referring to his worship of Hindu God Vishnu at this place. It is a city in the Indian state of Tamil Nadu, 72 kilometres from Chennai.*

It is located on the banks of the Vegavathy River. In Hindu theology, Kanchipuram is one of the seven Indian cities to reach final attainment. The city houses Varadharaja Perumal Temple, Ekambareswarar Temple and Kamakshi Amman Temple, and is a holy pilgrimage site for both Saivites and Vaishnavites. It is well known for its handwoven silk sarees and most of the city's workforce is involved in the weaving industry. It is the headquarters of the Kanchimada, a Hindu monastic institution believed to have been founded by the Hindu saint and commentator Adi Sankaracharya, and was the capital city of the Pallava Kingdom between the 4th and 9th centuries.

Kanchipuram has been chosen as one of the heritage cities for HRIDAY (Heritage City Development and Augmentation Yojana) scheme of Government of India.

Arulmighu Meenakshi Amman College of Engineering (AMACE) is one of the earliest self-financing colleges to be started in 1985-86 by the Meenakshi Ammal Trust. It is located in Vadamavandal Village of Cheyyar taluk of Tiruvannamalai district and is just 15 kilometres from Kanchpuram and so is identified with it. It is affiliated to Anna University. All its programmes are approved by AICTE and accredited by NBA. Mr. A.N. Radhakrishnan, M.A., D.Com. is the Managing Trustee. He was a Senior Lecturer in Commerce for over three decades in the State Institute of Commerce Education (SICE), under the Department of Technical Education, Government of Tamil Nadu. His rich experience in teaching was instrumental in starting Educational Institutions with Engineering, Medical and Para Medical courses.

To join AMACE, we left Trichy on Monday, June 9, 2003 in my Maruti Omni which was driven by Rajaratnam. Before we left, we sent our luggage in a lorry with Kaliaperumal and Nelson.

We reached AMACE around 8 p.m. I joined duty on Wednesday June 11, 2003.

On the following Saturday June and I went to the SBI in Kanchipuram and deposited my retirement money. The Bank manager, Mohan, was a very kind man. Whenever we visited the bank to withdraw money he would make us sit in his room and send his staff to bring fresh notes. We received royal treatment and it made us happy.

Slowly, I got accustomed to the teaching environment in the college and settled down in the department to execute my duties. N. Prabhakar was the senior most faculty and he was acting Head till I took over. He was happy to be relieved of his responsibilities. He was a good person, respected by all. The laboratories were well equipped and we had a faculty strength of 12.

I had my Maruti with me and used it to commute between Kanchipuram and Chennai. We purchased a new LG 29" TV, as desired by June and some light weight furniture in Kanchipuram. The house had three bedrooms, three toilets, a big hall and a kitchen. The master bedroom was air conditioned. The house had all the modern amenities and was too big for the two of us.

Routine work went on smoothly with the cooperation of all the faculty members of the department and the administrative staff of the college including the Principal.

Accreditation by NBA - March, 2004

The immediate concern for the Managing Trustee was to get programmes in Civil, Mechanical and Electronics Engineering to be accredited by NBA. I was specifically appointed for it.

I was made the coordinator for NBA accreditation because of my previous experience in REC. I started working earnestly, filling up the form and creating the necessary documents for all the three departments. After submitting the form successfully, I prepared PowerPoint presentations for all the departments. We worked continuously for two weeks even on Sunday to prepare ourselves for the anticipated NBA team's visit

They visited us for three days in March 2004. I presented the details of the Civil Engineering programme first followed by the Mechanical and Electronics Departments. The Head of Electronics Departments was a visiting faculty and his presentation did not go well. On the final day, the NBA team hinted that Civil and Mechanical were likely to get accreditation but not Electronics Department.

The official results came after two months. As hinted earlier, the Electronics Department did not receive accreditation. The Head of the Electronics Department was relieved immediately. It was the practice in some private colleges that as soon as NBA accreditation process was successful they would relieve the heads. But I was not relieved of my duties.

Creation and Clearance of Misunderstanding - July 2004

When the academic session 2004-05 started, I thought of restricting my teaching hours to 3 days a week as my son-in-law had joined Ranbaxy in Gurgaon in May 2004 and my wife had to stay in Chennai with Shymala's family.

I got approval for my request from the Secretary of the Trust and I thought he would inform the Chairman. But he forgot. When the Chairman came to know from the Principal that I was coming only for 3 days, he got angry and issued a relieving order.

After seeing that order, I went to his office in Chennai to apologize for not informing him about my request.

But when I met him in his office in Chennai, he never gave me a chance to speak and said that he felt sorry for his action and would withdraw his order. **Destiny** made the Chairman withdraw his own order which he would normally never do. I continued till July 11, 2007.

Chief Superintendent, Anna University Examinations - 2005 to 2007

When Balakrishnan, former Director, Department of Technical Education, Government of Tamil Nadu, became the Principal, he appointed me as the Chief Superintendent of Anna University Examinations. Usually, the Principal himself would be the Chief Superintendent and would be assisted by one of the Head of Departments unofficially. But Balakrishnan had full faith in me. It was a very tedious and highly responsible job. I had Deepa (Physical Education), Mythili (MCA), Sumathi (MCA) and Chitra (Placement) to assist me in all the activities connected with examination cell. I had covered November 2005, May 2006, November 2006, and May 2007 examinations.

Promotions to the Faculty - 2006

Prof. V. R. Rajamanickam joined as Director in 2005 when Balakrishnan was the Principal. Rajamanickam was very sincere and hard working. Both tried to implement many policies for the betterment of the college. Promotions for the faculty was one such thing. A selection committee was formed which included experts from outside colleges and industry. Interviews were conducted. Vijayakumar who was junior at AMACE but senior by profession was promoted to Assistant Professor overlooking Prabhakar, Sumathi, Kumar and Rao. Prabhakar was the most deserving candidate because of his experience. But he was promoted at a later date. This made the faculty members react in a hostile manner towards Vijayakumar and he resigned. Few faculty members also resigned due to resentment over this issue.

College Day Function - 2007

Dr. C. V. Jayakumar joined as Principal, after Balakrishnan, in 2006. He wanted to organise a College Day celebration. The practice of organising college day celebrations had been discontinued for a few years. We decided to have a cultural program at the end of the function. We formed teams and had a few rehearsals and for the final one June also came. Deepa coordinated the entire event. The college day function went off very well including the cultural program.

After the function Jayakumar told Rajamanickam and me that he felt that there may be a clash between the students. After saying this, he took his ailing mother to the Meenatchi Hospital, run by the Trust of our college, in Kanchipuram.

I returned home and was relaxing with June. Suddenly, I saw a few students running to the Director's house on the first floor. As the Director came down, he asked me to accompany him. As we approached the hostel, we saw a few second-year students standing outside the hostel with sticks and stones while the third year students were inside the hostel. We informed the Principal and he rushed back to the college. We tried to pacify them till 1 a.m., and then returned home. After few hours of calm, a fight broke out again at 5 a.m. Immediately, a decision was taken to close the college and hostel for a few days. There was an enquiry about this under my Chairmanship. Things returned to normal after a week.

Other Notable Contributions

Report Preparation and Coordinating Visits

I prepared all the reports and applications for continuation of affiliation to Anna University, and for approval of all programmes by AICTE on an annual basis. I also coordinated all the visits by different bodies.

Motivating the Students to Participate in Design Competitions - 2005

For the first time, I started the placement programme for the Civil Engineering Department. I motivated and guided the final year Civil Engineering students to participate in the National level design competition. One group of students cleared the state and zonal level and reached the finals held in Calcutta. The team won the third prize at the National level finals. Another feather in my cap.

National Conference - 2006

I co-ordinated a two-day National Conference on "New Frontier in Civil, Mechanical and Electronics Engineering", held in March 2006.

Addition of Universal Testing Machine

I added a universal testing machine to the Strength of Materials laboratory

Paper Publication - 2005

I attended an International conference on "Tsunamis, Disaster Management and Coastal Area Development" organized by the

Madras Development Society, Chennai on June 30 and July 1 and presented a paper on "Managing Calamities and Disasters Effectively and Efficiently".

Case of a Weak Student, Shobha - 2006

Shobha was a final year student in Civil Engineering during the academic year 2005-2006. She had arrears in 5 papers and she became nervous. Her mother came from Trichy and talked to June and me about Shobha's plight and requested me to tutor and help her. I started to teach her in our house. Since she didn't drink coffee, June used to give her milk to drink. I was a staunch believer in the miracles of Jesus, so I took Shoba and her uncle to the "Jesus Calls Prayer Tower" in Chennai and prayed for her success in the examination. She cleared 3 of the arrears in the November semester examination along with her regular papers and the remaining 2 arrear papers along with regular papers in the May examinations and got 64 %. This was a miracle and became the talk of AMACE.

Outreach Activity - 2004

I served as Chief Examiner in the central valuation of Anna University examinations held in Thanthai Periyar Government Engineering College, Vellore.

Personal Life

60th birthday (Shashti Poorthi) Celebration - August, 2003

We decided to celebrate my 60th birthday on a small scale in Trichy inviting only close relatives since I was recovering from a mild heart attack.

__Shashti Poorthi__ is a Hindu ceremony to celebrate the 60th birthday of a male, akin to the renewal of marital vows. This term is derived from Sanskrit word, shasthi abda poorthi, in which Shashti means sixty; abda means year; poorthi means completion. It marks completion of half the years of one's lifetime according to Hinduism. The sixtieth year in one's life is a significant milestone, memorable turning point, a touching reminder of the rich, mellowed life that would unfold in the years to come. The Hindu calendar has 60 years that repeat themselves after every 60 years in a sequence. The sages and the rishis of lore have acknowledged the sanctity of the sixtieth year and have drawn out elaborate rituals to mark this special event.

They looked at it as rebirth and suggested the repetition of those rituals performed at one's birth. The Shasti Poorthi Shanti should be performed in the sixty first year and in the same month and day of birth according to the Indian Zodiac. The choice of the place to carry out this tradition could be a pilgrim town, a temple, a river bank or even one's residence. As part of the celebrations the couple's children perform their parents' second wedding.

We did not print any invitation and we orally invited the close relatives.

June and I, accompanied by my sister, performed a special pooja in the Tirukkadaiyur Temple, located at a distance of about 150 kilometres from Trichy.

Tirukkadaiyur Amritaghateswarar Abhirami Temple *is dedicated to the God Shiva in his manifestation as Kalantaka (Sanskrit: "Destroyer of Death") and his wife Parvati in her form as Abhirami (Sanskrit: "Lovely One"). It is located in Thirukkadaiyur (Thirukadavur), 21 kilometres East of Mayiladuthurai, Tamil Nadu. This temple is particularly associated with Shiva saving his devotee Markendeya from death and the tale of saint Abirami Pattar, a devotee of the presiding Goddess.*

It is one of the 275 Paadal Petra Sthalams, where three of the most revered Nayanars (Saivite Saints) Appar, Suntharar and Tirugnana Sambhandar have sung the glories of this temple. People perform Shasti Poorthi on completion of their 60 years, Bheemaradha Shanthi on completion of 69 years, Sadabishegam at the beginning of 80th year of their Star Birthday, Ayush-Homam for children to rid any future astrological difficulties arising from Navagrahas and Mirthunja-Homam to get relief from illness and save life.

We had a function in the Vincent Gardens, Trichy. Shyamala, Alex and Amenda made all the arrangements. We cut a big cake. Rev. Richard Reid prayed and blessed us. Amenda composed a song and played her composition on her violin. I gave a toast to June and Amelia. But Amelia, as usual, remained aloof during the celebration. About 150 people attended the function. It ended with a grand dinner.

Alex's New Job - May, 2004

When Alex accepted the job in Ranbaxy, Gurgaon in May 2004, Shyamala decided to stay in Chennai for one more year to continue Amenda's studies. We used to visit Chennai on the weekends.

In AMACE the hostel mess was good. Whenever June was held up in Chennai, I had my food in the mess. There were a few provision shops in front of the AMACE campus from where we bought our provisions and vegetables. There were also a few roadside eateries which served dosas and parottas. In addition, there were good hotels in Kanchipuram including two branches of Hotel Saravana Bhavan. June and I loved the snacks made there. Usually, I would take the bus to Kanchipuram to get food from there.

We had cable TV connection but unfortunately 50% of the time we did not get any reception.

Once, I got a severe toothache and the doctor in Kanchipuram referred me to a doctor in Chennai and after controlling diabetes, the tooth was extracted.

Amelia, Dinky, Darrel, Shyamala, Amenda, Alex, Joshua, Alex's mother and my sister visited us at different times. Tamil Arasi and Anjalai worked alternately in Chennai and Kanchipuram.

In the meantime, my uncle Padmanaban purchased a house in Padmanabhanagar, Adyar, Chennai and we all attended the house warming ceremony.

Shyamala's Life in Chennai - 2003 to 2005

Shyamala tutored some children in Chennai. This included Anupriya whose family became an integral part of our lives. She also became acquainted with Suresh from UK Travels. He also became close to our family and catered to our needs in an efficient manner.

Amenda's Credentials

Academics

Amenda studied VIth standard and VIIth standard in St. Patrick's Higher Secondary School and secured I[st] rank in both classes. Since she left Chennai in July 2005, I collected her proficiency certificate for VII standard. She also bagged two awards for best instrumental player. (Violin)

Language Issue

Amenda studied Tamil as the second language during VIth and VIIth standard in Chennai. She had studied Tamil in I[st] standard before moving to USA. In USA, she had been out of touch with the Tamil language for about five years. It was just a matter of time before

Amenda started scoring more than 90% in Tamil also. But when Shyamala decided to move to Gurgaon, the problem of second language arose again. Amenda did not know a word of Hindi so she had to opt for French. We found a French teacher in Chennai and arranged special coaching for Amenda.

Violin

I told you earlier that Amenda learnt violin in USA from James Preston. She continued her violin lessons in Chennai with Jayakumar master. Jayakumar master was an exceptional violinist and a very good teacher. He was the violinist, first in Maestro Ilayaraja's music group and then in Oscar winner A.R. Rahman's music group. She wrote the London Trinity School of music exam in Grade III violin in 2004 and passed with distinction (94%) and won the P. Subbarayan Memorial Prize for getting the highest mark in instrumental music and Dhanraj Memorial Cup for highest mark in practical violin.

Trinity College London (TCL) is an international exam board based in London, England. Trinity offers qualifications across a range of disciplines in the performing arts and English language learning and teaching. The board conducts exams in over 70 countries.

Trinity College London was founded as the external exams board of Trinity College of Music (known today as the Trinity Laban Conservatoire of Music and Dance), and began offering exams in music to external students in 1877.

In 2004, Trinity College London's performing arts examinations division merged with the external examinations department of the Guildhall School of Music and Drama to form the Trinity Guildhall examinations board. The name Trinity Guildhall was dropped in 2012, and renamed The Trinity College London brand.

Trinity College London offers graded musical qualifications for musical theory and for performance in string instruments, singing, piano, electronic keyboards, brass, woodwind instruments and percussion. The grading begins with the Initial Grade, and then are numbered from Grade 1 to Grade 8 in increasing difficulty. Candidates are rated under three categories – the performance of musical pieces, technical work such as scales, and supporting tests such as sight reading and improvisation. Candidates are graded on a scale from 1 to 100, with 60 being the pass mark.

TCL also offers foundation, intermediate and advanced certificates in music. TCL also offers diplomas in music at three levels - Associate (ATCL), Licentiate (LTCL) and Fellowship (FTCL).

Sports

She continued to play football and started tennis lessons.

Joshua's First Tonsure

As per Indian custom, we did his first tonsure in a saloon and visited the Catholic Church in Besant Nagar. Joshua freaked out and as a result got a few nicks here and there.

Joshua Starting his School

Joshua started attending Princess Naik Play School which was close to our home. He was quite a mischievous child. He would throw everything out of the window. In the middle of the night he would get up from the cot, open the refrigerator and drink water.

Shyamala Leaving Chennai to Settle in Gurgaon - 2005

When Shyamala decided to leave for Gurgaon in July 2006, I booked train tickets for Shyamala, Amenda, Joshua, June and Dinky. For the return trip, I booked fight tickets for June and Dinky. We booked Agarwal Packers and Movers for the household goods and the car (my Maruti Omni, which we decided to give them).

After booking the train tickets I wanted to give them to Shyamala but she asked to me to keep them and give them to her on the day of the travel. I was under the belief that I had booked the Tamil Nadu Express which would leave at 10 p.m.

On the day of travel (Saturday), we were casually seeing a movie "Mumbai Express" on the DVD player. It was around 2 p.m., and everyone was relaxed as the train was at 10 p.m. Suddenly, I remembered the tickets. When I started talking about the tickets again Shyamala wanted to take them later. But I did not know what compelled me to take out the tickets and glance at them. I was shocked to realise that I had booked tickets in the Grand Trunk Express which would leave at 4.45 p.m. When I made this known to Shyamala, she became very angry and started yelling. Amenda and Joshua ran out of the room confused. June and Dinky could not say anything. Darrel had gone out to meet his friend. Shyamala continued her ranting saying she would not go to Gurgaon. All of us were confused and upset. After 10 minutes, Shyamala calmed down and Dinky pacified her. Then Shyamala conceded. Everyone started getting ready. I booked two cars from UK Travels, I called Darrel and asked him to come directly to the station. We informed Anupriya's parents about the change in train timings. They were coming to the station for a small send off and also to provide dinner for the travel.

By 3.30 p.m., everything was ready. The taxis had arrived and we all left for Central Station. They boarded the train by 4.15 p.m. Darrel also arrived on time. Anupriya and her family also came and that too with the food. It was really a wonder that they could prepare everything at such short notice. We waited till the train departed from the station and then proceeded towards the exit. Then it hit me that none of us had purchased a platform ticket. To our ill luck we were asked for platform tickets. Anupriya's uncle was a policeman in the Tamil Nadu Police Department. He showed his ID and we were let off. I sighed in relief.

The next day, I packed the remaining things, which were at home, into a van and proceeded to Kanchipuram. Before leaving, I returned the house keys to the person in charge as the house owner was from Coimbatore.

Return of June and Dinky from Gurgaon

Darrel went back to Trichy. After helping Shyamala settle in Gurgaon, June and Dinky returned to Chennai. From the airport, Darrel picked up Dinky and left for Trichy and I took June to Kanchipuram.

Settling in Gurgaon

Shyamala and Alex rented House No. 8, in sector 40, near NH 8. Amenda was admitted to the VIIIth standard in Ryan International School affiliated to the Central Board of Secondary Education (CBSE) and she took French as the second language. Joshua was admitted in the same school in the Montessari I which had a campus for elementary wing near our house itself. Again, language was a problem and Shyamala and Alex put him in the Excelsior American School in the Montessari II in June 2006 since the school had the environment of an American school.

Amenda's Trips for Violin Examinations

Amenda had to fly from Delhi to take her Grade VI Violin examination in Chennai in 2005. June and I booked a guest house in Chennai. She was coached for three or four days by Jayakumar before she took the examination. She passed with merit (79%). She won three prizes namely: Music Director Kalyan Prize, Hindle Manuel Sight Reading Cup and Ist prize for highest marks in Instrumental music.

She came again in 2006 for her Grade VII examination. She passed with merit (80%) and bagged the music director Kalyan Prize.

Since she could not find a violin instructor in Gurgaon, she would regularly speak to Jayakumar on the telephone. She practiced mainly through oral instructions.

Arumuga Rajan's Marriage - October 27, 2006

Uncle Padmanaban's only son, Arumuga Rajan (we call him Raja), is lawyer practicing in the Madras High Court. His marriage was fixed on October 27 in Raja Rajeshwari marriage hall in Chennai. June started to help aunty and uncle in the various activities of the marriage. She bought a beautiful black sari and I bought her a pair of diamond earrings (first gift from me after 39 years of marriage). Just two days before the marriage, the North-East monsoon became vigorous and heavy rains started lashing Chennai. I travelled up and down between Kanchipuram and Chennai for attending pre-marriage functions and college work. June stayed for almost 15 days in Chennai in uncle's house.

It rained continuously and heavily from the afternoon of October 26 flooding the streets of Chennai making it difficult to travel on the road. The marriage activities were performed with difficulty.

On the morning of 27th, June, Pappa and I went to bring the bride from her uncle's house in Chennai to the marriage hall. We went in a car in the pouring rain and somehow brought the bride without any hitch. By this time, water had reached up to the entrance of the marriage hall. The kitchen became flooded. By 9 a.m., the rain water started subsiding preventing flooding of the marriage hall. It was an unforgettable marriage for everyone. It was the last marriage attended by June which she enjoyed the best.

Why did you decide to leave Kanchipuram for Gurgaon?

Shyamala joined Salwan Public School in Gurgaon as a Chemistry teacher in March 2007. Even though B.Ed. is the minimum qualification along with a post graduate degree, Shyamala was given the job without a B.Ed. (Bachelor of Education) degree because it is her gift to be recognized as a person having potential talent in any endeavour she undertakes.

In the meantime, Prakash, eldest brother of Alex, was diagnosed with brain cancer. Prakash had two sons. His second son, Prince, had just completed the 10th standard board examination and was waiting to join 11th standard. At Shyamala's suggestion, Alex and Shyamala decided to bring Prince to Gurgaon to complete his higher secondary schooling. But, in Gurgaon, 11th standard had already started in April. By the influence of Shyamala, the Principal admitted him in July 2007 in the 11th standard.

Shyamala found it difficult to simultaneously work and look after the three children. In early 2007, Alex and she asked us to come to Gurgaon so that it would be helpful to all of them.

After giving some thought, we told them that we would come in July 2007 after completing all the work at AMACE.

This is the background for leaving Kanchipuram for Gurgaon. After all, our purpose was that we should be useful to others wherever we are.

Leaving Kanchipuram - July 12, 2007

Since we had decided to leave Kanchipuram in July 2007, I gave my resignation letter with 3 months' notice period. The Principal, Director and the Managing Trustee accepted it even though they desired that I continue with them. My relieving date was fixed as July 11, 2007.

By July 10th, I completed all the academic and administrative work. As usual, Kaliaperumal and Tamilarasi came to assist us in vacating the house and June distributed few things to Amelia aunty, Dinky, Pappa and Tamilarasi. The department and the college gave me a farewell party. On the morning of July 12th, we left the AMACE campus by taxi for my uncle's house in Chennai. After staying the night in their house we left by Rajdhani Express on July 13 at 6.15 a.m., for Delhi.

The journey was very nice and we reached Nizamuddin railway station, New Delhi by 11.30 a.m., and Alex came to pick us up.

After spending 64 years in South India, you were going to live in North India. What were your feelings?

After all, we were not going to live alone there, we were going to live with my daughter's family and that too we were going for a purpose. We were quite happy.

Above all, I got a chance to perform many things for the first time in my professional life which was unexpected.

Wherever you went you had many special things to do. I am eager to know about your life in Gurgaon.

I never expected that God would put me again in a place where He wanted me. I got a job with great responsibility and new achievements brought me quite a few recognitions. In my personal life, among many good things I had, the one which gave all of us joy and pride was Amenda getting admitted in All India Institute of Medical Sciences (AIIMS), New Delhi. AIIMS is a dream institute for any student aspiring to study medicine.

But along with so many good things, the worst tragedy happened on November 6, 2010 when June suddenly passed away.

Oh! Very sad to hear that. Your life has been a mixture of happy and sad moments.

Around Me

Let us go through the major events that took place during this period.

India

Politics

Founding of Janata Dal (United), 2003 - Janata Dal (United) or JDU was formed with the merger of the Sharad Yadav faction of the Janata Dal, the Lok Shakti Party and the Samta Party on October 30, 2003. JDU party's mentor and patron was the veteran socialist leader George Fernandes. It is present only in Bihar and Jharkhand.

XIVth Indian General Elections, 2004 - The general elections were held on April 20, April 26, May 5 and May 10 in 2004 to elect the 14th Lok Sabha. INC fought under United Progressive Alliance (UPA) and BJP fought under National Democratic Alliance (NDA). INC (UPA) won 218 seats. (INC 145; RJD 21; DMK 16; PMK 6; MDMK 4; NCP 9; others 17). Outside support was 117 (Left Front 59; BSP 19; SP 36; others 3), National Democratic alliance (NDA) won 181 seats. (BJP 138; Shiv Sena 12; Biju JD 11; Shironmani Akali Dal 8; others 12).

Manmohan Singh became Prime Minister, 2004 - Manmohan Singh, a technocrat, took the oath as the Prime Minister of India on May 22, 2004. Sonia Gandhi became the Chairperson of UPA.

Visit of Manmohan Singh to USA and the Frame Work for the Nuke Deal, 2005 - Manmohan Singh visited USA during July 15 to 21, 2005 when George W. Bush was the President. India agreed to separate its civil and military nuclear facilities and to place all its civil nuclear facilities under International Atomic Energy Agency (IAEA) safeguards and in exchange, US agreed to work toward full civil nuclear cooperation with India.

Name change from Pondicherry to Puducherry, 2006 - The name Pondicherry was officially changed to Puducherry on September 20, 2006.

Visit by George Bush, 2006 - At the invitation of Dr. Manmohan Singh, U.S. President George W. Bush visited India during March 1-3, 2006. The joint statement issued focused on the efforts of the two countries for economic prosperity and trade, energy security and clean environment, innovation and the knowledge economy, global safety and security and deepening democracy and meeting international challenges. They also emphasised their agreement on civil nuclear cooperation.

Birth of the Maharashtra Navnirman Sena Party (MNS), 2006 - This is a Maharashtrian Nationalist Party based in Maharashtra and operates on the motto "Sons of the Soil". It was founded on March 9, 2006 in Mumbai by Raj Thackeray after he left the Shiv Sena party due to differences with his paternal cousin, Uddhav Thackeray, and to his side-lining in major decisions like distribution of election tickets.

Reopening of Nathu La Pass, 2006 - Nathu La is an open trading border post between China and India; the others being Shipkila in Himachal Pradesh and Lipulekh (or Lipulech) in Nepal. Sealed by India after the 1962 Sino-Indian War, Nathu La was reopened on July 6, 2006 following numerous bilateral trade agreements.

Agreement between India and Russia to develop FGFA, 2007 - Following the success of the BrahMos project, Russia and India agreed in early 2007 to jointly study and develop a Fifth Generation Fighter Aircraft (FGFA) programme.

Space Technology

Launching of 10th PSLV with 4 satellites, 2007 - On January 10, 2007, 10th Polar Satellite Launch Vehicle put four satellites into orbit. The PSLV-C7 blasted off into space at 9.24 a.m., from the spaceport at the Satish Dhawan Space Centre in Sriharikota, 160 kilometres from Chennai.

Return of SRE-1, 2007 - Indian spacecraft SRE-1 successfully completed a twelve-day orbital test flight, making India one of the few nations to return a craft from orbit.

Bombings and Death Toll

54 were people killed in the Mumbai twin bombings on August 25, 2003, 62 in Delhi on October 29, 2005, 28 in Varanasi on March 7, 2006, 200 in train bombings in Mumbai on July 7, 2006, 68 in train (Delhi-Lahore) bombings near Panipat on February 18, 2007 and 16 in Hyderabad Mecca Masjid bombing on May 18, 2007.

Accidents

Mandher Devi Temple Stampede, 2005 - 291 pilgrims were killed in the stampede on January 25, 2005 in the Mandher Devi Temple, Wai, Maharashtra.

West Bengal Train Disaster, 2006 - Five people were killed in a train accident (suspected terrorist act) in West Bengal on November 20, 2006.

Others

Shooting in IISc. Bangalore, 2005 - The shooting occurred on December 28, 2005 at the Indian Institute of Science (IISc), Bangalore, killing Prof. Munish Chandra Puri of IIT Delhi.

Nandigram Violence, 2007 - It was an incident in Nandigram, West Bengal where the Communist Party of India (Marxist) forcefully tried to acquire land for SEZ (Special Economic Zone). Farmers of the locality were adamant that they did not want to give up their land and agitated under the banner of Bhoomi Raksha Committee. The governor was in air and no contact was available. So, the police entered the Nandigram area and violence erupted. In the police shootings, at least 14 villagers were killed and 70 wounded. This incident played an important role in the politics of West Bengal for the next few years. Mamata Banerjee and her political party widely mentioned this issue along with the political war cry 'Ma Mati Manush' in their election campaigns.

Tamil Nadu

Arrest of Jayendra Saraswathi, 2004 - Jayendra Saraswathi, seer of Kanchi Mutt, was arrested on November 12, 2004 in Mehboob Nagar, Hyderabad in connection with the murder of Sankararaman, the manager of Varadharaja Perumal Temple in Kanchipuram, Tamil Nadu on September 3, 2004 in the premises of the temple. Later, Vijayendra Saraswathi, another seer was also arrested.

XIIIth Tamil Nadu Elections, 2006 - The XIIIth Legislative Assembly election was held on May 8, 2006 for all 234 constituencies. The contest was between two major alliances in a seat sharing agreement, the AIADMK alliance and the DMK alliance. DMK alliance won 163 seats (DMK 96; INC 34; PMK 18; CPI(M) 9; CPI 6). AIADMK alliance won 69 seats (AIADMK 61; MDMK 6; VCK 2).

Karunanidhi became Chief Minister, 2006 - M. Karunanidhi was sworn in as Chief Minister of Tamil Nadu for the fifth time on May 13, 2006.

Birth of Desiya Murpokku Dravida Kazhagam (DMDK), 2005 - Desiya Murpokku Dravida Kazhagam (DMDK) is a regional political party formed by Tamil film actor Vijayakanth Naidu in Tamil Nadu, along the lines of the regional Dravidian political parties on September 14, 2005 in Madurai.

Kumbakonam School Fire, 2004 - The fire accident happened in a school in Kumbakonam town, Thanjavur district. A total of 94 students of the primary section of the Krishna English Medium School were burnt to death in their classroom as the thatched roof caught fire on July 16, 2004.

Tsunami in Tamil Nadu, 2004 - More than 1,500 people were killed and hundreds more went missing when tsunamis triggered by a massive earthquake (the biggest in four decades at 8.9 on the Richter scale), near the Indonesian islands of Sumatra slammed into the southern peninsular coast of India on the morning of Sunday,

December 26, 2004. According to estimates, there were 750 deaths in Nagapattinam, 250 in Kanyakumari, 200 in Cuddalore, 150 in Chennai and 100 in Puducherry.

Killing of Veerappan, 2004 - Koose Muniswamy Veerappan, born on January 18, 1952 was a notorious Indian brigand and dacoit. He was active for nearly 30 years in the scrub lands and forests in the states of Karnataka, Kerala and Tamil Nadu. On October 18, 2004, Veerappan and two of his associates were killed by the Tamil Nadu Special Task Force headed by K. Vijay Kumar.

World

Politics

ASEAN Business and Investment Summit, 2003 - The Prime Minister Vajpayee attended the ASEAN Business and Investment Summit during October 5-7, 2003 in Bali, Indonesia. ASEAN's efforts towards greater economic integration were given a deeper dimension with the successful convening of the inaugural ASEAN BIS.

George W. Bush Became US President, 2005 - George W. Bush was elected as US President for the second time and he took office from August 20, 2005.

Execution of Saddam Hussein, 2006 - The execution of Saddam Hussein took place on December 30, 2006 at the joint Iraqi-American military base Camp Justice in Kazimain, a northeastern suburb of Baghdad. He was sentenced to death by hanging, and convicted of crimes against humanity by the Iraqi Special Tribunal for the murder of 148 Iraqi Shi'ites in the town of Dujail in 1982, in retaliation for an assassination attempt against him.

Gordon Brown Became PM of UK, 2007 - James Gordon Brown, Scottish-born British Labour Party politician, became the Prime Minister of the United Kingdom on June 27, 2007 after Tony Blair.

Space Technology

Spirit (Rover) landed in Mars, 2004 - Spirit or MER-A (Mars Exploration Rover – A) or MER-2, is a robotic rover on Mars, active from 2004 to 2010. It landed successfully on Mars at 04.35 Ground UTC on January 4, 2004, three weeks before its twin, Opportunity (MER-B), landed on the other side of the planet. Its name was chosen through a NASA-sponsored student essay competition.

Huygens landed on Saturn's Moon Titan, 2005 - Huygens was the first atmospheric entry probe that landed successfully on Saturn's moon Titan in 2005. Built and operated by the European Space Agency (ESA), it was part of the Cassini–Huygens mission. The probe was named after the Dutch 17th century astronomer Christiaan Huygens, who discovered Titan in 1655.

Launching of New Horizons, 2006 - New Horizons, an interplanetary space probe was launched on January 19, 2006 from Cape Canaveral Air Force Station directly into an Earth-and-solar escape trajectory with a speed of about 16.26 kilometres per second. It was part of NASA's New Frontiers Program engineered by the Johns Hopkins University Applied Physics Laboratory (APL) and the Southwest Research Institute (SwRI), with a team led by S. Alan Stern. The role of the spacecraft was to perform a flyby study of the Pluto system.

China's Anti-Satellite Missile Test, 2007 - On January 11, 2007, China conducted an anti-satellite missile test. A Chinese weather satellite, the FY-1C polar orbit satellite of the Fengyun series, at an altitude of 865 kilometres with a mass of 750 kg was destroyed by a kinetic kill vehicle traveling with a speed of 8 km/s in the opposite direction.

Climate Change

UNFCCC, COP 9, Milan, 2003 - The ninth COP was in Milan, Italy during December 1-12, 2003. There were 22 decisions and 1 resolution. The focus was on the institutions and procedures of the Kyoto Protocol and on the implementation of the UNFCCC.

UNFCCC, COP 10, Buenos Aries, 2004 - The tenth COP was held in Buenos Aries during December 6-17, 2004. There were 18 decisions and 1 resolution. COP 10 discussed the progress made since the first Conference of the Parties 10 years ago and its future challenges, with special stress on climate change mitigation and adaptation.

IPCC Third Assessment Report, 2005 - The Third Assessment Report (TAR) was completed in 2001 and consists of four reports, three of them from its working groups covering the scientific basis, impacts, adaptation, vulnerability and mitigation of climate change and a synthesis report.

UNFCCC, COP 11, Montreal, 2005 - The eleventh COP was held in Montreal, Quebec, Canada during November 28 to December 9, 2005. There were 15 decisions and 1 resolution. It was the first Meeting of the Parties (CMP 1) since their initial meeting in Kyoto in 1997. It was one of the largest intergovernmental conferences on climate change and marked the implementation of the Kyoto Protocol.

UNFCCC, COP 12, Nairobi, 2006 - The twelfth COP was held in Nairobi, Kenya during November 6-17, 2006. There were 9 decisions and 1 resolution. Decisions were adopted to mitigate climate change and help countries adapt to the effects. There was agreement on the activities under the "Nairobi Work Programme on Impacts, Vulnerability and Adaptation", as well as on the management of the Adaptation Fund under the Kyoto Protocol.

Sports

XXVIII Olympiad, Athens, 2004 - The 2004 Summer Olympic Games were held in Athens, Greece, from August 13 to 29, 2004 with the motto "Welcome Home". It marked the return of the games to the city where they began in 1896. A new medal obverse was introduced at these Games, replacing the design by Giuseppe Cassioli used since the 1928 Games.

Death

Death of Yasser Arafat, 2004 - Yasser Arafat, the President of the Palestinian National Authority and Chairman of the Palestine Liberation Organization, died unexpectedly on November 11, 2004, 75 years of age, after a short period of illness.

Bombings and Death Toll

192 people were killed in the Madrid train bombings in Spain on March 11, 2004, 52 in train bombings in London on July 11, 2005, 135 in Baghdad bombing in a market on February 3, 2007 and 32 people in Virginia Tech shooting in USA on April 16, 2007.

CHAPTER - 13

Life in Gurgaon, Part I - July 2007 to November 2010

ABSTRACT

Me

The details of our arrival in Gurgaon (2007), joining Ansal Institute of Technology (2007) and Institute of Technology and Management (2008), Amenda's violin examinations (2008), death of Prakash (2009), Amenda's 10th and 12th board examinations (2008 and 2010), Amenda's credentials, Joshua's change of school (2010), Amenda's medical entrance examinations (2010), Amenda's admission in AIIMS (2010), Shyamala's trip to Australia (2010), Alex's move to Daiichi Sankyo (2010), change of house for June and me (2010), Diwali and June's last night in this world (2010) are presented.

Around Me

In India, the major events were Pratibha Patil as President (2007), IVF in AIIMS (2007), visit of Iranian President (2008), completion of IGMDP (2008), Nuke Deal and vote of confidence (2008), launching Agni missile III (2008), Abhinav's gold in Beijing Olympics (2008), Mumbai attack (2008), 10 satellites in single launch (2008), launching Chandrayan I (2009), water found on Moon (2009), Prithvi II Missile (2009), 15th general elections and Manmohan Singh continuing as Prime Minister (2009), Meira Kumar becoming first woman Speaker of Lok Sabha (2009), launching of anti-surface missile Dhanush (2009), launching of Radar Imaging Satellite 3 (2009), launching of Project to ID 1.2 Billion people (2010), Putin's visit (2010) and India finishing second in Common Wealth Games, New Delhi (2010).

In the World, the major events were the meeting of North and South Korean leaders for the second time (2007), climate change conference (2007), Benazir assassinated (2007), Nepal becoming democratic (2008), Russian new President Dmitri Medvedev (2008), Phoenix Lander on Mars (2008), US-Iraq forces agreement II (2008), Global food and financial crisis (2008), China's manned satellite (2008), defeat of Tamil Tigers (2008), Bill Gates's retirement (2008), Big Bang experiment (2008), Obama becoming President of US (2009), Israel's Palestine peace plan (2009), Copenhagen Summit (2009), Bing search engine (2009), death of Michael Jackson (2009) and David Cameron as Prime Minister of UK (2010).

You have shifted from the state of Tamil Nadu (Nadir) to the state of Haryana in the North Capital Region (NCR). Please tell us about your life in Gurgaon.

Reaching Shyamala's House, Gurgaon

Alex brought us home in his new Alto and after unloading the luggage we had our lunch.

Gurugram (formerly Gurgaon) is a city in the Indian state of Haryana and is part of the National Capital Region of India. It is 32 kilometres southwest of New Delhi and 268 kilometres southwest of Chandigarh, the state capital. Since 2011, witnessing rapid urbanisation, Gurgaon has become a leading financial and industrial hub with the third-highest per capita income in India. The city's economic growth story started when the leading Indian automobile manufacturer Maruti Suzuki India Limited established a manufacturing plant in Gurugram in the 1970's. Today, Gurugram has local offices of more than 250 Fortune 500 companies. It is known for high rise buildings and shopping malls. In addition to road, rail and air transport it has metro and rapid metro also. The name-change to Gurugram came from a proposal by the Chief Minister of Haryana, Manohar Lal Khattar, on April 12, 2016.

Shyamala was staying in a three bedroom individual house on the ground floor. It had a big hall cum dining space, one small pooja space, two attached bathrooms and one common bathroom. We parked both cars in the open yard in front of our gated house. The staircase by the side of the house led to two floors above us. Both families had small children. Alex, Shyamala and Joshua occupied the master bed room. Amenda had her own bedroom so that she could study without disturbance. Prince and Alex's mother occupied the smaller bedroom.

June and I occupied the hall which was converted into a bedroom. The dining space served as both the living room and dining hall.

Searching for a job

Amenda was studying in 10th standard in Ryan International School, Joshua was in 1st standard in Excelsior American School and Prince was studying in 11th standard in Salwan Public School. Shyamala was working as a teacher in Salwan Public School and Alex was working in Ranbaxy. June and Alex's mother helped in cooking. I just helped in taking the children for Karate classes. With great difficulty, I transferred the deposits from SBI Kanchipuram to SBI in Sector 31 due to lack of residence proof. After about 10 days of our stay both June and Shyamala felt that I could try for a teaching job in self - financing private Engineering Colleges in Gurgaon. In the meantime, Alex's mother went back to Coimbatore. I was just about to complete 64 years on August 24, 2007. I went in person to World College of Technology and Management, and Dronacharya College of Engineering but got no positive response. I sent my resume by mail to Institute of Technology and Management, Gurgaon.

Getting Job in Ansal Institute of Technology, Gurgaon (AITG)

I visited Ansal Institute of Technology in sector 55 on August 22 where I got the first favourable response.

I met the Registrar and he took my CV to the Deputy Director. In less than five minutes they called me for a discussion and immediately offered me the post of Deputy Registrar, Examinations. When asked about my expected salary, I humbly replied that I had been getting consolidated salary of Rs. 25,000 earlier. They agreed to pay me the same amount. They asked me to join at the earliest and I joined duty on August 24, on my 64th birthday. I just had a break of 42 days. I had one teaching course in Mechanics of Structures. I was also provided with an Executive Assistant. My experience as Chief Superintendent of Examinations, Anna University clinched this job for me.

I introduced a decent system of conducting the examinations and devised a good seating plan. When I visited the college after four years, they told me that they were following the same system that had been developed by me.

There was no Civil Engineering Department. They followed a special system of education in which students could study for two years at AITG and then complete their UG degree in Engineering at a University in USA.

The timings were very inconvenient, 9.00 a.m., to 6.30 p.m., and 6 days a week.

I left the house at 7.30 a.m., and returned by 8.30 p.m. I travelled in shared autos and mini bus. During the Diwali semester break, I went to Chennai.

They conducted an international conference during December 2007. I was one of the lucky people to interact with a Nobel Laureate and ask him a question. After the conference, there was a party in a farm house and I danced along with the other faculty.

During the next even semester, I was given two courses, Strength of Materials and Mat lab. Online feedback by students was favourable to me.

Call from Prof. Nakra, Institute of Technology and Management, Gurgaon (ITM)

Institute of Technology and Management (ITM), now known as The NorthCap University, is situated in the heart of Gurgaon in sector 23-A. It was started in the year 1996 by Educate India Society. But, the Bachelor of Technology in the Civil Engineering programme was started in July 2007. They required Civil Engineering faculty from July 2008. Prof. Nakra, a distinguished Professor retired from IIT Delhi was the Head of the Department of Mechanical Engineering and at the same time in charge of recruitment of faculty in Civil Engineering. He received my CV from Prof. K. K. Choudhary another retired Professor from IIT Delhi.

After going through my CV, Nakra invited me to ITM for discussions. When I went to ITM for the first time in April 2008, I was made to sit in the reception area and Nakra came personally and took me to his cabin. We discussed about ITM and about my willingness to join as faculty. Then we went to the Principal Rakesh Ranjan and discussed about the total emoluments which came out to be Rs. 49,000 per month. The designation would be Associate Professor. Then we went to meet the governing body members. Avdhesh Mishra, one of the governing body members, spoke to me and asked me when I could join. I replied that I could join on May 9, after completing my responsibilities at AIT, Gurgaon. When he asked about the date 9, I said 9 suits me as per numerology. He smiled and asked me to join on May 9, 2008. A letter of intent was issued to me on the same day. Before I could join I was in touch with Nakra regarding purchase of laboratory equipment.

I went home and discussed this with June and Shyamala and both were happy. But there was slight hesitation on my part wondering how I would establish the entire department at my age and at a new place. But June and Shyamala encouraged me to take it up.

Joining ITM - May 9, 2008

I gave one months' notice at AIT and immediately the Director sent word through others to find out the reason and whether I needed more salary. I told them that I was planning to go back to Tamil Nadu. I thought if I told them the real reason they may try to spoil it. The Director also called me to his office but he did not ask me anything directly. Anyway, I got relieved on May 7, 2008 and after resting for one day, I joined ITM on May 9, 2008 as planned.

__Institute of Technology and Management, Gurgaon__ was started in 1996 by Educate India Society, affiliated to Maharshi Dayanand University, Rohtak. It became an autonomous institute in 2009 and it was elevated to a Private University by the Haryana Government in 2010 and the name was changed to The NorthCap University in the year 2015.

Setting Up the Laboratories

I was given a cabin in the Department of Mechanical Engineering. H. K. Mishra, retired Director, Indian Telephone Industries, joined the department just before me.

I made plans to set up the Concrete, Surveying and Structural Analysis laboratories. I was made Chairman, Purchase Committee for procuring a Universal Testing machine. I successfully purchased and installed it in the Strength of Materials laboratory under the Department of Mechanical Engineering. Before the classes could start in July 2008, I had set up the Concrete, Surveying and Structural Analysis laboratories. Two rooms on the second floor of the main building were allotted for Structural Analysis and Engineering Geology laboratories. One room was allotted in the workshop area for Concrete and Surveying laboratories.

Faculty Recruitment - July to September, 2008

We selected Dr. A. K. Mishra, specialized in Geology, Hydrology and Remote Sensing, as Lecturer in July 2008 and Niragi Dave with Master of Technology in Structures as Lecturer in September 2008. A. K. Mishra set up the Engineering Geology laboratory.

Inauguration of SPACE, Professional Society - November 27, 2008

A Civil Engineering professional society, SPACE (Society in Pursuit of Advances in Civil Engineering) was started on November 27, 2008 initiated by a second-year student, Sakshi Gupta. It was inaugurated by A.P. Singh of Larson and Toubro Ltd, New Delhi.

Establishment of the Department of Civil Engineering - December, 2008

A function was arranged in December 2008 to launch the Department of Civil Engineering and Principal Rakesh Ranjan informed me that I would be the Head of the Department. H. K. Mishra was upset because he thought he would be the Head since he had joined ITM before me.

I went to thank the governing body members. Avdhesh Mishra came out of his chamber and when I said thanks for making me the Head, he just took my right hand and put it on his heart and said, "Professor, you would be doing great things here. Wish you all the best." I and others in the veranda were surprised by his gesture.

Strike by Students - February, 2009

In the even semester of 2008-09, in February 2009, Niragi complained that two students in her class harassed her by asking questions repeatedly in spite of answering them. Mishra and I told her that we would make an enquiry and ask the students to apologise. But she did not agree with us and made a written complaint to the disciplinary committee. After the initial inquiry, the two students were suspended for a week. The same week, some students of other branches were also suspended. When leaving the college on Friday, the day of their suspension I met the two suspended students outside the college campus and I told them not to worry about attendance or the classes missed. The students seemed to be satisfied. When we came on Monday, everything was normal in the morning session. When the afternoon session started all the students left their classes and assembled near the main gate shouting slogans.

Unfortunately, the next day, they converted this into a strike and the worst part was that the strike was led by the two suspended students of Civil Engineering Department. It continued for a week and was resolved after a lot of efforts by the administration.

Recruitment of Faculty - 2009 to 2010

Dr. V. Gayathri, who had specialized in Geotechnical Engineering from IIT Delhi, came to see Nakra along with her husband Narayanan in November 2008. After an interaction, Nakra sent her to meet me. I took her resume and briefed her about the department and ITM. Gayathri said that she would be able to join only after six months due to domestic issues. She finally attended the interview towards the end of April 2009 and joined as Associate Professor on May 4, 2009. She set up the Soil Mechanics and Foundation Engineering laboratory in a new room allotted in the workshop area.

In July 2009, Col. (retd). H.S. Dhull, with a specialization in Environmental Engineering from IIT Roorkee was appointed as Lecturer. He set up the Transportation Engineering laboratory in the Concrete laboratory itself.

Vaishali Sahu, who had specialized in Environmental Engineering from IIT, Roorkee, joined as Lecturer on September 9, 2009 and she set up the Environmental Engineering laboratory in a new room in the workshop area.

Dr. Ram Karan Singh, specialized in Water Resources and Environmental Engineering from BITS Pilani, was appointed as Professor in January 2010. In the same month Prachi Sohoni with specialization in Structures joined as lecturer. She set up the Computer laboratory in one half of the Engineering Geology laboratory in 2011. By the end of academic year 2010-11, we had six laboratories - Soil Mechanics and Foundation Engineering, Environmental and Surveying, Concrete and Transportation - located in the workshop area and three laboratories - Structural Analysis, Engineering Geology and Computer - in the main building.

ITM became Autonomous - July, 2009

ITM became autonomous from July 2009 under Maharshi Dayanand University. A new curriculum was designed and approved, initially by the Board of Studies and then by the Academic Council.

Presentation to Governing Body - December, 2009

I presented the report of the department and the future plan of the department in the form of PowerPoint slides to the members of the governing body on December 11, 2009 with a timeline. All but consultancy projects, mentioned as future plan, had been completed.

Pay revision and Anomaly - 2010

Sixth pay commission scales were implemented at ITM from April 2009 but with monetary benefit from July 2009. My basic was fixed in the Assistant Professor scale instead of in Associate Professor scale of Pay. As usual I waited for a year and brought this to the attention of the governing body through Avdhesh Mishra in June 2010. Immediately, Mishra took out a paper and asked me "Krishnamoorthi Saab, how much you want your basic salary to be in the Associate Professor scale?"

I was caught unawares but still I managed to say, "Sir, as per your wish."

The order came in September 2009 that I would be paid the new revised salary from the month of October 2010. June was very happy to see the order which showed that my revised total emoluments had crossed the six-figure mark for the first time in my career.

But, she did not live to see the salary being paid into my account.

ITM Elevated as University - July, 2010

Based on its track record, ITM was elevated to private university status by the Government of Haryana in 2009 and started functioning as a university from July 2010.

Starting of Ph.D. Programme - July, 2010

Ph.D. programme in Civil Engineering was started in July 2010 and two scholars joined the programme, one of them was Vaishali Sahu, our own faculty.

Amenda's Violin Examinations - November 2007 and 2008

Amenda passed her VIII grade violin examination with merit (72%) in 2007 and got the first prize. She also obtained her Performance Certificate in violin with merit (80%) in 2008.

Death of Prakash, Alex's Brother - January 2009

Just before the practical Board examinations in February 2009, Alex's brother Prakash, who was suffering from cancer, passed away on January 30 only a day after Alex visited him. Shyamala took Prince to Coimbatore for the funeral and after completing the formalities Alex, Shyamala and Prince returned to Gurgaon. It was a very sad moment for all of us and more so for Prince at the sudden loss of his father. Prince wrote his examinations and I coached him for Pre-Medical Entrance Examinations. He did not qualify in the first round and later joined a Dental College in Madurai.

Uncle Padmanaban's 50th Wedding Anniversary - September, 2009

Uncle Padmanaban and aunty Shantha celebrated their 50th wedding anniversary in September 2009. Padmanaban is a very successful lawyer practicing criminal law in Chennai. He was first based in Trichy. He has won many cases by his candid arguments and sound knowledge of law. Shantha is a multitalented lady who excels in administration, cooking, writing, painting and dancing. They are blessed with Priya, a lawyer, married to Chellappa (Retd). Principal, settled in Trichy, Bala, a medical doctor married to Annadurai, an Engineer settled in USA, Devi, a medical doctor married to Sudhir, settled in USA, Rani, a doctorate in Psychology married to (late) Mohanraj, settled in Chennai, Kala, a medical doctor married to Vaithianathan, an Engineer settled in USA, Arumuga Rajan, a lawyer married to Anitha settled in Chennai and Gayathri married to Selvaraj, a businessman settled in Singapore. Unfortunately, their daughter Prahada passed away at a young age. They have granddaughters, Sukanya, Sharanya, Tanya, Maya, Priyanka, Varsha, Ambal, Krithika, Ananya and grandsons, Vijay, Santhosh, and Shrawan.

Joshua's Change of School to DPS Gurgaon - March, 2010

Joshua completed third standard in Excelsior American School in March 2010 and was admitted in Delhi Public School, sector 45, Gurgaon in fourth standard from March 2010. He did exceedingly well in both academics and extracurricular activities in the Excelsior American School.

Amenda's 10th and 12th Board examinations 2008 and 2010

Amenda scored 92% in the 10th Board examinations in 2008 and she was admitted in Delhi Public School (DPS) Vasant Kunj, New Delhi for her 11th and 12th standards. Amenda scored 96.7% in the 12th Board examinations in 2010 with a 100% in Chemistry

Amenda's Other Credentials

Amenda received many awards in school like Academic Genius, Scholar Badge Proficiency, and Best Girl. She was conferred the Times NIE (Newspaper in Education) Award by Times of India in 2007. She was the recipient of National Science Talent Examination Scholarship in 2008 and Kishore Vaigyanik Protshan Yojana (KVPY) Scholarship in 2009. She was among top 35 students from India to qualify for Indian National Biology Olympiad and was awarded gold medals in 2009 and 2010. She attended training at Homi Bhabha Centre for Science Education for the same.

Amenda's Entrance Examinations for MBBS Programme - May - June 2010

Amenda joined Aakash Coaching Institute, Delhi in 2008 for medical entrance exam coaching. She received 50% waiver in her tuition fees since she secured first rank in the entrance examination.

Amenda cleared the preliminary level examination of AIPMT and secured All India 16th rank in the final level. She also secured 5th rank in the Delhi quota entrance examination. She was waiting for the result of AIIMS. In the meantime, she joined Maulana Azad Medical College, Delhi. When the results came for AIIMS, she got the 30th rank and was eligible for admission into AIIMS under General category.

June's Happiest Moment

June wanted Shyamala to become a doctor but she chose science stream instead. June wanted Amenda to do medicine and when she got selected in AIIMS, June was the happiest person. I have never seen June so happy in 43 years of my life with her.

Amenda's Admission in AIIMS - August, 2010

Amenda cancelled her admission in Maulana Azad Medical College and joined the prestigious AIIMS in August 2010.

All India Institute of Medical Sciences (AIIMS), New Delhi was conceived by the dreams of Nehru and Amrit Kaur (Health Minister) and the recommendations of the Joseph Bhore Committee through a proposal which found favour with the government of New Zealand. A generous grant from New Zealand under the Colombo Plan made it possible to lay the foundation stone of AIIMS in 1952. AIIMS was finally created in 1956, as an autonomous institution through an Act of Parliament, to serve as a nucleus for nurturing excellence in all aspects of health care. It is situated in Ansari Nagar, New Delhi.

Shyamala's Trip to Australia – September, 2010

Shyamala was sponsored by Salwan Public School to attend the 6th International Students Science Fair in 2010 in Australia along with four students. The fair was held during September 13 to 18, 2010, in Adelaide, Australia. The students made a presentation on "Ethno pharmacological Studies using Paspalum Scorbiculatum as Anti- Diabetic Agent". More than 12 countries across the world participated in it.

Purchase of Ranbaxy by Daiichi Sankyo, Japan - 2008 to 2010

Daiichi Sankyo Company Ltd. was founded on September 28, 2005 through the merger of Daiichi Pharmaceutical and Sankyo. Its head office is in Tokyo, Japan. It Purchased Ranbaxy Laboratories Limited in 2008 and Alex became an employee of Daiichi Sankyo from 2010.

Change of house for June and Me – October, 2010

June and Shyamala did not get along sometimes due to small misunderstandings. Earlier, Mr. Balan Nair, an astrologer, had indicated that mother and daughter staying together for a long time should be avoided. June wanted, at least, to live separately in Gurgaon itself since I could not leave my job. It was only a minor misunderstanding and it did not require such a big decision. I was trying to pacify her but could not succeed. As soon as Amenda got a medical seat in AIIMS in 2010, she became more adamant and without a choice and against my conscience I started looking for a house close to the present one. I consoled myself that I also needed more space for my work. I felt that it would be better to be a little apart so that the affection would be more. This was the message given in the Tamil movie "Samsaram Athu Minsaram" by the director Vishu. I got a furnished three bedroom house in Jalvayu Vihar, B-86 on the second floor. (Normally, I would not have considered No 86 since I don't want 8 in my house or vehicle- just a superstition). There were quite a few bad omens.

One of the worst was the milk boiling function. On that day, it was raining heavily and we were not able to light the gas to boil the milk. I tried to change the regulator but we failed. We left the house without doing the ceremony which is a must for anyone moving into a house for the first time.

Anyway, we shifted on October 6, Wednesday and within two to three days my daughter also shifted to B-65 which was one block away from us. Then June started helping to settle Shyamala's house as our house did not require much arrangement. I had lot of space in the new house to do my own work.

Everything went on smoothly.

Dinner for Amenda's Friends

A dinner party was arranged for Amenda and her new friends at AIIMS. June enthusiastically prepared the dinner for all.

Commonwealth Games - October 3 -14, 2010

We purchased a new 32 inches TV Sansui, put Tata Sky dish connection and enjoyed the Commonwealth Games 2010 held in

New Delhi. Saina winning Singles Title in Badminton was the highlight of the games. Later, we came to know how the games were marred by corruption charges.

Diwali and June's Last Night in this World - November 5, 2010

Diwali came on November 5, 2010. Before Diwali day they used to show trailers of various programmes and one of them was the famous Pattimanram by Solomon Pappaya in which a new speaker, Seshadri, was to talk about old age homes.

June, after seeing the trailer, told me that we should not miss that.

On Diwali day, she got up early and started to make breakfast along with Bonda, Vadai and Sulium. Then she asked me whether we could give breakfast to our neighbour and I agreed. I was surprised because she would not voluntarily do such things for unknown people. Then she carried everything herself and handed over the food to the neighbour. Later, my daughter's family came and we all had breakfast together. Then we all sat to watch Pattimanram on Sun TV. That was the first time we all watched this type of programme together. When the programme ended, we started to wash the utensils. As both of us were washing in the kitchen, June told me the speech by Seshadri was touching. Again, this was unusual of June because she had never shared her opinion openly in 43 years.

We went to Naivedyam Hotel in Gurgaon for lunch. After lunch, we went to Sector 31 market where June and Shyamala did some shopping and then returned home. As usual I went to B-86 and June stayed back in Shyamala's house. She called me for coffee and after drinking coffee, again, I went back. Then we had dinner at Shyamala's house and I returned home again. Around 9.30 p.m., June returned along with Joshua and watched TV for some time while I worked in my room. Suddenly, I looked into the hall, no one was there and the light was switched off. I saw both June and Joshua sleeping in the bedroom.

June would never go to sleep without telling me. Again, it was strange.

I never thought that would be the last night June would be spending in this world with us.

Very sorry to hear about that. What happened?

I will tell you.

Around Me

Let us go through the major events that took place during this period.

India

Politics

Pratibha Patil became 12th President of India, 2007 - Pratibha Devisingh Patil (born December 19, 1934) became the first woman President of India on July 25, 2007 after Abdul Kalam.

Visit of Iranian President Mahmoud Ahmadinejad, 2008 - Iranian President Mahmoud Ahmadinejad arrived in New Delhi on Tuesday, April 29, 2008 on a brief visit to review the progress on trilateral gas pipeline and bilateral liquefied natural gas project.

Nuke Deal and Vote of Confidence, 2008 - The Indo-US civilian nuclear agreement was met with stiff opposition by political parties and activists in India. The Indian Government survived a vote of confidence on July 22, 2008 by 275 - 256 after the Left Front withdrew their support to the government.

XVth Indian General Elections, 2009 - India held general elections to the 15th Lok Sabha in five phases between April 16 and May 13, 2009. There were four fronts consisting of United Progressive Alliance, National Democratic Alliance, Third Front and Fourth Front. Manmohan Singh was the Prime Ministerial candidate for UPA and L. K. Advani for NDA. UPA won 262 seats (INC 206; TMC 19; DMK 18; NCP 9; others 10;), NDA won 159 seats (BJP 116; JD(U) 20; Shiv Sena 11; RLD 5; Shironmani Akali Dal 4; TRS 2; AGP 1), Third Front won ˉ79 seats (BSP 21; CPI(M) 16; Biju JD 14; AIADMK 9; TDP 6; CPI 4; others 5) and Fourth Front won 27 seats (SP 23; RJD 4). Others won 16 seats.

Manmohan Singh became Prime Minister for the second time, 2009 - Manmohan Singh was sworn in as Prime Minister for the second time on May 22, 2009. He became the first Prime Minister since Jawaharlal Nehru in 1962 to be re-elected after completing a full five-year term.

Meira Kumar Became First woman Speaker of the Lok Sabha, 2009 - Meira Kumar became the first woman Speaker of the Lok Sabha when she was elected on June 4, 2009. She is the daughter of former Deputy Prime Minister and prominent Dalit leader, Jagjivan Ram.

Putin's Visit to India, 2010 - India and Russia signed a nuclear co-operation agreement, to build nuclear reactors in India, with Russian help. The agreement came at the end of talks between Russian Prime Minister Vladimir Putin and Manmohan Singh, in New Delhi during March 2010.

Space Technology

Completion of IGMDP, 2008 - On January 8, 2008, the DRDO stated that the strategic Integrated Guided Missile Development Programme was completed with its design objectives achieved since most of the missiles in the programme had been developed and inducted by the Indian Armed Forces.

Launching of Agni Missile III, 2008 - On May 7, 2008 India again successfully test fired Agni III missile. This was the third consecutive test. Agni-III has a range of 3,500 km, and can take a warhead of 1.5 tonnes.

10 Satellites in single launch, 2008 - India launched 10 satellites into orbit in a single launch on April 29, 2008 which became a world record. Polar Satellite Launch Vehicle (PSLV-C9) successfully put all the 10 satellites into orbit on April 30, 2008.

Launching of Chandrayaan-1, 2008 - Chandrayaan-1 was India's first lunar probe. It was launched by the Indian Space Research Organisation in October 2008, and operated until August 2009. The mission was a major boost to India's space program, as India researched and developed its own technology in order to explore the Moon. The vehicle was successfully inserted into lunar orbit on November 8, 2008.

Water on the Moon, 2009 - Inconclusive evidence of free water ice at the lunar poles was accumulated from a variety of observations suggesting the presence of bound hydrogen. In September 2009, Chandrayaan-1 detected water on the Moon and hydroxyl absorption lines in reflected sunlight.

India Tests Nuclear Capable Prithvi-II Missiles, 2009 - India, successfully, test fired its indigenously developed nuclear capable Prithvi-II missile on October 12, 2009 from a mobile launcher from launch complex-3 of the Integrated Test Range (ITR) at Chandipur. It has a strike range of 350 kilometres.

Launching of Anti-Surface Missile Dhanush, 2009 - Dhanush, the ship-based anti-surface missile was successfully launched from a naval vessel, INS Subhadra in the Bay of Bengal, off the Orissa coast on December 13, 2009. The missile was fired by Indian Navy personnel as part of user training exercise.

Launching of Radar Imaging Satellite 2, 2009 - RISAT-2 or Radar Imaging Satellite 2, was launched aboard a PSLV-CA rocket on April 20, 2009 from the second launch pad at the Satish Dhawan Space Centre. It was built by the Israel Aerospace Industries. It has a day-night, all-weather monitoring capability. Potential applications include tracking hostile ships at sea that could pose a military threat.

Launching of Project to ID 1.2 Billion People, 2010 - India's project assigning a unique 12-digit number to each of its 1.2 billion people was launched in 2010. The project seeks to collect fingerprint and iris scans from all residents and store them in a massive central database of unique IDs.

Science and Technology

First IVF in AIIMS, 2007 - Keeping the interest of women's health the first state of the art In Vitro Fertilisation (IVF) Research Centre was established at the Department of Obstetrics and Gynaecology of All India Institute of Medical Sciences (AIIMS) in February 2007.

Sports

Abhinav Bindra, first Indian, to win Gold in solo event of Olympics, 2008 - In his third Olympics, Abhinav Bindra had shot himself to the pinnacle of Indian sporting glory by gunning down a gold medal in the Olympics. He was the first Indian to win a gold in any Solo Event in the Olympics.

XIX Commonwealth Games, India, 2010 - The 2010 Commonwealth Games were held in Delhi, India, from October 3-14, 2010. A total of 6,081 athletes from 71 Commonwealth nations and dependencies competed in 21 sports and 272 events, making it the largest Commonwealth Games to date. The final medal tally was led by Australia. The host nation India achieved its best performance ever at the Games, finishing second overall.

Bombings and Death Toll

42 people were killed in twin bomb blasts in Hyderabad on August 25, 2007, 63 in nine bomb blasts in Jaipur on May 13, 2008, two in nine bomb blasts in Bangalore on July 25, 2008, 56 in 21 bomb blasts in Ahmedabad on July 26, 2008, 81 in 18 bomb blasts in Assam on

October 30, 2008, six in three bomb blasts in Guwahati on January 1, 2009, and 17 in a bomb blast in Pune on February 13, 2010.

Accidents

146 people were killed in the Naina Devi temple stampede in Bilaspur, Himachal Pradesh on August 3, 2008, 5 in the collapse of a bridge being built to carry Delhi's metro trains, on July 12, 2009. Rajashekara Reddy, Chief Minister of Andhra Pradesh was killed in a helicopter crash on September 2, 2009 and 63 in Ram Janki temple stampede in Kunda, Uttar Pradesh on March 4, 2010.

Natural Calamities

149 people were killed in severe cyclonic storm Aila on May 23, 2009 in India and 17 soldiers in a huge avalanche in Kashmir on February 8, 2010.

Terrorist Attack.

Mumbai under Attack, 2008 - In November 2008, 10 members of the Lashkar-e-Taiba, an Islamic militant organisation based in Pakistan, carried out a series of 12 coordinated shooting and bombing attacks lasting four days across Mumbai. The attacks began on Wednesday, November 26 and lasted until Saturday, November 29, 2008, killing 164 people and wounding at least 308.

World

Politics

North and South Korea Leaders Meet for the Second Time, 2007 - On October 2, 2007, South Korean President Roh Moo-hyun walked across the Korean Demilitarized Zone travelling to Pyongyang for talks with Kim Jong-il. The two sides reaffirmed the spirit of the June 15 Joint Declaration and had discussions related to the advancement of South-North relations, peace on the Korean peninsula, common prosperity of the Korean people and unification of Korea.

Russian New President Dmitri Medvedev, 2008 - Russian New President Dmitri Medvedev had his inauguration on May 7, 2008. He was preceded by Vladimir Putin.

Nepal Holds Historic Election, Monarchy Abolished, 2008 - A general election for the Constituent Assembly was held in Nepal on April 10, 2008. The Unified Communist Party of Nepal (Maoist) or CPN(M), placed first in the election with 220 out of 575 elected seats. After months of power-sharing discussions and deliberations, CPN(M) Chairman Prachanda was elected as Prime Minister in August 2008.

Obama Became President of USA, 2009 - Barack Hussein Obama (Democratic) became the 44th President of the United States on Tuesday, January 20, 2009 after George W. Bush. He was the first African American to hold the office and the first President born outside the United States.

Sri Lanka Tamil Tigers Defeated, 2009 - Beginning on July 23, 1983, there was an intermittent insurgency against the government by the Liberation Tigers of Tamil Eelam (the LTTE, also known as the Tamil Tigers), which fought to create an independent Tamil state called Tamil Eelam in the north and the east of the island. After a 26-year military campaign, the Sri Lankan military defeated the Tamil Tigers in May 2009, bringing the civil war to an end.

David Cameron became Prime Minister of UK, 2010 - David Cameron was sworn in as Prime Minister of UK on May 11, 2010. He was preceded by Gordon Brown.

Climate Change

The UN Climate Change Conference, Indonesia, 2007 - The Bali Climate Change Conference brought together more than 10,000 participants, including representatives of over 180 countries with observers from intergovernmental and nongovernmental organisations and the media. Governments adopted the Bali Road Map to reach a global climate deal. The Bali Road Map includes the Bali Action Plan to enable the full, effective and sustained implementation of the Convention through long-term cooperative action, now, up to and beyond 2012, with the aim of reaching an agreed outcome and adopting a decision at COP15 in Copenhagen.

Copenhagen Climate Summit, 2009 - The 2009 United Nations Climate Change Conference or Copenhagen Summit, was held at the Bella Center in Copenhagen, Denmark, during December 7-18. The conference included the 15th Conference of the Parties (COP 15) to the United Nations Framework Convention on Climate Change (UNFCCC) and the 5th Meeting of the Parties (MOP 5) to the Kyoto Protocol. According to the Bali Road Map, a framework for climate change mitigation beyond 2012 was to be agreed there.

Science and Technology

The Large Hadron Collider, Big Bang Experiment Inaugurated, 2008 - The Large Hadron Collider (LHC) was built by the European Organization for Nuclear Research (CERN) between 1998 and 2008 in collaboration with over 10,000 scientists and engineers from over 100 countries and hundreds of universities and laboratories. It lies in a tunnel, 27 kilometres in circumference and 175 metres deep, beneath the France–Switzerland border near Geneva, Switzerland.

Microsoft Launch Bing Search Engine, 2009 - Bing.com, the new search engine was officially launched on June 1, 2009 by Microsoft.

Bill Gates Retired from Microsoft, 2008 - For 33 years, Bill Gates worked to make Microsoft into a software juggernaut. From modest beginnings, Gates rose to become the world's richest man. From pushing and helping to develop DOS and the PC to defining the modern operating system with Windows, Gates has left an unparalleled mark on the face of technology in the world today. On Friday, July 25, 2008 after 33-years, Gates clocked in his last work day with the company.

Space Technology

Phoenix Lander on Mars, 2008 - Phoenix was a robotic spacecraft on a space exploration mission under the Mars Scout Programme. The Phoenix lander descended on Mars on May 25, 2008. Mission scientists searched for environments suitable for microbial life on Mars, and researched the history of water there.

China Manned Satellite Shenzhou-7, 2008 - Shenzhou 7 was the third human spaceflight mission of the Chinese space programme. The Shenzhou spacecraft carrying the three crew members was launched on September 25, 2008.

Benazir Bhutto Killed in Suicide Attack, 2007 - The assassination of Benazir Bhutto occurred on December 27, 2007 in Rawalpindi, Pakistan. Bhutto, twice Prime Minister of Pakistan (1988–1990; 1993–1996) and then leader of the opposition Pakistan People's Party, had been campaigning ahead of elections scheduled for January 2008. Shots were fired at her at Liaquat National Bagh, and a suicide bomb was detonated immediately. She was declared dead at Rawalpindi General Hospital. Twenty-four other people were killed by the bombing.

Natural Calamities

85,000 were killed in Myanmar due to cyclone Nargis on May 5, 2008, 70,000 in China Sichuan Earthquake of Magnitude 8 on May 12, 2008, 1,00,000 in Haiti rocked by scale 7.0 earthquake on January12, 2010,

War

Israel Propose Palestine Peace Plan, 2009 - In June 2009, reacting to President Obama's Cairo Address, Israeli Prime Minister Benjamin Netanyahu declared conditional support for a future Palestinian state but insisted that the Palestinians would need to make reciprocal gestures and accept several principles: recognition of Israel as the nation-state of the Jewish people; demilitarization of a future Palestinian state, along with additional security guarantees, including defensible borders for Israel.

US-Iraq Status of Forces Agreement II, 2008 - The US-Iraq Status of Forces Agreement was signed by President George W. Bush in November 2008. It established that US combat forces would withdraw from Iraqi cities by June 30, 2009 and will be completely out of Iraq by December 31, 2011. Jalal Talabani was the President and Nouri Al-Maliki was the Prime Minister of Iraq.

Others

Global Food Crisis, Rice Price Rise, 2008 - World food prices increased dramatically in 2007 and the 1st and 2nd quarter of 2008 creating a global crisis and causing political and economic instability and social unrest in both poor and developed nations. The initial causes included droughts in grain-producing nations and rising oil prices.

Global Financial Crisis, 2008-2009 - The world experienced a global financial crisis during 2008 -2009.

Death of Michael Jackson, 2009 - On June 25, 2009, Michael Jackson died of acute propofol and benzodiazepine intoxication in his house on North Carolwood Drive in the Holmby Hills neighbourhood of Los Angeles.

CHAPTER- 14

Death of June - November 6, 2010

Abstract

Me

The details of my wife's death and the holy rituals connected with it are presented.

I know this is the most difficult part for you to narrate. Please tell us about the sudden passing away of your wife June and her last rites.

The morning of Saturday November 6, 2010 dawned like any other day. But most of the people would not have got up after celebrating Diwali the previous day. I got up at my usual time 5.30 a.m., and started the day with my prayers. After that I continued with my college work. I saw June going from the bedroom to the kitchen. I looked at the time. It showed 8 a.m. She had told me the previous day that she would get up late by 8 in the morning.. Normally she would first come and say hello to me and only then do anything else. But that day, she deviated from her routine. After some time, I went to the kitchen to throw the bread, which had expired, into the dust bin. I saw the milk boiling and she was washing some vessels. Usually I would tap her back or hug her. I did not do the usual thing and also, I did not say anything to her and returned to my work.

By 8.15 a.m., I heard some screeching noise and I tried to locate from where it came. I saw Joshua also getting up and looking and finally when I went to the kitchen I saw June lying on the floor below the sink with one leg flat and the other leg folded up and the dust bin pushed away. I thought she might have fainted. I put her on my lap and sprinkled water on her face. But she gasped deeply and that seemed to be the end. I rang Shyamala and within a few seconds Alex and she came running and they tried to give her CPR but it was all over. We called the duty doctor from the nearby Shivam Hospital and he declared her dead. Everything was over in 15 minutes.

It took some time for us to recover. She was laid out in the hall on a cot and we started to inform our near and dear ones.

My sister, my uncle's daughter, Priya, and my aunty Amelia from Trichy joined my aunty Shantha in Chennai and they landed by night. June's sister, Dinky, and Darrel, also came from Trichy. Donella and Ricky came from Hyderabad and Denys came from Dubai. Amenda, who had gone to Dewas, Madhya Pradesh, for the Diwali holidays, also returned. By 10 p.m., all the near and dear ones reached our home for her viewing.

Nobody could believe that she had passed away. We discussed whether to take her to Trichy or do the last rites in Gurgaon itself. We decided to cremate her in Gurgaon.

My sister Vasantha told all of us what June shared with her earlier when we were leaving Kanchipuram for Gurgaon in 2007. She told my sister, "Akka (sister), we are going far away to Gurgaon. Supposing I die there, what will they do? Will I be cremated as a Hindu or buried as a Christian?" June further added, "Anyway Akka I would like my last rites to have a combination of both Hindu and Christian customs just as I had in my marriage." None of us could hold back our tears and we decided to do everything she wished for.

Alex's friend, Dr. Sam, was helpful in getting the coffin. Alex's friends, Shyamala's friends and my friends helped a lot. It looked as though she was sleeping peacefully. Many of us did not sleep the whole night and it soon dawned. We were contemplating electrical cremation but the facility was only in Delhi and we decided to cremate her in a burial ground near IFFCO Chowk in Gurgaon itself. Ricky managed to shift her from the coffin to a stretcher smoothly and we left the house by 1 p.m., with June in an ambulance on November 7, Sunday. Just before we left, my colleague from REC Trichy N. Krishnamoorthi and his wife Manonmani came all the way from Trichy with a garland. June was lucky to have a garland from Trichy, her home town.

A small crowd of about 50 gathered to watch her cremation just like a small crowd of 200 watched her getting married. I lit the pyre and within a short time June was cremated. All the visitors left one by one and I wanted to be there till the fire stopped and had died down but it was not allowed. We left June to be alone.

She had helped every one of us when we were ill and hospitalized. She helped her father, Amelia, Darrel, Dinky, my mother, Shyamala, and me. She never gave a chance to any one of us to serve her. She had a good death but it was too early and too sudden.

Sometimes I used to tell her, "June, I want to see whether you would be fighting with me the same way when you are in your 80's." I lost the chance of seeing that.

We collected the ashes the next day and discussed about the immersion of ashes in holy rivers. At that time, my colleague Niragi's husband Kalpesh suggested that Ganges at Ganga Ghat was about 250 kilometres from Gurgaon and we could immerse her ashes there. Then we booked two taxis and started by 2 p.m.

We reached the Ganga Ghat by 5 p.m., and hired a boat to the middle of the Ganges. There we performed a small pooja and immersed the ashes. June's body took birth in Trichy where the Cauvery River flows and her ashes were immersed in the Ganges thereby connecting Cauvery and Ganges. The real project of connecting Ganges and Cauvery is yet to find its birth.

Somehow, we found Tamil poojaris (pandits for pooja) in Delhi, through my colleague Gayathri's husband Narayanan. The first pooja after the cremation and immersion of ashes was performed in our house by Ramesh Gurukkal and his group.

Then, we planned to immerse the ashes in Cauvery River in Trichy and Rameshwaram, two sacred places. We also wanted to have a Memorial Service in a church and a gathering with near and dear ones to pay tributes and place her ashes in the grave of her mother in Trichy according to Christian practice.

After making a detailed plan we left Gurgaon.

On Saturday morning (November 20) at 9 a.m., we had a Memorial Mass at St. Mary's Cathedral, Melapudhur, Trichy, keeping the ashes in the church and then went to the cemetery in Marsingpet road and placed June's ashes in her mother's grave at 10 a.m. When were about to close the grave, there was a sudden powerful light, similar to the one seen by Moses (as written in the Bible). On Sunday morning (November 21), 8 a.m., we went to the River Cauvery near Amma Mandabam, Trichy and immersed the ashes there.

On the same day, we organized the gathering to pay tributes (Down the Memory Lane) to June at SRM (Royal Southern) Hotel, Race Course Road, Kajamalai, Trichy at 11.30 a.m. This function was attended by about 150 people all very close to June. A PowerPoint show, prepared by Amenda, on the life of June starting from her childhood through marriage to death was presented. Before that, Amenda, Ammu (Anandaraj's wife) and Rev. Richard Reid gave the eulogy. Lunch was also arranged at 12.30 pm. A memoir booklet was prepared by Shantha aunty in June's memory.

In Loving Memory of June (By Amenda)

God's blessing to our world, she was our June
Our only sorrow is her departure too soon
A heart of gold reflected in her deep, thoughtful, kind eyes
A lifetime of memories that shall never die
Prefect grandmother, wife…
Aye, she has taught us many a lesson through her exemplary life
Unwavering visage reflecting serenity and calm
Her loving voice to us a smoothing balm
Her soul has imprinted upon our souls
Through her mere presence when we needed a console
Her never resting nimble fingers
Created masterpieces that still linger
In body, you have left us…to grieve
But your powerful memory gives us the fortitude to believe
That immortal, yes, immortal you are in spirit,
As you forever live on through all our lives that your very existence lit.

That night around 7 p.m., we started for Rameshwaram. It was a very long trip. It rained throughout the night and there were long stretches of darkness and isolation. Somehow, we reached Rameshwaram by 12.30 a.m. There we took a room and rested.

Monday early morning we left for the Indian Ocean and immersed the ashes. We then travelled to Madurai Airport for our trip back to Gurgaon.

***Asthi Visarjan (Immersion of Ashes in the Holy Rivers)** is a Hindu custom. Hindus cremate the dead bodies. The remnant of the dead bodies is in the form of ashes which Hindus immerse in holy rivers like the Ganges. If it is not possible to come all the way to the Ganges, people immerse them in rivers close by. The meaning of asthi is left over bones or some collected ashes and visarjan is to immerse them in holy rivers. It is believed that through the immersion of their ashes the departed soul enjoys remaining in heaven multiple times* *to thousand years. There is a scientific reason also for this. In India river waters are used for irrigation and since this asthi is rich in phosphates, the level of phosphates in water increases and this in turn increases the fertility of the land. Ultimately, the elements of the body return to nature after death.*

30th day ceremony was conducted on December 7, which coincided with my mother's death anniversary. First Christmas and New Year 2011 without June came and went. First anniversary ceremony was conducted on October 27, 2011.

Tributes to June

Smooth Switchover

Brought up as a Catholic Christian, June switched over easily to adopt the culture of Hinduism. She became an expert in following the rituals of marriages and deaths. Of course, we celebrated the festivals of Hindus and Christians.

Expert Cook

She did not know cooking when she got married. But she became an expert in cooking simply by observing my mother and aunts. My grandfather had never given any certificate for my mother or my aunts for their delicious cooking but after staying one week in Calicut with us in 1968, he mentioned openly to everyone that June cooked very well.

She attended a course at Food Craft Institute, Thuvakkudi, Trichy and got a certificate. She used to try her hand at different types of recipes. She could whip up the world's most delicious food.

Effortless Nursing

She was an excellent nurse to all of us whenever we fell ill. She looked after her father when he fell sick in 1977 for more than two months. She took care of her foster mother Amelia when she had a heart attack in 1980. She stayed with my mother in the hospital for a week when my mother had a heart attack in 1986. She stayed in the hospital, without coming to the house, for more than two months when my daughter Shyamala was undergoing treatment for her burn injuries in 1995. Finally, she took complete care of me for 10 days when I had to be treated for a mild heart attack in 2003.

But she never gave us a chance to nurse her when she passed away without a warning.

Perfect Homemaker

She kept the house neat and tastefully decorated. Her garden, both in Calicut and Trichy campuses, drew appreciation from all the people.

Genius in her Own Way

She had a good knowledge of medicine and engineering gained just by reading and observing. She could locate faults in a car, electric circuits at home or find the cause for any ailment.

Interest in Sports, Entertainment and Reading

She was very interested in watching sports and games, movies, television and reading novels. She had been a sprinter and represented her school in athletic events. She played shuttle and carrom like a pro.

Selfless, Honest and Trustworthy

She was known for her selflessness, honesty and trustworthiness throughout her life.

She belonged to all Generations

She belonged to all generations, be it her own age group or the fast-paced world of her grandchildren.

Sharp Memory

She had a sharp memory. She could remember birthdays and anniversaries and small details of the past.

Astrological Coincidence between June and Me

When we wanted to start a computer business, we went to Balan Nair, a famous astrologer in Karaikudi. He made our horoscopes based on date, time and place of birth. He told that we have been husband and wife in our earlier births also. Both of us had the same Star Rohini, Rishaba Rasi and Kadaga Lagnam. It is very rare for any couple to have such a coincidence.

Popular Among our Family and Friends

Everyone in our family wanted her in all their functions. She was the confidante of most of my relations and friends. She would be in the pen tholzhi (like maid of honour) in all my family weddings. Even for M.G. Ramachandran, former Chief Minister of Tamil Nadu and Sivaji Ganesan, famous film actor, fish curry and fish fry were prepared by her whenever they visited Trichy.

She always used to pack the mementos for the chief guests in the college functions.

Healthy

She had never fallen sick for even a single day but later she became diabetic with high blood pressure for which she had been taking medication.

She was Bold and Never Expressed her Feelings

She was bold and not afraid of anything. She never used to show her happiness or sadness. She kept her emotions to herself but was there for everyone in their need.

Death also Listened to Her

She wanted to have a peaceful death before mine and death also obeyed her wish. She had her wish of dying as a Sumangali (married woman and not a widow).

Overall, June was the epitome of a good daughter, sister, wife, mother, aunt, mother-in-law and the best grandmother

Oh! She seems to be very gifted lady. Just like her self- respect marriage in 1967, you had given her a combination of Hindu custom of cremation and ashes immersion and Christian custom of memorial service and ashes burial. In addition, you arranged a gathering to glorify her. Very rarely such things happen in this world.

Mmm. It is all God's plan. I should thank God for giving such ideas and for giving strength to do everything in a grand manner without a hitch.

She died young and suddenly. How did you take it?

It was the greatest shock. The first time I saw her was sudden and her passing away was also sudden. Everyday a flashback runs in my mind starting from the first day I saw her to the day she lay on my lap and breathed her last.

These are my thoughts everyday

>"They said time would ease the pain
>Every day, I still feel the same
>I wake every morning reaching for her
>My pillow soaked with tears like the morning dew."

I take this opportunity to offer my apologies to her for all the times I hurt her.

CHAPTER - 15

Life in Gurgaon, Part II - November 2010 Onwards

ABSTRACT

Me

The details of my professional life (2010-18), Amenda's gold medal (2012), death of Darrel Nigli (2012), Vasantha's heart attack (2012), shifting to house in sector 15 (2012), one year stay of Alex, Shyamala and Joshua in Tokyo (2013-14), Amelia's accident (2013), arrival of Aomame and Tengo (2014), Joshua's win in History Bowl Asian Championship (2014), Amelia shifting to Gurgaon (2014), Ramaiyan's accident (2015), death of Amelia (2015), Amenda's admission into MD (2016), death of Ramaiyan (2016), my retirement from ITM (2016), Joshua's credentials, 25th wedding anniversary of Alex and Shyamala (2017), closing of Daiichi Sankyo and new job for Alex (2017), shifting to own apartment (2018) and visiting faculty role for me again (2018).

Around Me

In India, the major events were hunger strike by Anna Hazare (2011), India's population touching 1.2 billion (2011), Mamata becoming first woman Chief Minister of West Bengal (2011), Pranab Mukherjee becoming President (2012), gang-rape in Delhi (2012), hanging of Kasab (2012), end of telegram service (2013), 16th general elections (2014), BJP's government and Narendra Modi becoming Prime Minister (2014), birth of Telengana state (2014), Nobel Prize for Kailash (2014), Aam Admi Party's first win (2015), death of Kalam (2015), demonetization (2016), Goods and Services Act (2017), Ram

Nath Kovind becoming President (2017), visit of Japanese Prime Minister (2017), Rahul Gandhi becoming President, INC (2017), launching of PSLV-C37 with 104 satellites (2017), Heads of ASEAN Nations in the Republic Day celebrations (2018), verdict on Fodder Scam (2018), death of Vajpayee (2018) and Kerala floods (2018).

In Tamil Nadu state, the major events were 14th Assembly elections (2011), Jayalalithaa becoming Chief Minister (2011), Jayalalithaa's conviction in DA case (2014), Jayalalithaa's acquittal (2015), 15th Assembly elections (2016), Jayalalithaa becoming Chief Minister (2016), Jayalalithaa's death (2016), events after Jayalalithaa's death (2016), pro Jallikattu protests (2017), new entries in politics (2017-2018) and death of Karunanidhi (2018).

In the World, the major events were the killing of Osama bin Laden (2011), end of US mission in Iraq (2011), landing on Mars (2012), death of Mandela (2013), cloning of human stem cells (2013), Xi Jinping becoming President of China (2013), Li keqiang becoming Prime Minister of China (2013), US-Cuba relation breakthrough (2014), Obama continuing as President of US (2014), possibility of rocket reuse (2015), climate change deal (2015), Britain votes to exit EU (2016), Bolt's triple-triple in Olympics (2016), Mother Teresa's Sainthood (2016), Obama visiting Hiroshima (2016), Trump becoming President (2017), North Korea's missile tests (2017), ceasing of participation by US in the Paris Agreement on Climate Change (2017), Trump-Kim Summit (2018) and Imran Khan becoming Prime Minister of Pakistan (2018).

After completing all the rituals connected with the death of your wife June, how did your life go on?

After completing all the rituals, I re-joined duty. I also vacated my house and started to live with my daughter's family at B-65, Jalvayu Vihar, Gurgaon.

How did you overcome your grief?

I don't know if one can overcome grief. Time is said to be a healer but grief after sometime is still a dull ache in the heart.

In the immediate few days one overcomes grief by indulging in the mundane ceremonies associated with the death. It becomes compulsive to make plans and arrangements almost willing your mind to forget sorrow. Once the ceremonies are done away with actual loss strikes its ugly head. Every sound, food and smell become a constant reminder of the loss. But in my case, I was surrounded by my family members. I used to think that my grandchildren or my daughter might be grieving more. This helped me in hiding my emotions and emerging strong for them. But with time I accepted the loss thinking June was in a better place. And it was God's design to take her away as He needed her more than me. Then, life goes on. I do the things which would make her feel proud of me.

Professional

Workshop on "Climate Change" - March 14-15, 2011

When June passed away, Bhanu Neupane of UNESCO, New Delhi, asked me if the workshop needed to be postponed.

I said no and we decided to stick to the original dates. We started to send our brochures across the country and abroad. The workshop was the first of its kind to be organized in ITM, in association with a world organization like UNESCO. International experts included Dr. Michael Van der Valk, Member Secretary, IHP Committee, UNESCO, Netherlands and Er. Ganesh Shah, former Minister of Environment, Government of Nepal. There were also experts from the government and the private sectors of India.

R. K. Singh's Visit to USA - May 2011

Prof. Ram Karan Singh attended an international conference on "Climate Adaptation Research and Understanding through Social Sciences" organised by the University of Michigan's School of Natural Resources and Environment, in Ann Arbor, Michigam, USA and presented a paper on "Clean Development Mechanism (CDM) and Land Filling: Study of the Municipal Waste Processing Complex at Ghajipur, Delhi". He also wanted to visit Michigan Technological University, Alberta. I prepared a short PowerPoint presentation about the Department of Civil Engineering and he shared it with the Faculty of Civil Engineering and they showed interest to work with us.

I was Elevated as Mentor - July 2011

After ITM became a University, I could not continue as Head of the Department because of the age constraint. Prof. Ram Karan Singh was made the Head of the Department from July 1, 2011 and I was elevated as Mentor of the Department. I was given a contract for two years which was unprecedented. ITM also created the post of Mentor for a former Head of the Department for the first time.

Internship by Students from Germany - 2011 - 2012

A letter was received from Viktoria, a third-year student of Civil Engineering, Kassel University, Germany through Governing Body member Avdhesh Mishra, expressing interest to carry out project work and internship at ITM. Prof. Ram Karan Singh consulted me and I told him to go ahead. We completed all the formalities and Johanna, Viktoria's classmate came first between October - December 2011 and Viktoria came between January - March 2012. They successfully completed their respective projects.

Indo-US bilateral Workshop with Michigan Technological University, USA - March 5-6, 2012

A proposal was submitted by June 30, 2011 to the Indo-US Science and Technology Forum, New Delhi for organizing a two-day workshop in association with Michigan Technological University, USA on the topic "Global Challenges: Climate Change, Water, Environment and Society" during March 5-6, 2012.

The proposal was peer reviewed by a team from India and a team from USA. Based on recommendations of both teams, a revised proposal was submitted and it was approved on December 31, 2011.

The workshop was organized in a successful manner. Besides experts from India, it also included Professors Bruce Sealy, Alex Mayer, Amlan Mukherjee, and David Watkins from Michigan Technological University, USA and Richard N. Palmer from Massachusetts University, USA. The total attendance was around 110.

It was completely sponsored by Indo-US Science and Technology Forum, New Delhi.

Application for National Board of Accreditation (NBA) - November, 2012

An application for accreditation of B. Tech. Civil Engineering programme by NBA was submitted in November 2012.

Civil Engineering Conference "iSPACE" - March 4-5, 2013

Under the professional society SPACE, an international conference on Civil Engineering, iSPACE (i for intelligent) was organized during March 4-5, 2013. Prof. Bruce Sealy of USA, who earlier attended the Indo-US workshop and Prof. Brechen of Kassel University, Germany (by the efforts of our internship student Viktoria) attended the conference making it a truly international one. It was sponsored by DST and CSIR.

Emeritus Fellow - April, 2013

When I was to complete 70 years of age in August 2013, ITM made me an Emeritus Fellow with effect from April 1, 2013. I was on contract up to May 31, 2014. I had to take one course and was under the provision "freedom of the house" (no punching for attendance).

Initiation of M.Tech. Programme - July, 2013

M.Tech. in Civil Engineering was started in July 2013. Even though the minimum strength was not reached for the full-time course, 95 % of the seats were filled up for the part time programme.

NBA Visit - July, 2013

NBA visited ITM in July, 2013. The total marks obtained by the Department of Civil Engineering was the highest (72.4%). Departments of EECE, CSE and ME did not cross 70%. All the programmes were accredited from November 8, 2013 for two years provisionally.

I was in charge of NBA in the Department of Civil Engineering, REC Trichy, AMACE, Kanchipuram and ITM, Gurgaon when each of them applied for accreditation for the first time. I was successful in Civil Engineering Department getting the first rank in all attempts.

Prof. Ram Karan Singh Leaving - July, 2013

Immediately after the visit of NBA, Dr. Ram Karan Singh was relieved on July 31, 2013 on his request. The next senior faculty, Dr. V. Gayathri, was made the Head of the Department. Some faculty like Isha Verma, Amit Munjal, Mudit Mishra, Manimohan, T. Choudhry, Tanvi Gupta, Garima Srivastav, Ankit Pachouri, Rohit Poyil, Geetha Varma, P. Verma worked for one or two years and left. Some faculty like Vaishali Sahu, Lokesh Choudhary, Shubam Bansal, Megha Kalra and Diptendu Roy continue to teach there.

Dr. Mathiyazhagan Joined ITM - December, 2013

One day, when I was talking to Avdhesh Mishra, he asked me to get teaching faculty from Tamil Nadu especially for the Department of Mechanical Engineering. I immediately searched the internet for contacts in REC Trichy. I got the mobile number of Noorul Haq, who was well known to me and was the Head of the Department of Production Engineering. I immediately contacted him. He said that he had a Research Scholar, Mathiyazhagan, who had just submitted his Ph.D. thesis. I got the number of Mathiyazhagan and asked him to send his CV.

Then, I handed over the CV to Avdhesh Mishra. An interview was conducted and he was selected for the post of Associate Professor (designate). After convincing his parents he joined ITM in December 2013. After his joining, we became very close friends. He got married to Preeti who has a Ph.D. in Microbiology.

Mathiyazhagan is doing fine academically with a lot of research publications. I drew a plan for his house in Neyveli in Tamil Nadu. My sister and I visited his house during its construction in 2016 and with the help of his father went to Vadalur Vallalar Ramalinga Adigalar Sathya Gnana Sabai, a Temple of Wisdom, for the first time. He recently switched over to Amity University, Noida.

Head In-Charge Again - July, 2014

When Gayathri resigned and was relieved on July 10, 2014, I was made acting Head of the Department.

R & D projects

Two R&D projects were sponsored by the DST one in Geotechnical Engineering and the other in Environmental Engineering.

Ghoshal Joining and Leaving - September 2014 to July 2015

Dr. Ghoshal joined ITM on September 1, 2014 as Professor of Civil Engineering and he was relieved on July 24, 2015. I helped him a lot in running the Department. Prof. Ghoshal has M.E. and Ph.D. degrees in Offshore Structures. He has also specialized in Computer Science. He has written a number of textbooks related to Computer Science and Information Technology. He used to make a lot of educational models and he won the first prize in the Macona Competition in December 2014.

Amit Srivastava became Officiating Head - July 25, 2015

Dr. Amit Srivastava was made Officiating Head of the Department of Civil Engineering under my guidance.

NAAC visit

NAAC team visited ITM for the first time during May 9-11, 2016 to accredit the University.

Personal

Amenda's Gold Medal - October, 2012

Amenda received gold medal for Anatomy from Pranab Mukherjee, the President of India in October, 2012.

Death of Darrel - October 18, 2012

Darrel Nigli was my co-brother. He developed complications in liver and kidney in August 2011. He was in and out of Aarthy Hospital, Cantonment, Trichy and finally breathed his last, on Friday, October 18, 2012, at the age of 67. Shyamala and I went to Trichy and attended his funeral.

Tributes to Darrel Nigli

Darrel Nigli was born on December 3, 1945 as the eldest son to his parents, Steven Bernard Nigli and Doughty Nigli. He studied in Holy Cross High School, Tuticorin and Campion High School, Trichy. He had a diploma in Mechanical Engineering from Nachimuthu Polytechnic, Pollachi. He joined as chargeman in the Mechanical and Millwright division of the Golden Rock Workshop in 1967. He retired on December 3, 2005 as Senior Section Engineer. He was sent on deputation to Sri Lanka for two years during 1984-86 for construction of railways in Sri Lanka. He was married to Eugenia (Dinky), June's sister, on May 29, 1971 in Trichy. He was the proud father of Donella (Hyderabad) and Denys (Dubai) and grandfather of Ryan and Kyle.

He was honoured with the President's Award (Railway Board) for his meritorious service.

He helped his mother to educate his sister Deana (medicine) and brothers Dazzel (diploma), Daley (Arts) and Don (Arts).

He was a very intelligent man. He worked hard for the railways and rarely took leave of absence from work. He was a master of many subjects including general knowledge. He excelled in mind games like chess and scrabble. He was straightforward and bold in conveying his feelings and criticisms.

My Sister's Heart Attack - November, 2012

My sister, Vasantha, had a mild heart attack in November 2012. She recovered quickly and was back to normal after treatment in Githanjali Medical Centre, Puthur, Trichy.

Shifting of House - December, 2012

Shyamala started to take tuitions while working in the school. As the number of students increased, for want of more space we shifted our house to sector 15, part I in December 2012. She also resigned from her job.

Alex's Trip to Japan - April, 2013

Alex was selected to go to Tokyo, Japan on deputation for one year by his company. Alex and Shyamala asked me whether I could manage being alone for one year in the same house if they arranged for a maid servant to cook for me. I said yes and then Alex accepted the offer from his company. I thought it was a nice opportunity for Alex which should not to be missed.

Shyamala taught the maid servant, Sushmita, to cook South Indian food. She also wrote the recipes in Hindi and English and hung them in the kitchen so that it could be referred to when required.

Shyamala's passport had expired and she had to renew it. Alex and Shyamala went to Japan for a week in March 2013 as a pre-visit to choose an apartment and also a school for Joshua. They availed one year leave for Joshua from his school, DPS, and paid the full fees for the academic year 2013-14.

Amenda went to Trichy and brought aunty Amelia, to stay with me so that we could be company for each other.

Alex, Shyamala and Joshua left Delhi on March 31, 2013 for Tokyo. Joshua joined India International School Japan in VIIth standard. The school followed the CBSE syllabus. He took Japanese as his second language.

Visit of Dinky and Ryan - May 2013

Dinky and her first grandson, Ryan, visited us during April-May 2014 for a short holiday of 10 days.

Amelia leaving Gurgaon - June, 2013

Aunty Amelia started giving trouble from the end of May. She also acted as if she lost her memory. I did not have any choice but to take her and leave her in Trichy in June.

Alex's Visit to India and Amenda's Visit to USA - October - November 2013

During the mid-year vacation, Shyamala and Joshua came on October 23, 2013 to Gurgaon to see Amenda off to USA. She went to USA for one month to do her elective. Alex came on October 26 and Alex's mother came from Coimbatore on October 25. Joshua's 12th birthday was celebrated on October 26 after which Amenda took her flight.

The third anniversary ceremony for June was conducted on Monday November 4.

Alex, Shyamala and Joshua left on November 6 for Tokyo after the completion of their mid-year vacation.

Visit of Mangayarkarasi and Balaji - November, 2013

Mangayarkarasi aunty (Govindarajan's wife) visited me in Gurgaon along with Balaji, her sister Gandhi's first son for three hours.

Amelia's Accident in Trichy - November, 2013

Amelia aunty fell down in her house on Friday, November 8, 2013 and broke her hip. She was admitted to Sundaram Hospital, Puthur and all her friends took care of her. Dinky was in Hyderabad and I asked her to go to Trichy and help her. Amelia was operated on Wednesday and she recovered slowly. But she needed a nurse 24x7 at least for a few months. When she was discharged on November 20, she was put in an old age home for which Dinky made all the arrangements. I paid all her expenses for the hospital and old age home and for Dinky's upkeep and it came to around Rs. 4.0 lakh. After extensive physiotherapy, she was able to walk with a walking stick.

My Visit to Japan - December, 2013

During my winter vacation, December 25, 2013 to January 1, 2014, I visited my daughter's family in Tokyo, Japan. Amenda was also there. She stopped over in Tokyo for a month on her way back from USA. It was peak winter in Tokyo similar to North India. I travelled by Air India. I visited most of the important places. The discipline of the people is to be admired. I liked the washrooms very much which were provided with sensors to make toilet seats warm.

Sukanya's Marriage - February 20, 2014

I attended the marriage of Sukanya, first granddaughter of Uncle Padmanaban on Thursday, February 20, 2014 in Trichy. I also visited Amelia aunt in the old age home after her accident.

Return of Alex to India - April. 2014

Alex and Shyamala returned from Japan in March 2014 after completion of deputation. Joshua re-joined DPS in class VIII. Shyamala started taking tuitions again.

Shifting of Amelia from Old Age Home to her Home - April, 2014

After their return from Japan, Shyamala visited Trichy and shifted

Amelia to her home from the old age home. A maid servant was arranged to be with her 24x7.

Arrival of Aomame and Tengo, the Puppies - April, 2014

One day, in April 2014, Amenda and her friend Ajmeera visited a dog shelter near AIIMS and found two new born puppies, one male and the other female of the same mother. They felt pity for the puppies and adopted them, one for Amenda and one for Ajmeera. They kept them for a week in their hostel rooms but found it difficult to manage them. Then Alex, Shyamala and Joshua went to the hostel and brought them to our house in a cardboard box. Joshua was stealthily taking them to the master bedroom. He knew I did not like dogs and he tried to hide them from me. Amenda named them Aomame (female) and Tengo (male).

I am a person who never liked pets. I avoid going to houses if they have dogs.

But I slowly got attached to the puppies. I searched the internet just to know about dogs. I started to tell my friends and relatives about these dogs. They are a part of our family. I wrote about them in a blog.

Joshua Winning in the Asian Championships in Hong Kong - June, 2014

When Joshua was studying in Japan, he represented his school in the team event of the International History Olympiad at zonal level in March 2014. His team and another team from the same school won the event and qualified to represent Japan in the Asian Championship to be held in Hong Kong during June 2014.

Although Joshua had returned to India, his coach-Ted Wysor had asked him, through email, to join his team for the Asian championship, junior level. Shyamala and Alex decided to send him to Hong Kong. First Alex thought he would accompany Joshua but due to work pressure he could not go. Both of them asked me whether I would go. Without hesitation, I accepted and decided to accompany Joshua.

Then I started collecting questions from previous years and Joshua and I practiced diligently.

First Asian championship of the International History Olympiad was hosted by Sha Tin College, Hong Kong during June 14-15, 2014. 35 schools from Asia registered for the event. They had booked our accommodation at Royal Park Hotel, Hong Kong. Alex got us a Forex Card with Hong Kong dollars.

We left Delhi on Thursday, June 13, 2014 and reached Hong Kong. We went to the hotel and informed them about our booking. They gave us a room and after having brunch we took a nap. By 5 p.m., the team mates from Tokyo arrived and after they settled down, we went out for sightseeing. The next day as well, we went for sightseeing.

On the first day of the tournament, History Bee, an individual event, was conducted. In that Joshua narrowly missed entering the finals. His teammate won the runner's up position.

On the second day, the team event was conducted. There were 14 teams from different countries and Joshua's team entered the semi-finals and again lost by a narrow margin. Joshua and his team won the third prize. I was very happy because our efforts did not go to waste and any win at international level is a great achievement.

Amelia Shifting to Gurgaon - November, 2014

After the accident, Amelia found it very difficult to manage alone in her Trichy house even though she had a maid servant and so many friends to look after her. She called Shyamala in the month of November 2014 and asked her to take her to Gurgaon permanently. She also said that she was willing to wind up everything in Trichy. We were hesitating a little since she might not keep her word. But Amenda convinced us that we do not say NO if anyone asks for our help. So, Shyamala went to Trichy and brought Amelia to Gurgaon once and for all. Later, I went and completely vacated the house and it was rented out.

Amenda's Internship - January, 2015

Amenda completed her course work for MBBS and she started her internship (house surgeon) from January 1, 2014. They had to spend three months in a village and she selected the first three months to work in Ballabgarh, Chainsa and Dayalpur. One weekend Alex, Shyamala, Amelia and Joshua visited Amenda along with Aomame and Tengo.

Ramaiyan's Accident - March 15, 2015

When my sister went to Selvam's Kula Deivam Temple on Sunday March 15, 2015, my brother-in-law, Ramaiyan, got down from his apartment in Bharani Towers, Srinivasanagar, Trichy, on to the road, and was knocked down by a two-wheeler. Those who were nearby took him to Githanjali Medical Centre which was close by. My brother-in-law gave Vasantha's number to inform her, but she could not pick up the phone. She came to know after a long time and all came rushing to the hospital.

Ramaiyan's eldest son Sekar and his family insisted that Ramaiyan be taken to CSI hospital, Woriyur. He was shifted to CSI hospital.

It was also a hip injury like Amelia's and Dr. Samson, surgeon in Orthopaedics operated on him but Ramaiyan developed complications just before the surgery.

After the surgery, he was able to walk with a walker for just two days. The surgery had failed and he was never able to walk again. He developed a mild heart condition, along with vomiting and hiccups. He was in and out of the hospital several times and was bed ridden. My sister arranged physiotherapists for home visits but nothing worked. Finally, she arranged for Mohan, a care giver, to assist him. Mohan had excellent experience with invalids. Ramiayan was very comfortable with him.

Manoj Kumar's Marriage - September, 2015

I attended my sister Vasantha's eldest grandson, Manoj Kumar's, marriage which was conducted in September, 2015 in Trichy. As Ramiayan could not attend the marriage my sister also did not attend it. But Manoj and his wife visited Ramaiyan and Vasantha on the same day to get the blessings of their grandparents.

Death of Amelia - October 24, 2015

Amelia aunty was doing fine till the night of October 23, 2015. In the middle of the night she called Shyamala as she felt uncomfortable. Shyamala attended to her and asked whether she should take her to the hospital. Amelia aunt said no and asked Shyamala to go back to sleep. I got up at 7 a.m., on Saturday, October 24, 2015, and wanted to use the washroom. Amelia aunt's bedroom had no door and it was close to the washroom. As I was entering I just peeped in to her room and I saw her lying on the bed in an unusual position. I immediately became concerned and touched her. I knew she had passed away. I woke up Shyamala and Alex. We called an ambulance and took her to Shivam Hospital where the duty doctor declared her dead and put the time of death around 6 a.m.

In the meantime, I called my auto driver, Javed, and asked him about CSI churches nearby. He said he knew one. I asked him to go the church (Church of Epiphany, Civil Lines, Gurgaon) and talk to the Pastor. The Pastor then called me and I asked whether Amelia could be buried as per Protestant Christian customs. He obliged and agreed to conduct the funeral ceremony. Alex and Shyamala brought Amelia back home and by that time Amenda had also joined us. Alex and I met the Pastor who helped us to make all the necessary arrangements for the burial.

We informed all our close relatives and friends but we knew that no one would be able to make it.

She had a peaceful death just like her sister, Rachel, my mother and my wife.

Tributes to Amelia

Her Life

Amelia was born on April 25, 1933 in Trichy. Her parents were Henry Morton and Edith Morton. She was the second of five children. Her siblings were her older sister Rachel, younger sister Ada and two younger brothers James and John. Her father went to Iraq to fight in the Second World War and her mother passed away when her youngest brother, John, was two years old. So, the children were brought up by Amelia's uncle (father's elder brother), who worked in the Mechanical and Millwright Shop, Golden Rock Workshop and her aunt Mabel Emma Morton. They lived in the Railway quarters. They did not have children of their own. After his retirement, they shifted to a house called Pepper Water Castle in Beemanagar. Amelia's uncle became a victim of black magic (seivinai) and passed away. Mable started to work in Pudukkottai Palace in order to take care Pudukkotai Maharaja's five children. They never received any news about Amelia's father and they assumed that he had died in the war. Rachel got married to Lionel Narcis on June 23, 1948. Lionel was working in the railways as a crane operator. He was a paying guest in the same house.

Suddenly tragedy struck them. One Sunday, when Mabel had gone to church, their house caught fire and all the children escaped by running out of the house. All their belongings were burnt down. Mabel had deposited some money in the post office but they got back only 25% of their deposit as the necessary papers were lost in the fire. They rented a house behind the Nalwazhi Hospital in Heber road, Beemanagar. In this house, June was born on June 24, 1949.

Nalwazhi Hospital was owned by Dr. W.G.P. Thomas, a retired army doctor. When he came to know about Mabel's family, he was willing to train Amelia as a nurse in his hospital. Mabel, Rachel and Lionel were not willing for this but Amelia wanted to help the family and so she joined Nalwazhi Hospital and Dr. Thomas taught her everything about nursing, gynaecology and obstetrics. Amelia was very intelligent and quickly learnt everything. First Amelia was given a room in the hospital itself. Later she rented the house next to the hospital and brought Mabel and her sister's three children June, Rodney and Dinky to stay with her. She decided to be a spinster. She was happy to look after her sister's children. She also brought her elder sister Rachel to work in the hospital. Rachel and her husband were living in Subramaniapuram. In the meantime, her younger sister Ada got married and went to Podanur. John joined the Indian Army and James became a lorry driver.

Amelia built her house in Raja colony, Beemanagar. The house was occupied in 1986. She kept the rented house as well. When her sister Rachel passed away in her sleep on July 15, 1989, she was very upset. She could not manage the hospital alone. She closed the hospital and decided to sell the house and get an apartment. She took residence in the apartment in 1994.

By the year 2005, she had exhausted all her savings and the Vasavi Chit Fund cheated her. She was struggling for money and she refused to accept any help from us. After discussing a few options, Shyamala suggested that she would buy the house at government price, give Rs.1 lakh as advance and pay the remaining as instalments of Rs. 3800 per month for 120 months. Amelia could continue staying in the house. In addition, I was contributing Rs. 2000 to Rs. 5000 for her expenses monthly.

When she met with a hip accident, she decided to wind up and come to Gurgaon to be under the care of Shyamala and Alex.

Her Profession

In her profession, she had a lot of patients and every one of them liked her. She was gifted by God to have developed such skills without formal education. She was very dedicated to her profession. Sometimes she would work for two days continuously without any rest. She was the biggest source of strength to the hospital.

Godmother

Amelia became a godmother to June and me. When we did not know where to stay after our marriage, she readily agreed for us to stay in her house. From that time onwards, she took care of us till her retirement.

Character

Amelia was a very simple person. She derived pleasure by giving to others. She was selfless.

Sports Interest

She was interested in tennis, football and cricket. She knew all the players. She would read newspapers thoroughly.

Amenda Joining M.D. - January, 2016

Amenda wanted to do the three-year MD/MS in AIIMS itself. She wrote her entrance examination for AIIMS on November 1, 2015, just one week after the death of her nana Amelia. She also wrote JIPMER and Post Graduate Institute (PGI), Chandigarh entrance exams. She was interested in Orthopaedics or Gynaecology. Counselling for AIIMS came first and she confirmed her seat for M.D. Gynaecology and Obstetrics. Even though she got 22nd rank in PGI, Chandigarh, she did not attend the counselling because she wanted to study in AIIMS only.

She joined M.D. Gynaecology and Obstetrics in AIIMS from January 1, 2016.

Sharanya's Marriage - January 29, 2016

I attended Padmanaban's second granddaughter, Sharanya's, marriage in Trichy on January 29, 2016.

Joshua's OCI Card - 2016

Since Joshua is an American citizen by birth, his PIO (Persons of Indian Origin) card had to be changed to Overseas Citizen of India (OCI) card. The PIO was valid up to 16 years of age and OCI is for life time. Alex and Shyamala successfully got the OCI card for Joshua.

Aadhar card - 2016

All of us received the Aadhar card in the year 2016.

Death of Ramaiyan - March 1, 2016

My brother-in-law, Ramaiyan, was very upset over his bed ridden condition and he cried to everyone why God was not calling him to relieve his pain. On Monday February 22, 2016, he was finding it difficult to breathe and asked my sister to take him to the hospital. He was in the hospital for a week and he was discharged on Monday, February 29. When he came back to the house he was not himself. Early next morning at about 4.30 a.m., my sister got up and saw him struggling to breathe. She called her daughter, Pappi, who was sleeping in the other room. Both sat by his side and saw him slowly going down and he finally breathed his last. A doctor was brought home and he was pronounced dead.

My sister informed everyone and they started coming to pay their last respects to him. There was a very big crowd and they had to continuously clear the garlands. They cremated him by 5 p.m., on the same day in an electric crematorium. I could reach their house only by 9.30 p.m. They gave the ashes the same day and Punniajanam was done the same night.

The Karumathi function was held on Tuesday February 14 which Shyamala attended.

Tributes to Ramaiyan

Ramaiyan was born on April 3, 1934 in Thanjavur. His parents were Venkatachalam and Pushpavalli Ammal. His father was a school teacher. He died at age of 32 due to jaundice, when Ramaiyan was 13 years old. Ramaiyan had one elder and two younger sisters. Her elder sister was married soon after his father's death. After passing SSLC, Ramaiyan joined as a clerk in the Thanjavur Municipal Office in 1952. He got his two younger sisters married. Then he married my sister Vasantha on September 5, 1963. Through his hard work, he became a Manager in the Trichy Municipality in the year 1973. He wrote the department examination and was promoted as Municipal Commissioner. He retired as Municipal Commissioner in the year 1992 from Rajapalayam. He served in many places in his professional capacity.

He was a very hardworking official and honest person. Municipal service is known for corruption but Ramaiyan was an exception. He knew the rules and regulations by heart. I have never known a more straightforward man.

He had helped many people without expecting anything in return. He helped Shyamala and Alex in purchasing Amelia's apartment and another apartment in Udhaya Flats. He helped Rani in a property dispute and helped her recover her rightful inheritance after the death of her husband Mohanraj. He also worked in A. G. Eye Hospital to help Kumararaj and Anandaraj. He was the proud father of Chandrasekar, Selvaraj, Ramesh (late) and Premalatha and grandfather of Manoj Kumar, Praveen, Shwetha and Samyuktha.

Relieved from The NorthCap University - May 31, 2016

When I completed 72 years of age, I was relieved from the post of Emeritus Fellow from the NorthCap University on May 31, 2016.

On the day of my retirement, the faculty of the Department of Civil and Environmental Engineering gave me a farewell lunch and a few gifts. Brig. Sharma, Pro-Vice-Chancellor extended his welcome for me to be associated with the University. Avdhesh Mishra, the member of Governing Body thanked me for everything I had done in the university for eight years from May 2008.

Entering 50th Year of my Teaching - October 2016

As there was no faculty to teach Water Resources Engineering and Fluid Mechanics at NorthCap University they sent me a SOS to be a visiting faculty and teach the two courses. I readily obliged them. This is the third time I was recalled. First time it was in REC Trichy for the post of Chairman, Transport Committee, second time in AMACE, Kanchipuram when the Managing Trustee revoked his own order of relieving me as faculty.

I worked as Emeritus Visiting Faculty in the NorthCap University in the July-December session of 2016-17. On October 16, 2016, I entered the 50th year of my teaching.

Joshua's credentials in Academics and Extra-Curricular Activities

Academics

Joshua always excelled in academics and received a "Scholar Badge" every year. He scored a perfect 10 (out of 10) in his standard 10 board examination in 2017.

Competitive Examinations

He passed with merit in various competitive examinations like PSAT examination, ASSET, National Science Olympiad, International Math Olympiad, National Science Talent Search Examination and is a recipient of the prestigious Haryana State Scholarship.

He cleared the prestigious KVPY national scholarship examination with an All India Rank of 351 in 2017.

He scored 1460 out of 1520 in the PSAT examinations held in 2016 and 1480 in 2017 and was awarded the Highly Commendable Performance certificate.

Piano

He has cleared up to 8th Grade Piano examinations (both theory and practical) conducted by Trinity College London with Distinction/Merit.

Sports

He won a bronze medal in the Delhi State Jeet Kune-Do (Martial Art) championship in 2008.

He won the IInd place in Table Tennis in CBSE cluster competition in 2015-16 and won the bronze medal in the Haryana State Taekwondo Championship in 2016. He will again be taking part in Haryana State Taekwondo Championship in 2018 as he was selected at the district.

He was awarded Black Belt by Taekwondo Academy of India in 2016 under the authority of World Taekwondo Federation and International Taekwondo Academy, South Korea.

My Visit to Trichy - January to March 2017

I visited Trichy to attend Ramaiyan's first death anniversary and stayed for a month with my sister for the first time. We visited all the temples in and around Trichy and also stayed in Pappi's house for a week. For the first time, we visited Vadaloor and had a darshan of Vallallar Ramalinga Swamigal.

25th Wedding Anniversary - February 10, 2017

Shyamala and Alex celebrated their 25th wedding anniversary in Gurgaon on February 10, 2017. On the same day. my sister and I attended a Mass at 6 a.m., in St. Mary's Cathedral Church where Shyamala and Alex got married 25 years ago. Blessings were given to Shyamala and Alex in the Mass.

Closing of Daiichi Sankyo - January 31, 2017

The Japanese pharmaceutical company Daiichi Sankyo was on a mission since April, 2016 to refine its R&D operations, and in that pursuit closed its Indian research facility in January, 2017.

New job for Alex - June 12, 2017

Alex joined as Professor in the Department of Biotechnology, Manav Rachna International University, Faridabad on June 12, 2017.

Shyamala as Private Tutor

I was very much disappointed when Shyamala lost her opportunity to be an engineer or doctor. I did not show my disappointment but as I was driving to the club tears were dropping from my eyes. I did not feel like stopping them. But after she started to take home tuition in Chemistry and biology during the past 5 years, she has earned a great name for herself and she is much sought after teacher in Gurgaon and Delhi. She works hard to make her students perform well in the board examinations and other entrance examinations. Every year she teaches about 50 to 60 students. I am very proud of her.

Family Trip to Trichy - April, 2018

Alex, Shyamala and the children made a trip to Trichy to attend the wedding of Prasana (eldest son of his late brother Prakash) in Tanjavur on April 27, 2018.

Shifting to Own Apartment - May 2018

We shifted to our own apartment in Sare Homes, Phase 3, T070402 in sector 92, Gurgaon on May 26, 2018. We had the traditional Milk Boiling Ceremony on May 25. Alex and Shyamala had booked it in 2010. The apartment was offered for fit-out in November 2017. We took over the apartment and started the interior decoration. A joyful occasion for all of us. Eugenia (Dinky) came from Trichy to help with the transition.

Priyanka's Marriage - June 3, 2018

I attended the marriage of Priyanka, granddaughter of Padmanaban in Chennai on June 3, 2018. She was one of the flower girls in Shyamala's wedding.

Visiting Faculty - From July, 2018

Accepting the invitation from the Department of Civil and Environmental Engineering, the North Cap University, I am taking two courses as visiting faculty from July 2018.

Oh! Again it has proved that God has put you where He wanted and you have delivered great things with his blessings. Now can you share your role in the success of others?

Around Me

Let us go through the major events that took place during this period.

India

Politics

Hunger strike by Anna Hazare, 2011 - The Anti-Corruption Movement gained momentum from April 5, 2011, when Anna

Hazare began a hunger strike at the Jantar Mantar in New Delhi to press the government for enacting the Jan Lokpal Bill.

Mamata Banerjee the First Female Chief Minister of West Bengal, 2011 - Mamata Banerjee was sworn in as the first woman Chief Minister of West Bengal, on May 20, 2011. Banerjee founded the party All India Trinamool Congress (AITMC or TMC) in 1997 and became its chairperson, after separating from the Indian National Congress.

Pranab Mukherjee, 13th President of India, 2012 - Pranab Mukherjee was sworn in as the 13th President of India on July 25, 2012.

XVIth General Elections, 2014 - The general elections were held for all 543 parliamentary constituencies in nine phases during April 7 to May 12, 2014. It was the longest election in the country's history. The average election turnout was around 66.38%, the highest ever. UPA and NDA were the two main fronts who fought the election. NDA won 336 seats (BJP 282; Shiv Sena 18; TDP 16; Shiromani Akali Dal 4). UPA won 60 seats (INC 44; NCP 6; RJD 4; Jharkhand Mukti Morcha 2; IUML 2). Others won 144 seats (AIADMK 37; AITMC 34; CPI(M) 9; CPI 1; YSR 9; TRS 11; SP 5). Independents won 3 seats.

Narendra Modi became 15th Prime Minister of India, 2014 - Narendra Modi was sworn in as the 15th Prime Minister of India on May 26, 2014. The ceremony was noted by the media for being the first ever swearing in of an Indian Prime Minister to have been attended by the heads of all SAARC countries.

Birth of Telengana, 29th State, in India, 2014 - Telengana, the 29th state in India, was born on June 2, 2014 under the Andhra Pradesh Re-organisation Act, 2014.

Delhi Legislative Assembly Election's Results, 2015 - Aam Aadmi Party secured 67 of 70 seats, and formed the government in New Delhi. Arvind Kejriwal became the Chief Minister. The remaining three seats went to BJP.

Demonetization of all Rs.500 and Rs.1,000 Bank Notes, 2016- On November 8, 2016, the Government of India announced the demonetisation of all Rs. 500 and Rs.1,000 banknotes of the Mahatma Gandhi series. The government claimed that the action would curtail the shadow economy and crack down on the use of illicit and counterfeit cash to fund illegal activity and terrorism.

Population

India's population of 1.21 Billion, 2011 - India's population rose to 1.21 billion people over the last 10 years - an increase by 181 million, according to the new census released.

Seven Billionth Baby Born, 2011 - A baby girl, born to 23-year old Vinita and Ajay at a local Community Health Centre at 7.20 a.m. on the outskirts of Lucknow, was welcomed as the seven billionth baby in the world.

Goods and Services Tax (GST), 2017- Goods and Services Tax (India) Act came into force on July 1, 2017.

Ram Nath Kovind became President, 2017 - Ram Nath Kovind was sworn in as 14th President on July 25, 2017 after Pranab Mukherjee.

Visit by Japanese Prime Minister, 2017- Shinzo Abe, Prime Minister, Japan visited Ahmedabad on September 13 and 14 for bilateral talk and signed many agreements including Bullet train project connecting Ahmedabad and Mumbai.

Rahul Gandhi became Congress President, 2017 - Rahul Gandhi, son of Rajiv and Sonia Gandhi became President, Indian National Congress on December 16, 2017.

10 Heads of ASEAN Nations attend Republic Day, 2018 - 10 leaders from the Association of Southeast Asian Nations (ASEAN) namely Halima Yacob, President, Singapore, Najib Razak, Prime Minister, Malaysia, Joko Widodo, President, Indonesia, Prayuth Chano-O-cha, Prime Minister, Thailand, Nguyễn Xuân Phúc, Prime Minister, Vietnam, Hun Sen, Prime Minister, Cambodia, Rodrigo Roa Duterte, President, Philippines, Thongloun Sisoulith, Prime Minister, Laos, Htin Kyaw, President, Myanmar, and Hassanal Bolkiah, Sultan, Brunai and Prime Minister attended the 69th Republic Day functions on January 26, 2018.

Others

Gang Rape in Delhi, 2012 - The 2012 Delhi gang rape case occurred on December 16, 2012 in Munirka, in South Delhi. A 23 year old female physiotherapy intern was beaten, gang raped, and tortured by six men in a private bus in which she was traveling with her friend. Eleven days after the assault, she was transferred to a hospital in Singapore for emergency treatment, but she died two days later. All the accused were arrested and charged with sexual assault and murder.

Supreme Court's Verdict on Delhi Gang Rape Case, 2013 - The Supreme Court upheld the Delhi High Court and trial court decision to award death to all four convicts in the December 16, 2012 gang rape and murder.

Hanging of Mohammed Ajmal Amir Kasab, 2012 - Mohammed Ajmal Amir Kasab was a Pakistani militant and member of the Lashkar-e-Taiba Islamist group. He took part in the 2008 Mumbai terrorist attacks in Maharashtra, India. Kasab was hanged on November 21, 2012 at 7.30 a.m., and buried in Yerwada Jail in Pune.

Nobel Prize

Shared 2014 Nobel Peace Prize for India's Kailash Satyarti - The 2014 Nobel Peace Prize was shared between Kailash Satyarthi of India and 17-year old Malala Yousafzai of Pakistan for their struggle against the suppression of children and young people and for the right of all children to education.

End of Telegram Service

Dot, Dash, Full Stop: Telegram Service Ends, 2013 - On July 15, 2013, one of India's oldest communication services, the telegram became history. Financial constraints forced the Bharat Sanchar Nigam Ltd., to wind up the telegraphic service, which would be remembered mainly as a historically inexpensive but relatively quick method of sending alerts related to births, deaths and emergency situations

Deaths

Death of A. P. J. Abdul Kalam, 2015 - Former President Abdul Kalam, widely acclaimed as the "People's President", passed away after collapsing during a lecture at the Indian Institute of Management, Shillong on July 27, 2015. Mr. Kalam, the country's 11th President, between 2002 and 2007, was one of India's most eminent scientists, and had the unique honour of receiving honorary doctorates from 30 universities and institutions. Apart from leading the Indian Space Research Organisation's satellite launch Development Programme, he headed the country's Integrated Guided Missile development programme for many years.

Death of Atal Bihari Vajpayee, 2018 - Atal Bihari Vajpayee, former Prime Minister died on August 16, 2018. He served three terms as the Prime Minister of India: first for a term of 13 days in 1996, then for a period of 13 months from 1998 to 1999, and finally, for a full term from 1999 to 2004. A member of the Bharatiya Janata Party (BJP), he was the first Indian Prime Minister who was not a member of the Indian National Congress party to have served a full five-year term in office. Vajpayee authored several works of both prose and poetry. He was conferred India's highest civilian honour, the Bharat Ratna, in 2015.

Bombings and Death Toll

8 people were killed on November 21, 2010 in Aurangabad due to a bomb blast, 26 killed on July 13, 2011 in Mumbai due to three bomb explosions, 17 killed on February 21, 2013 in Hyderabad due to two blasts, 3 injured on February 13, 2012 in New Delhi due to bomb explosion in the car of the wife of Israeli Defence Attaché and 1 killed on May 1, 2014 in Chennai due to low intensity bombing in a train.

Natural Calamities

110 people were killed in a 6.9 earthquake on September 18, 2011 in the Kanchenjunga Conservation Area, near the border of Nepal and the Indian state of Sikkim, about 12 million people were affected due to severe cyclonic storm Phailin on October 10-11, 2013 in Odisha, 124 people were killed due to severe cyclonic storm Hudhud on October 12, 2014 in Eastern India, 11 people killed in 6.7 earthquake in Imphal on January 4, 2016 and 24 people killed due to Cyclone Vardah in Tamil Nadu on December 12, 2016.

Kerala Floods, 2018 - Beginning on August 15, 2018, severe floods affected the south Indian state of Kerala, due to unusually high rainfall during the monsoon season. Over 483 people died. The Indian government had declared it a level 3 Calamity, or "calamity of a severe nature". It is the worst flood in Kerala after the great flood of 99 that happened in 1924.

Accidents

67 people were killed in Lalitha Park residential building collapse on November 15, 2010 in New Delhi, 106 in the stampede in Sabarimala on January 14, 2011, 90 in the fire in AMRI Hospital,

Kolkata on December 9, 2011, 2 by Italian Merchant vessel on February 15, 2012, 9 in collapse of five-storey building under construction in Goa on January 4, 2014, 5 in the crash of military transport aircraft near Gwalier, on March 28, 2014, 24 in Beas River disaster in Himachal Pradesh, on June 8, 2014, 24 in the fire in GAIL gas pipeline in Nagaram,Andhra Pradesh, on June 27, 2014, 200 in landslide in Malin on July 30, 2014, 27 Pilgrims in Stampede at Pushkar Ghat in Rajahmundry on July 15, 2015, 30 in Uttarakhand cloudburst on July 2, 2016, 24 in stampede in Varanasi on October 15, 2016, 22 in SUM hospital fire in Bhubaneswar, October 17, 2016, 150 in train accident near Kanpur on November 20, 2016 and 290 children at BRD Medical College, Gorakhpur due to lack of oxygen on August 30, 2017.

Space Technology

The following test firing and launchings were made.

Agni 1, a strategic ballistic missile, with a range of 700 km, November 26, 2010, Agni V with a range of 5500 km, April 19, 2012, Indian Regional Navigation Satellite System, July 1, 2013, Mangalyan, a space probe to orbit Mars, November 5, 2013, GSAT-14, a communication satellite, January 5, 2014, PSLV-C23 rocket with 5 foreign satellites, June 30, 2014, Prithivi II missile with a range of 350 km, November 14, 2014, signing of NASA-ISRO Synthetic Aperture Radar Mission to launch a satellite in 2021, the Crew Module Atmospheric Re-entry Experiment (CARE) on December 18, 2014, Astra, active radar homing beyond visual range air-to-air missile, March 18, 2015, Polar Remotely Operated Vehicle, March 26, 2015, IRNSS-1D, March 28, 2015, induction of Akash Missile system in Indian Army, May 5, 2015, communication satellite GSAT-6, August 27, 2015, ASTROSAT, first space laboratory, September 28, 2015, RLV-TD, reusable shuttle, May 23, 2016, PSLV-C34 with 20 Satellites in a single flight, June 22, 2016, PSLV-C37 with 104 satellites from seven countries on February 15, 2017.

Scams

Fodder Scam Case, Judgement, 2018 - A special CBI court sentenced RJD chief Lalu Prasad Yadav to three and half year jail term in the second case of Fodder scam on January 6, 2018 and a five-year term in the third case on January 24, 2018.

Tamil Nadu

Politics

XIVth Tamil Nadu Assembly Elections, 2011 - The fourteenth Legislative Assembly election was held on April 13, 2011 to elect members from 234 constituencies. There were two major fronts: AIDMK Front and DMK Front. The ruling party DMK's Front consisted of 8 parties and AIADMK Front consisted of 11 parties. AIADMK Front secured 203 seats. (AIADMK 150; DMDK 29; CPI(M) 10; CPI 9); DMK front secured 31 seats. (DMK 23; INC 5; PMK 3).

Jayalalithaa Became Chief Minister for the Third Time, 2011 - Jayalalithaa was sworn in as the Chief Minister of Tamil Nadu for the third time on May 16, 2011.

Jayalalithaa Convicted by the Special Court, 2014 - On September 27, 2014, the Special Court convicted all the four accused in the disproportionate assets case. Jayalalithaa was sentenced to four years imprisonment under the Prevention of Corruption Act and fined Rs. 100 crore. The three co-accused were all sentenced to four years imprisonment and fined Rs. 10 crores each. It also meant that Jayalalithaa was disqualified as an MLA and as Chief Minister, and she would not be able to contest elections for 10 years. Jayalalithaa was moved to Parappana Agrahara prison. Requests for a VVIP cell and medical treatment were denied. The three co-accused were also jailed in that prison.

O. Pannerselvam became Chief Minister, 2014 - O. Pannerselvam was sworn in as the Chief Minister of Tamil Nadu on September 29, 2014 after Jayalalithaa was imprisoned.

Bail for Jayalalithaa and Others, 2014 - The four sought bail, pending an appeal, and this was granted on October 17, 2014. It was stipulated that the appeal must be completed within three months.

Acquittal of Jayalalithaa, 2015 - Jayalalithaa and her associates were acquitted of all charges in the DA case by the Karnataka High Court Judge, Kumarasamy, on May 11, 2015.

Appeal to Supreme Court, 2015 - Karnataka Government moved the Supreme Court against Jayalalithaa's acquittal on June 23, 2015.

XVth Tamil Nadu Assembly Elections, 2011 - The fifteenth Legislative Assembly elections were held on May 16, 2016.

AIADMK led by Jayalalithaa won the elections. AIADMK won 134 seats DMK 89; INC 8. Jayalalithaa was sworn in as Chief Minister on May 23, 2016

Jayalalithaa's Death - Jayalalithaa died on December 5, 2016 after being hospitalized for more than two months. As per medical report, she died of heart attack.

Events after Jayalalithaa's Death, 2016 to 2018 - O. Panneerselvam was sworn in as the Chief Minister on the night of December 5, 2016. Sasikala was elected as the General Secretary by the General Council of AIADMK on December 29, 2016 and as the Chief Minister by the AIADMK MLAs on February 5, 2016. O. Panneerselvam resigned as the Chief Minister. Opposition to Sasikala was started by O. Panneerselvam and his supporters on February 7, 2016. There was also some delay from the Governor's side. On February 14, the Supreme Court set aside AIADMK general secretary V.K. Sasikala's acquittal by the Karnataka High Court in the Jayalalithaa disproportionate assets case and "restored in full" the trial court conviction of September 2014. Before going to Parapana Agrahara Prisons in Bengaluru on February 15, Sasikal appointed T. T.V. Dinakaran, her nephew, as the Deputy General Secretary AIADMK. She also elected Edapadi Palanisamy as the leader of the AIADMK Legislature Party and he was sworn as Chief Minister on February 16, 2016.

Pro-Jallikattu Protests, 2017 - It refers to numerous leaderless apolitical youth groups protesting in January 2017 in large groups in several locations across Tamil Nadu, with some sporadic smaller protests taking place across India, as well as overseas. The chief motivation of the protest was against the Supreme Court's order to ban jallikattu a traditional Tamil bull taming sport, which is held during Pongal

After several days of protests, jallikattu was finally legalised locally on January 23, when the Government of Tamil Nadu passed a bill to amend the PCA Act.

T. T. V. Dinakaran Won the R. K. Nagar By-Elections, 2017- T.T.V. Dinakaran, as an independent, won the R.K. Nagar Assembly by-elections, held on December 24, by more than 40000 votes defeating AIADMK and DMK candidates.

Rajinikanth's Entry in Politics, 2017 - Actor Rajinikanth confirmed, on December 31, 2017, his entry into politics, to form a party and fight elections

Party Launched by Kamal Haasan, 2018 - Actor Kamal Hassan launched his party "Makkal Needhi Maiam" on February 22, 2018 in Madurai.

Party Launched by T.T.V. Dinakaran, 2018 - R.K. Nagar MLA T.T.V. Dhinakaran announced his new political party "Amma Makkal Munnetra Kazhagam" (AMMK) on May 18, 2018 in Madurai.

Death of Karunanidhi, 2018 - M. Karunanidhi, five-time Tamil Nadu Chief Minister and DMK President for nearly 50 years, died at 6.10 p.m., on August 7 after battling infection and age-related ailments for 11 days at the Kauvery Hospital in Chennai. Affectionately called "Kalaignar" (artiste and man of letters), he was 94. He played multiple roles from championing social justice, to being a die-hard proponent of the Tamil language, from shaping the Dravidian movement to being a lifelong warrior for Sri Lankan Tamil cause.

World

Politics

Obama's Second Term, 2013 - Obama won the elections in 2012 and continued as President of US from January 20, 2013.

Xi Jinping became President of China, 2013 - Xi Jinping became the President of China on March 14, 2013 after Hu Jintao.

Li Kegiang became Prime Minister of China, 2013 - Li Kegiang became the Prime Minister of China on March 15, 2013 after Wen Jiabao.

Nelson Mandela Died at 95, 2013 - On December 5, 2013, Nelson Mandela, died at the age of 95 after suffering from a prolonged respiratory infection.

US - Cuba Relations Breakthrough, 2014 - President Obama ordered the restoration of full diplomatic relations with Cuba and the opening of an embassy in Havana for the first time in more than a half-century as he vowed to "cut loose the shackles of the past" and sweep aside one of the last vestiges of the Cold War.

Obama Visited Hiroshima, 2016 - President Obama visited Hiroshima, Japan, making a brief but historic visit to bolster an important ally and remind the world of the dangers of nuclear weapons. He visited the Hiroshima Peace Memorial Museum and signed the guest book.

Britain Voted to Exit the EU after Referendum, 2016 - Britain voted to leave the European Union in 2016. The stunning turn of events was accompanied by a plunge in the financial markets, with the value of the British pound and stock prices plummeting.

Theresa May became Prime Minister of UK, 2016 - Theresa May became the Prime Minister of UK on July 13, 2018 after David Cameron.

Donald Trump became President of US, 2017 - Donald Trump of the Republican Party was sworn in as the 45th President of US. He was preceded by Barack Obama

North Korea's Missiles and Nuclear Weapons Tests, 2017 - In 2017, the country launched 23 missiles, including its first intercontinental missiles that it said had a long enough range to reach the United States mainland. Their first missile was fired on February 11, 2017 which flew over the Sea of Japan as the new US President Donald Trump met with Japanese Prime Minister Shinzo Abe at Trump's Mar-a-Lago resort in Florida. In April, as Trump prepared to meet his Chinese counterpart, President Xi Jinping, North Korea fired another ballistic missile off the coast of the Korean Peninsula. The Hwasong-14 launched on July, 4 (Independence Day of USA), 2,800 kilometers above the Earth, before splashing down in the sea off the Korean Peninsula.

Trump - Kim Summit, 2018 - Donald Trump met with North Korean Supreme Leader Kim Jong-un on June 12, 2018, in Singapore, in the first summit meeting between the leaders of the United States of America and the Democratic People's Republic of Korea (North Korea). They signed a joint statement, agreeing to security guarantees for North Korea, new peaceful relations, reaffirmation of the denuclearization of the Korean Peninsula, recovery of remains of soldiers and follow-up negotiations between high-level officials.

Imran Khan became Prime Minister of Pakistan, 2018 - Imran Ahmed Khan Niazi of Pakistan Tehreek-e-Insaf became the 22nd Prime Minister of Pakistan on August 18, 2018. He was a former cricketer.

War

Killing of Osama Bin Laden, 2011 - Osama Bin Laden, the Founder and Head of the Islamist group Al-Qaeda, was killed in Pakistan on May 2, 2011, shortly after 1.00 a.m., PKT by United States Navy SEALS. (Naval Special Warfare Development Group).

US Military Formally Ends Mission in Iraq, 2011 - The US military mission in Iraq formally ended its assignment on December 15 in a small ceremony at Baghdad Airport as the last US troops prepared to leave the country.

Climate Change

Environmental Performance Index (EPI), 2010 - India ranked 123rd in 2010 EPI, while Iceland leads the world in addressing pollution control and natural resource management challenges.

Climate Change Deal Reached by about 200 Countries, 2015 - The 2015 United Nations Climate Change Conference, COP 21 or CMP 11 was held in Paris, France, from November 30 to December 12, 2015. The conference negotiated the Paris Agreement, on the reduction of climate change, the text of which represented a consensus of the representatives of the 196 parties attending it.

US Decision on Paris Agreement, 2017 - On June 1, 2017, US President Donald Trump announced that the US would cease all participation in the 2015 Paris Agreement on climate change mitigation. Trump stated that "The Paris accord will undermine (the US) economy", and "puts (the US) at a permanent disadvantage".

Space Technology

Landing of Mars Rover, Curiosity on Mars, 2012 - After executing a flawless landing sequence, NASA's new Mars rover, Curiosity, reached the surface of its new home. "We are wheels down on Mars," was the official word from mission control.

Space X Lands Rocket Successfully, Makes Reuse Possible, 2015 - Space X's Falcon 9 rocket successfully landed on solid ground at Cape Canaveral, Florida after traveling into space and back for the first time. It was a big first step toward reusable rockets.

Science and Technology

Scientists successfully Cloned Human Stem Cells, 2013 - 17 years after Dolly the sheep was cloned from a somatic cell, scientists applied the same technique to make the first embryonic stem cell lines from human skin cells.

Sports

Usain Bolt's "Triple-Triple", 2016 - The 2016 Summer Olympics (XXXI) were held in Rio de Janeiro, Brazil, from August 5, to 21, 2016. Usain Bolt ended his Olympic career by claiming an unprecedented "triple-triple" and his ninth gold. He is the only man to win all three sprint events at three Games

Mother Teresa Sainthood, 2016 - Mother Teresa was proclaimed a Saint by Pope Francis in a ceremony in the Vatican. Francis said St. Teresa had defended the unborn, sick and abandoned, and had shamed world leaders for the "crimes of poverty they themselves created".

Terrorist attacks

37 people died in the suicide bombing in Moscow Airport on January 24, 2011, 60 people in a wave of bombings in Iraq on August 10, 2011, 17 in four shooting attacks in Paris on January 7, 2015, 130 people in terrorist attacks in Paris on November 13, 2015, 32 in attacks in Brussels, Belgium on March 22, 2016, many in hospital bombings in Syria on April 22, 2016, and 29 due to an attack on a cafe in Dhaka on July 1, 2016

Natural calamities

Hundreds of people killed in Japan on March 10, 2011 due to a ferocious tsunami produced by one of the largest earthquakes, 600 in Van earthquake in Turkey on October 23, 2011, 195 people in Lushan earthquake (7.0) in China on April 20, 2013, 6300 people because of Typhoon Haiyan in Philippines on November 5, 2013 and 160 in an earthquake in Central Italy on August 24, 2016.

Worst Accidents.

On September 24, 2015 an event described as a "crush and stampede" caused deaths of over 2,000 pilgrims who were suffocated or crushed during the annual Haj pilgrimage in Mina, Mecca, Saudi Arabia.

CHAPTER-16

My Role in the Success of Others

You say that no matter how successful a person is, one should always help others. You said you have followed this belief. Can you share about that?

Everything is attributed to the day I started my first research project on "Water Resources Management".

As I required project assistants, I hired two of my former students of Civil Engineering, Jacob Soundararajan and Manivasagam. After working for a few months, Jacob left for USA for higher studies. I had given him a strong letter of recommendation. Manivasagam completed one year and he joined Indian Railways after clearing the Indian Railway Services Examination.

In the meantime, Rajendran, a diploma holder in Civil Engineering, joined along with Kannagi, a Civil Engineering graduate from REC itself. When Kannagi left, another diploma holder Balasubramanian was hired.

Govindan - Diploma Holder to Assistant Executive Engineer with a Master's Degree

Kannagi recommended Govindan, another Diploma holder in Civil Engineering, for a job on my project.

Even though vacancy was not there, I enquired about him. I came to know that he was fatherless from a young age. He had a blind mother and a younger sister. Naturally, I took pity on him and conveyed his case to the Principal. He was also sympathetic and asked me to take him under daily wages scheme if Govindan agreed. When I told Govindan about this, he was happy to accept. He started working on the project. He was very smart. To his luck Balasubramanian left for Bangalore and he was given employment.

After serving for two years, Govindan and Rajendran wanted to study part-time undergraduate degree programme in Civil Engineering at REC. But they were not eligible as they did not have first class in their diploma.

I took the case to the Principal Ilango and he was kind enough to waive the condition considering them as local candidates, according to my suggestion.

Govindan passed in first class and Rajendran in second class. Rajendran got a job in a private firm and left.

Then, Govindan was interested in pursuing a Master's degree and he completed part-time Master's degree in Water Resources Management. He passed this with first class as well and was hired as a teaching assistant in the Department of Civil Engineering.

Then, he got married and June and I attended the marriage. He started to write the state government competitive examinations. He cleared it in the first attempt and he was appointed as Assistant Engineer in the Highways Department of the Tamil Nadu Government.

Now, he has been promoted as Assistant Executive Engineer.

Babu - Diploma Holder to Postgraduate Degree

Babu was the son of Xavier, a mechanic in the Hydraulics Laboratory of the Civil Engineering Department. He had completed a diploma in Electronics and Communication Engineering. I wanted to give him a job in my project as computer operator. Even though my Head of the Department Kuppuswamy hesitated, I convinced him and hired Babu in the computer centre of our Department.

Then I encouraged him to do part-time undergraduate degree and post graduate degree at REC itself. He completed both with first class and he was offered a job in Wipro. After working for two years in India, he was sent to USA where he is working successfully.

Johnson - Civil Engineering Graduate to Associate Professor with Ph.D.

Johnson was a Civil Engineering graduate from Tanjavur, about 35 kilometres from REC campus. When he came to know about my project, he came to me for a job. He was doing part-time MBA in Bishop Heber College, Trichy.

When I said there was no vacancy, he replied that he would come every day from Tanjavur, help me in the project and leave in the evening for his classes. He added that he could do the job even without any salary. Even though I was hesitant, he pleaded and as usual I accepted his proposal.

For one year he worked on my project under this arrangement. He completed his MBA, got married and left for Canada. He finished his Ph.D. in business administration and he is now working as Associate Professor, Management Information Systems, Faculty of Management Administration, University of Regina, Canada. His wife Shanthi is Professor in the Faculty of Kinesiology and Health Studies. He has a son named Joshua.

He has a sister, Catherine, who is also a Civil Engineering graduate. I helped her to get a Lecturer post in the Department of Architecture and guided her in registering for the Ph.D. programme.

Usha

Usha was a diploma holder in Civil Engineering, who approached me for a job on the project. Like Johnson she also worked on my project for one year without any salary. I feel sad that I did not do anything great for her.

Pakkirisamy - Diploma Holder to Dean with Ph.D.

When I joined REC Trichy in July 1974, I was made faculty in charge of Hydraulics laboratory of the Department. Pakkirisamy, a diploma holder in Mechanical Engineering was the mechanic in the laboratory. After interacting with him for a few years, I suggested to him that he could do a part-time degree programme in Mechanical Engineering in REC itself. Based on my suggestion he joined the programme and passed B.E. in Mechanical Engineering in first class. Then I recommended to him to complete the master's degree also. When he completed his master's degree in first class, I encouraged him to do a Ph.D. To my surprise, he got his Ph.D. also and was appointed as Assistant Professor and later as Dean at REC, Trichy.

Workers on My Research Farm

On my research farm, there were a few labourers like Kaliaperumal, Nelson, Thangaraj, Doraimanickam, and Tirunavukkarasu who worked for a long time with me. I was able to get some of them permanent jobs and others temporary jobs in REC itself. As Chairman,

Transport Committee I had appointed a few drivers and conductors who are still working at REC.

Ram Mohan's Son - Education Problem

Ram Mohan is an astrologer practicing in Chennai. He is the son of Balan Nair, whom I consulted in 1983. I started consulting Ram Mohan not only for our family but also for relatives and friends. When we were in Kanchipuram in 2004, I called him on the phone to fix an appointment with him for some consultation. When he came on the line he seemed excited and told me "Sir, I was trying to contact you for the past few days but I could not since you had retired from REC. I have a problem. My son got admission in REC Surat, in Gujarat State and my wife does not want my son to be admitted there. You please come and solve this matter by convincing my wife. You are like my God, so please help me." I said, "Sir, don't worry. I will come and do the needful."

Then I discussed the matter with June. We knew that Bindu and her husband Chandramohan had studied in Surat. Bindu was in USA at that time but Chandramohan was in Chennai. I got Chandramohan's mobile number from Bindu and contacted him.

We told him about this matter and asked him whether he would accompany us to Ram Mohan's house to clear the doubts of Ram Mohan's wife. He readily agreed and we took him to meet Ram Mohan and his wife. Ram Mohan was so happy to see us and again said, "You have come like God." Then we allowed Chandramohan to talk to Ram Mohan's wife. After an hour, his wife told us that she was convinced to send her son to Surat. Ram Mohan was relieved.

His son joined Surat and came out in flying colours. Later he did his post-graduation in UK and is successful in his career.

Sundaram - Paper Boy to Swimming Coach

There was a boy named Sundaram, who delivered newspapers to all the houses in REC. He requested me for a job and I made him a club boy for our Officers' Club. After some time at his request I recommended him to the Officers' Club, BHEL and they employed him as the club boy. From there he went to Singapore for employment and returned as a swimming coach to the same Officers' Club, BHEL. He coached my granddaughter Amenda when she was 5 years old and she is an excellent swimmer now. He also became the swimming coach of REC.

Juliet Willets - Ph.D. Holder to Research Director and Professor

I told you about Juliet earlier whom I never thought I would meet again. But in the first week of January 2000, I received an email from her that she had come to Chennai and she would be staying there for a month. She mentioned her address in Chennai. June and I had already planned to visit Chennai during Pongal festival holidays (January 13-15) and stay with uncle Padmanaban. After telling June I left on January 14 to meet Juliet. After exchanging details, I casually invited her to uncle's house for lunch. First, she said no and as I started to leave she said she would like to come. Then I took her to my uncle's home and she had lunch and everyone liked her. She liked and appreciated our customs and food. She often visited Chennai in connection with her job.

In that year, she visited thrice and I met her all the times. She shared her fears about her unemployment, marriage and family. I took her to my friend, astrologer Ram Mohan, and he gave some predictions about her future. I also gave her a print out of computer predictions about her life. She seemed to be happy.

There was no contact for few years and suddenly I received an email in 2005 in which she stated that she had married the person she loved and she was carrying her first baby and had got a job as Assistant Professor in University of Technology, Sydney. As usual I replied to her wishing the best.

In 2013, I sent an email to her in connection with a conference which we had planned in March 2014. I came to know that the astrological predictions for her had come true. She had her own house, two children and a good challenging job. She said she was thankful to me.

Juliet Willetts is currently working as Research Director and Professor at Institute for Sustainable Futures, University of Technology, Sydney, Australia. Her husband's name is Steven Higson and her sons are William Higson (16 years) and Luke Higson (13 years).

Rajakkili's Problem on Joining REC

Rajakkili was our neighbour from 1982 and her husband Samikkannu was the doctor at REC, Trichy. After his sudden and unexpected death, she was offered a temporary job in REC. Balasubramanian was her younger brother who studied in REC Calicut. He started objecting to his sister going to work with thilak on her forehead. Normally, according to Hindu Custom, widows are not supposed to put thilak on the forehead. Rajakkili told June about this asked us to help her in this matter. We called both of them to our house and convinced Balasubramanian that it is harmless for working widows to put thilak to safeguard themselves from exploiters. Rajakkili never had a problem after that and she completed 26 years of service there.

Bindu's Problem in Marriage

When Bindu was studying in REC Surat, She fell in love with her senior Chandramohan of the same college. After their studies, they wanted to get married. But Bindu's family were not willing since Chandramohan was a Tamil from Sri Lanka. Bindu wanted us to solve this issue. Then June and I took her to Gopalakrishnan, another dependable astrologer in Trichy. After seeing the horoscope of Bindu and Chandramohan, he said that it is not advisable to have a marriage between them. Bindu started crying. Then, Gopalakrishnan said, " I have never changed my decision for any one. Seeing your plight, I am telling you about a solution. I will give you a prayer which you have to say every day. Then your future will be alright. Don't cry. Good luck."

She did everything she was asked and they got married in March 2004.

In addition to the above few examples, I have helped many students and counselled them in clearing their arrears, getting better jobs and going for higher studies.

It is nice to hear how you have been a source of help for so many people to come up in their life.

It is all God's plan which I executed.

You said that you help in a small way to alleviate the sufferings of the poor. Can you please elaborate?

I contribute to temples, churches and orphanages that look after the poor people. I contribute to non-governmental organisations (NGO) for education of children. I am a partner in Jesus Calls Ministry and through the contributions of partners they heal the sufferings of millions of people by prayers and work for the upliftment of the poor through Seesha (The Samiti for Education, Environment, Social and Health Action).

Very nice. Did you face any failures in your life?

Yes. I have had a few failures. These are some of the doors shut by God.

Destiny means accepting failures also.

CHAPTER 17

My Failures

What do you consider as your failures?

Not getting a Ph.D. Degree, not possessing own house and failed business ventures are some of the disappointments I faced in my otherwise satisfying and full life.

Ph.D. Degree

When I went to meet T. M. Narayanasamy to seek his blessings before joining REC Trichy, he advised me to earn a Ph.D. degree. At that time, they introduced QIP (Quality Improvement Programme) in which faculty would be deputed for doing M. Tech. or Ph.D. during which both salary and stipend could be claimed. It was a very profitable scheme but REC Principal Manisundaram was not magnanimous to implement the scheme and some of us including me suffered. After persistent efforts of Faculty Association, Manisundaram agreed to send one faculty from each department every year. When I applied for Ph.D. at IISc Bangalore in 1977, another faculty Janagarajan from my department also applied to IIT Madras. Janagarajan was the business partner of Nagaratnam, the Head of the Department and so Nagaratnam recommended his name to the Principal. I think Nagaratnam was selfish not to recommend me because he would not have anyone to help him in various academic activities. I got the admission at IISc Bangalore for Ph.D. but it was not approved since I was not officially sponsored by the Principal. **First failure.**

Then, I decided to do Ph.D. in REC, and registered under Dr. Ibrahim, Head of the Department of Chemical engineering in 1980. I started to collect literature and I spent 10 days at NEERI, Nagpur.

Within six months of my registration he resigned his post to join as Principal in an engineering college at Keelakarai. **Second failure.**

Afterwards, I got the Water Resources Management project and I got busy with it. Several other responsibilities were thrust on me and I could not even think about my Ph.D. degree.

When I joined AMACE in 2007, I filled up an application form to register for Ph.D. programme in Sathyabama University and on the day of my submission, Principal Balakrishnan called me and requested me to be Chief Superintendent, Anna University Examinations. This was a very responsible and time-consuming job. So, I dropped my idea of Ph.D. and I did not even submit the form. **Third failure**.

After joining ITM, I tried to register with IGNOU at the age of 67 years in 2010, but there were no suitable supervisors in my research area, I lost another opportunity. **Fourth failure.**

I have carried out 5 excellent projects, published papers, and organized short term courses and training programs benefitting the department, college, working staff and students. But I did not do Ph.D. for my own progress. Several students were benefitted by my recommendation letters and were accepted in prestigious universities abroad for higher studies and all of them have come up in life. **Destiny** was against me.

Possessing Own House

After my marriage Dr. Thomas said that he would help us financially to build our own house. My mother sold her diamond earrings, which she got from Dr. Daisy, and bought a plot in Mannarpuram. June and I decided on a plan for the house and made a model using chart paper. We dug a well and constructed a fence. But to our bad luck, Dr. Thomas died of heart attack on August 15, 1970. My mother then sold the plot. With that our dream for a new house got buried.

Also aunt Amelia wanted June to inhert her property and discouraged us from buying a house.

Thinking that we would possess a house one day, I did not feel the need to get our own house. I deeply regret that I could not fulfil June's dream of owning a home. I fully take the blame for this.

Business Adventures
Ziffer Data Management – 1983 to1985
Fourth Generation Computers

After 1971, the fourth-generation computers were built as the extension of third generation technology. The fourth-generation computers emerged with development of the VLSI (Very Large-Scale Integration) which gave rise to the microprocessor. The computers were designed by using microprocessors, as thousands of integrated circuits were built onto a single silicon chip. What in the first generation filled an entire room could now fit in the palm of the hand. The fourth-generation computers became more powerful, compact, reliable and affordable. They gave rise to the personal computer (PC) revolution. In 1981, IBM introduced its computer for the home user followed Apple in 1984.

Idea of Starting a Computer Business

My uncle Govindarajan had a strong business acumen. When the microcomputers of fourth generation started coming out in 1981, he thought micro-computer business would flourish. Around February 1983, he decided to establish a computer centre for teaching programming and data processing. His second son Anandaraj had completed B.Sc. Zoology and he required some opening to chart out his future. Govindarajan asked me whether I could be a partner and take up the teaching work in the evenings. I was neither aware of computers nor about running a business. But I agreed to his request. I did not know how to say no to my uncle who took care of me and educated me. Uncle was seeking a third partner who knew about computers and data processing. To our luck (or more so bad luck), uncle came across Balachander, who had just returned from Germany. Balachander was a Civil Engineering graduate and he knew about computers, computer programming and data processing. When my uncle told him about his idea he also agreed after some hesitation. Without knowing much about Balachander we ventured into the computer business. We did some survey about the computers and data processing job details. We estimated a budget for Rs. 6. lakh for purchase of computer and accessories, furniture, office maintenance and a technician for data processing. Each of us invested Rs. 1.0 lakh and we planned to get Rs. 3 lakh as bank loan. We prepared a partnership deed with Anandaraj, Balachander and Shanthi Krishnamoorthi as partners (I could not be official partner since I was a government employee). We decided to sign the deed in my uncle Govindarajan's house. First both Anandaraj and Balachander signed. When my wife started to sign, the pen refused to move smoothly and at the same time power went off. I thought that it was a bad omen. Others also would have thought the same but no one expressed it. Somehow June signed it and an application was submitted to Bank of Madurai branch at Thillainagar for a loan of Rs.3 lakh. Our application for a loan for doing computer business was first of its kind and many people tried to discourage us. But we insisted on getting the loan, and the papers were sent to their Head Office in Chennai. Before finalizing the sanction, we were called by the Head Office and once again we were discouraged. But our perseverance paid off and loan was sanctioned. There were so many indications for us to drop the idea but we never cared to take note of them. **Destiny.**

Bank of Madurai sanctioned our loan and Anandaraj and Balachander went to Bangalore to purchase a computer. We took the first floor of a house in June, 1983 on Tennur high road just facing the junction of Tennur road and Thillainagar road. We also employed a person for data processing. Balachander's wife, Sita, was the receptionist, Anandaraj was in charge of public relations and marketing, Balachander was for data processing and I for teaching of programming language BASIC. We started to register the students. About 100 students registered. The entire infrastructures like computer, printer, furniture, black board were all ready.

Three things happened which laid the foundation for the failure of our business.

Sri Lankan Ethnic War and Agitations in Tamil Nadu

In 1983, there was a big student uprising in the state on the Sri Lankan Tamils issue. The protests followed anti-Tamil riots in Sri Lanka. People from all walks of life joined the protests that broke out in almost every street corner in the state. In July 1983, students took out a procession in Trichy. Nagaraj was a government bus driver who was on duty on that fateful day. When the students in the procession refused to give way for the bus, Nagaraj lost his temper and drove the bus into the procession. At least three people were killed and one among them had registered in our centre. **Really, bad luck.**

Trichy Medical Association's Opposition to Manisundaram's Idea of Starting Government Medical College in Trichy

Manisundaram was the first Principal of REC Trichy from 1964 to 1982 and he also became the first Vice Chancellor of Bharathidasan

University in Trichy. Anandaraj contacted Manisundaram and requested him to allot the data processing work of the University to Ziffer Data Management and Manisundaram said he would look into it. We decided to invite him as the chief guest to inaugurate our centre and when we approached him, he readily agreed. The centre was inaugurated by him but at the time of switching on the computer, power supply failed. **Bad luck.**

In the meantime, Manisundaram wanted to start a government medical college in Trichy. My uncle Govindarajan and other members of Tiruchirapplli Medical Association opposed this. When Manisundaram came to know that the father of one of the partners of Ziffer Data Management was involved in opposing his idea of medical college, he just ditched us by not giving the order. **Bad luck.**

Later on, K. A. P. Viswanathan Government Medical College came to Trichy in 1997, inaugurated by the then chief minister of Tamil Nadu, Dr. M. Karunanidhi, in memory of Tamil scholar and businessman K. A. P. Viswanathan.

Business Data Processing Systems (BDPS) starting a Branch Close to our Centre

Just two days before our inauguration, BDPS started a similar venture in Tennur area just close to our centre. Being an established company they had an advantage over us. **Bad luck.**

Closing Down the Business

In spite of so much bad luck, we managed to get orders from SPIC and Trichy Distilleries and there were at least 20 students in every batch. But this was not sufficient. Moreover, Balachander started troubling Anandaraj and the clients. He wanted me to resign and work full time. He wanted to close down the centre. We tried to convince him but failed. After struggling for two years, we decided to sell the centre. Brilliant Tutorials was running successfully in Chennai and their owner showed interest in purchasing our centre. Since the price of computers had gone down, the sale price of the centre also came down. Somehow, we sold it and each of us paid Rs. 50000 to close the bank loan. So, the total loss for each of us was Rs.1.5 lakh. Until then I had never thought of starting a business or joining one as a partner. Without much thought, I joined this man Balachander in a risky venture. **Destiny.**

But with understanding partners and good luck, we could have become like Infosys which was started at about the same time.

Amway Business

Amway is a family company led by a diverse global management team that supports independent business owners and their goals.

Over 50 years ago, Steve Van Andel and Doug DeVos, dreamt of a better life for their families. They built a company 'Amway' on principles, people and products that have touched millions of lives around the world.

In 1959, Amway launched a business model based on the power of relationships.

I became a member in 2000 and I tried my best to build a prosperous business but was not successful. I incurred no loss in this venture.

Share Market Business

Twice, I entered Share Market business. Both the times it was ruined by stock scams - Harshad Mehta in 1992 and Ketan Parekh in 1999. I still have about 6 stocks which are not even listed and so it is a loss for me.

Failed Effort in the case of a Student

One of my final year student of Ist batch in ITM suffered from depression during the final year and in spite of my prayer and efforts he could not come out of it and committed suicide.

What are your feelings over these failures?

I feel sad sometimes for not being persistant in getting Ph.D. degree. But I feel really sad for not making any effort to get my own house which was my wife's dream because both of us were brought up in somebody else's homes. I can always console myself saying it is **Destiny**. Maybe, I am destined to fail in my personal needs. But I take it in the right spirit and I don't get bogged down.

But I am sad over your failures and I feel you don't deserve them. OK, shall we move on?

Sure.

CHAPTER 18

My Views on Major Events around Me

I would like to know your views on the major events that happened around you.

World War

I was born amidst the Second World War, which was triggered by Hitler. That war ended after the atomic bombing of two cities in Japan. I am pained even to write that more than two lakh innocent people lost their lives. In addition there was spread of genetic and chronic diseases and destruction of buildings. I am happy that a third world war has not come during these years. I am greatly relieved that the Cold War threat in the 60's, particularly the 13-day Cuban Missile Crisis involving Nikita Khrushchev, Kennedy and Fidel Castro ended without a war. But many wars have occurred during this period like Vietnam War and Korean War. The Middle East War occurred when Saddam Hussein came to power.

I would request the United Nations to take necessary steps to end the current wars involving Israel and Arab countries, India and Pakistan over Kashmir, Syrian War and others.

Terrorism

In the meantime, terrorism has emerged in most parts of the world and many countries have become victims of terrorism at one time or the other. The 21st century dawned with the worst tragedy when America's Twin Towers of World Trade Centre was attacked for which Osama bin Laden claimed responsibility.

Climate Change

When a hole was detected in the Ozone layer in 1985, the world woke up. It was predicted that temperatures would increase over the years in the planet leading to several other problems like erratic climatic conditions. Lot of efforts were taken to tackle the problems due to climate change. Intra-government Panel on Climate Change (IPCC) in 1988 and United Nations Framework Convention on Climate Change (UNFCCC) was formed. Assessment reports are prepared frequently by the IPCC and countries meet every year to monitor the situation and take suitable actions to tackle the climate change.

The world has to fight unitedly against two new challenges like terrorism and climate change threatening mankind for the past few years. I see that there are unified efforts to tackle climate change but such unified efforts are lacking for fighting against terrorism.

Technology Revolution

Computers, television and mobile phones have made most of the people their slaves. All these have made the world smaller. Enormous wealth of information is available on the internet. Many devices have been invented to help the engineering, medical, science, sports, arts and culinary areas.

My only desire, in the case of internet, is censoring of the contents.

Integration and Disintegration of Countries

After breaking the Berlin wall, East and West Germany united into one Germany in 1990. All the European countries were united into one European Union (EU) but UK voted to leave in 2016. Soviet Union was dissolved in 1991 after 69 years of existence from 1922.

Apartheid

I am happy that Apartheid, a system of racial segregation and discrimination that existed in South Africa from 1948, ended in the early 1990's. Apartheid was characterised by white supremacy, which encouraged state repression of the black population (African, Coloured, and Asian South Africans) for the benefit of the nation's minority White population.

Space Technology

Ever since the launching of artificial earth satellites Sputnik 1(1957) by the Soviet Union and Explorer 1(1958) by USA during the

International Geophysical year 1957-58, there have been several advancements in Space Technology made by different countries. Yuri Gagarin was the first human to travel in space and Armstrong was the first human to land on the moon in 1969. In addition to the moon, Mars was also included for the study. But still man is waiting to conquer it!

I wonder whether the money spent in these researches could have been used for the benefit of people in alleviation of poverty, and providing basic necessities like food, clothing, shelter and education so that every human being can live with dignity.

Olympics

This is one place where almost all the countries meet once in 4 years to exhibit their sports talent. Even here there was one boycott by the US block in 1980 and another by the Soviet Union block in 1984.

I feel such unity and sportsman spirit should be there in every area of conflict among countries.

Assassinations

The world has witnessed several assassinations The list include Mahatma Gandhi, Liaquat Ali Khan, John F. Kennedy, Martin Luther King, Robert F. Kennedy, Anwar Sadat, John Lennon, Indira Gandhi, Beant Singh, Benazir Bhutto and Rajiv Gandhi among several others.

India

Progress

India has progressed well in all areas under the different governments. INC was in power for 7 terms in majority and 3 terms under coalition. BJP had one full term with coalition and ongoing one was won by majority. In addition to these, there were two governments during 1989-91 and 1996-99. Each government has contributed to the progress of the nation.

But corruption at all levels has become the order of the day. Money has started to play the biggest role in elections. Terrorism has risen its ugly head causing too many deaths due to bombing. Crime against women and children (especially rapes) are on the rise.

I feel that amendment in the criminal laws, strict enforcement of the laws, treating the above crimes as non- bailable offences are need of the hour. Election rules and laws also require a few amendments.

We, the people, should work together to make India a corruption free nation.

War

India has periodic wars with Pakistan and a few wars with China.

I feel that every effort should be taken to end these wars once and for all, so that people of India and Pakistan can live in peace and harmony with each other.

Policies

I think that India requires a good National Educational Policy and a good National Water Policy.

I stress that India should make all efforts to connect the rivers Ganges with Cauvery which was mooted as early as 1960's by K. L. Rao. A model of the project is available in Vaigai dam, near Madurai in Tamil Nadu.

Let us hope that your vision comes true.

Next shall we talk about your hobbies?

I take the Bridge game as my second profession.

Reading novels, watching movies, playing games and listening to music are my hobbies.

What are your favourite novels and who are your preferred authors?

My favourite novels are *When Breath becomes Air* by Paul Kalanithi, *The Kite Runner* by Khaled Hosseni, *Harry Potter and the Philosophers Stone* by J. K. Rowling, *The Da Vinci Code* by Dan Brown. Chetan Bhagat, Erle Stanely Gardner, Agatha Christie, D. Jayakanthan, R. Krishnamoorthy (Kalki) and P. V. Akilan are some of my favourite authors.

What are your favourite movies?

I see a lot of movies in many languages. If I enjoy a movie I watch it many times. Some of my favourite actors are Charlton Heston, Charlie Chaplin, Elizabeth Taylor, Sivaji Ganesan, Mohanlal, Amitabh Bachchan, Kamal Haasan, Rajnikanth and Aamir khan.

What are your favourite games and who are your cherished sports persons?

Football, tennis, chess, carrom, table tennis and hockey are some of my favourite games. Cricket was my favourite but not anymore after the match fixing episodes and unnecessary hype. I can play football, chess, carrom, tennis and table tennis very well. My all-time favourites are Pele, Cristiano Ronaldo, and Lionel Messi in football, Rod Laver, Rafael Nadal, Chris Evert and Ramanathan Krishnan in Tennis, Gary Sobers, Budhi Kunderan, Gundappa Vishwanath, Tony Lock, Kapil Dev and Shane Warne in cricket, Bobby Fischer and Viswanathan Anand in Chess.

What's your taste in music?

I love all types of music, old and new. My favourite bands are the Beatles and ABBA. I like M. S. Subbulakshmi, T. M. Soundararajan, Balamurali Krishna, P. Susheela, L.R. Easwari, K.J. Yesudas, S.P. Balasubramanian, Latha Mangheskar, Asha Bhonsle, Mohammed Rafi, Jim Reeves, and so on. Among music directors, I like Viswanathan-Ramamoorthi, Ilayaraja, Shankar-Jaikishan, R.D. Burman and Harris Jeyaraj.

What are your views on astrology, numerology and Vasthu?

I have good experience with astrology and numerology. Both can be taken as a guidance to plan your life. But we have to take help of gifted and knowledgeable people, otherwise it would be a disaster. I do not have any experience with Vasthu and I have come to know that it can produce good results.

Finally, what are your views on spirituality?

I feel that there is one God even though we worship Him in different forms. If we all belong to one religion it would be fine. But practically it is not possible because no two human beings think alike. Everyone interprets life according to his own perceptions and experiences. But I feel that there should be harmony and not divisions due to religion. If God is love, then religion is about embracing all mankind.

Epilogue

You said that you very nearly went close to God through Ahilan. Can you elaborate on this?

In June 1998, a young man came into my room and introduced himself as Ahilan. He said "Sir, I have completed my Bachelor of Science (B.Sc.) degree in Agriculture from Tamil Nadu Agricultural University, Coimbatore. I am not having a job at present. I am married with two small children, one three years old and the other one year old. I came to know that you are carrying out a research project on "Water Management Studies for Paddy". I would like to get a job in your project."

I asked him about his family and his studies. I learnt that he was from a poor family and was fatherless like me. His wife held a small post in the DMK party at local level. He was from Namakkal which is about 90 kilometres from my college campus. I also learnt that he had come to see me directly after visiting Ahilandeswari Temple in Tiruvanai Kovil. I am very much attached to Namakkal because of Anjaneyar (Hanuman) Temple and Ahilandeswari Temple.

I said "My project is oriented towards irrigation water management and moreover, it is under the Department of Civil Engineering and we employ only Civil Engineering graduates. Even if I consider employing you, there is no vacancy at present."

He said "Sir, I can help in the agriculture part of the project and other field and office work. Please consider."

After a few seconds, I told him I would consider.

Then he said, "I have one request: Till I get a job, can I come daily and help you in your project?"

I said "How is it possible? You may have to spend at least Rs. 70 per day for your travel and food."

"That is not a problem, Sir. I will manage. Please permit me to come and help you."

I agreed.

He came daily for two months. When one of the project assistants, Rajendran, left, I gave him the job after convincing the Principal Dr. P. Aravindan. I also arranged accommodation in the REC hostel for him.

He helped me a lot in the day to day activities of the project. We started visiting various temples. In every temple, there was some miracle.

First, we went to a Kumbabishekam function in a Sivan temple in Tirunedungulam, 5 kilometres from the REC campus. A man was distributing Kungumam and Vibudhi. We were waiting for him but we lost sight of him. I asked Ahilan about this man and immediately he appeared from nowhere and gave us the prasad.

I took him to the Sri Aiyappan Temple in the Cantonment area in Trichy which was maintained by a committee headed by Kanagasabapathy who was my student at REC Trichy. After finishing Dharshan, we were taking the *prasadams* and I was telling Ahilan about Kanagasabapathy. In the next second, somebody tapped my back and it was Kanagasabapathy.

Next, I went to Vekkaliamman Temple in Woriyur, Trichy along with Ahilan, Bindu and my wife for the first time. After the completion of the pooja, they used to distribute Kungumam, Vibuthi and bunch of mixed flowers to the devotees. My wife prayed that she should get Talambu from the pandit. We were standing in the last and as the pandit was approaching, my wife saw that Talambu was getting over. But when her turn came, she got the Talambu. It was a miracle.

Wherever we went, we experienced such miracles.

We also visited Annamalaiyar Temple, Ramana Maharishi Ashramam, Seshadri Swamigal Ashramam and Visiri Swamigal Ashramam in Tiruvannamalai. Because of this I got employment in Arulmighu Meenakshi Amman College of Engineering located in Tiruvannamalai district.

He also introduced me to Sri Satguru Swamigal Ashramam in Trichy Cantonment. After our visit, the number of devotees grew in multiples and they have also constructed a school.

There was a lady sitting in a thatched shelter on the platform of the Tiruverambur Bridge near the road going to Kallanai for many years. Ahilan found out that her name was Thamayanthi and she had some power and we both visited her few times. Once, she saved us from a big accident near her place.

Then I wanted to test whether I had acquired any power. I checked a few times. When children cried in the bus or train, I used to pray for the suffering to go away and it worked miraculously. I became successful in solving problems of a few people through prayers. But I did not continue in a big scale due to preoccupation with my profession.

When he was with me, I visited Jerusalem and Bangkok. As I was leaving for Bangkok, he introduced me to Balakumaran, a famous writer in Tamil.

He was with me when I presented my final report in the review meeting of my project. My presentation and work was highly and openly appreciated. I also received a certificate of merit for the project from the AICTE.

I am sure that Ahilan had some divine power and he passed on a little of it to me. Due to my other commitments, I could not capitalise the opportunity to acquire more divine power,

From the happenings in your life, I can see that whatever was told by Balan Nair and Mata Amritanandamayi turned out to be true. You are the 'Adopted Son of God' and he has compensated whatever you had missed in life.

Finally, tell us what are your feelings about your life and what others can learn from your life.

Thoughts like loss of my father at such a young age and not being able to live with him still linger in my mind. Besides that, I have three feelings. I could have been a better grandson to my grandfather, better son to my mother and better husband to my wife.

I am not a big achiever but I can share my approach to life by which I did not earn a single enemy. I am truthful in responsibilities, honest in money matters, sincere, methodical, dedicated and hard working. I do not knowingly hurt anyone. I forgive easily without holding any grudges. I see both sides of the coin before believing facts. I am selfless also. I never hesitate to help others and above all I am a firm believer of God.

When you wake up in the morning, the question you ask yourself should be "What work should I start the day with?" and not "What shall I do today?"

I end with Lord Krishna's Gitaupadesam from the Bhagavat Gita:

Whatever happened, happened for the good;
Whatever is happening is happening for the good;
Whatever will happen will also happen for the good only;
You need not have any regrets for the past;
You need not worry for the future;
The present is happening;
What did you bring with you, which you think you have lost?
What did you produce, which you think destroyed?
You did not bring anything;
Whatever you have, you received from here;
Whatever you have given, you have given only here;
Whatever you took, you took from God;
Whatever you gave, you gave to Him;
You came empty handed;
You will leave empty handed;
What is yours today, belonged to someone else yesterday and
Will belong to someone else the day after tomorrow;
You are mistakenly enjoying the thought that this is yours;
It is this false happiness that is the cause of your sorrows;
Change is the law of the universe;
What you think of as death is indeed life;
In one instance, you can be a millionaire and
In the other you can be steeped into poverty;
Yours and mine, big and small erase these ideas from your mind;
Then everything is yours and you belong to everyone;
This body is not yours, neither are you of the body;
The body is made of fire, water, air, earth and ether
And will disappear into these elements;
But the soul is permanent-so who are you?
Dedicate your being to God;
He is the one to be ultimately relied upon;
Those who know of his support are forever free from fear, worry and sorrow;
Whatever you do, do it as a dedication to God;

This will bring you the tremendous experience of joy and life-freedom forever;

If every human being understands this philosophy, there will be no war but only peace on this earth.

I earnestly pray to God for such a thing to happen soon and I dream about an idyllic India and an epitome world.

Dare to Dream
Dreams Come True

www.ingramcontent.com/pod-product-compliance
Lightning Source LLC
Chambersburg PA
CBHW030102170426
43198CB00009B/460